Possessed

Possessed

The True Story of an Exorcism

Thomas B. Allen

iUniverse.com, Inc.
San Jose New York Lincoln Shanghai

Possessed
The True Story of an Exorcism

All Rights Reserved © 1994, 2000 by Thomas B. Allen

Published by iUniverse.com, Inc.

For information address:
iUniverse.com, Inc.
5220 South 16th Street, Suite 200
Lincoln, NE 68512-1274
www.iuniverse.com

ISBN: 0-595-13264-2

Printed in the United States of America

Contents

Prelude

In 1973, the Hollywood ballyhoo machine began to churn out publicity about "The Exorcist," a horror movie adapted from the best-selling book of the same title. The book and movie recounted the exorcism of a twelve-year-old girl who had been possessed by demons. The book had revived interest in the ancient mystery of diabolical possession. The movie, with its vivid special effects, did more. There was far more to the movie than the usual hokey horror. "The Exorcist" somehow reached deep into the unconscious and stirred up nameless fears.

Audiences at "The Exorcist" did more than scream and gasp, as they might at a typical horror film. People had nightmares and felt a terrifying, irrational presence of demons. Men and women who wanted to leave the theatre remained frozen in their seats. "I don't like horror movies, but I was utterly fascinated," said a man still shaken by what he had seen on the screen. "Here's this little girl turning colors and saying horrible, repulsive things. But I couldn't turn away, and I couldn't leave." A young woman came out of a theater and stood there, trembling. "I don't remember when I was so shook up," she said. "I come out here in the sunlight and I see people's eyes, and they frighten me." The movie broke attendance records and caused so many outbreaks of hysteria that, at some theatres, nurses and ambulances were on call. Moviegoers fainted or vomited. Many sought therapy to rid themselves of fears they could not explain. Psychiatrists were writing about cases of "cinematic neurosis."

Among the moviegoers were two priests, Father William S. Bowdern and Father Walter Halloran, members of the Jesuit community at St. Louis University. They went to see "The Exorcist" at a theatre in St. Louis, Missouri, a stolid Midwestern city better known for beer brewing and baseball than mysticism. It was in this city that Bowdern had performed a real exorcism, with Halloran assisting. That exorcism had inspired the movie.

Bowdern and Halloran did not like the movie. "Billy came out shaking his head about the little girl bouncing on the bed and urinating on the crucifix." Halloran remembers. "He was kind of angry. 'There is a good message that can be given by this thing,' he said. The message was the fact that evil spirits operate in our world."

Father Bowdern had always believed that he had driven a demon from a tormented soul. He also believed that revelations about the exorcism would help people understand the reality of evil. But Bowdern had promised his superiors that he would keep the exorcism a secret.

Although reports about the exorcism had circulated soon after Bowdern performed it in 1949, Roman Catholic Church officials had ordered him to remain silent. His role remained unknown, and Bowdern assumed that the exorcism would never be revealed. Then, some twenty years after he had first cried out, "*Exorcizo te!*——I cast thee out," Bowdern received a letter asking him about the exorcism.

The letter came from William Peter Blatty, who had read a newspaper account about an exorcism in 1949, while he was a student at Georgetown University in Washington, D.C. Georgetown, like St. Louis University, was a Jesuit institution. Through a mutual

Jesuit friend, Blatty wrote, he had learned about Bowdern's role as an exorcist. Blatty said he wanted to write a book about the exorcism and he asked for Bowdern's help.

"As you stated in your letter," Bowdern replied, on October 17, 1968, "it is very difficult to find any authentic literature on cases of possession; at least, I could not find any when I was involved in such a case. Accordingly, we (a priest with me) kept a minute account each day of the happenings each preceding day and night...Our diary would be most helpful to anyone placed in a similar position as an exorcist in any future date."

But Bowdern politely declined to give Blatty any help because, he said, he had been directed by Archbishop Joseph E. Ritter (later a cardinal) to keep the "the case," as he called it, unpublicized. He also feared that disclosure of the exorcism "would be most embarrassing, and possibly painfully disturbing to the young man" who was the subject of the exorcism.

Bowdern's lack of cooperation did not prevent Blatty from writing *The Exorcist*. But, at Bowdern's request, to further hide the identity of the boy, Blatty made the fictional victim a young girl. *The Exorcist*, which was published in May 1971, became an instant bestseller. *The New York Times* called it "a terrifying mixture of fact and fancy" and *Life* magazine hailed it as "hair-raising entertainment." In England, *The Sunday Express* said the novel was "a hypnotic combination of morality tale and supernatural detective story." The movie, launched on this tide of superlatives, was even more successful than the book.

Regan MacNeil, the devil-plagued girl of the book and movie, became the image of a human being in the grip of demons. Mention possession and what came to mind were movie scenes: Regan's writhing body and twisting head, Reagan's monstrous face spewing green vomit, a priest plunging to his death through a shattered window.

Hovering within the fictional character of Regan MacNeil was the boy who inspired the book and movie. The veneer of fiction covered a terrible reality. There had been a boy possessed. There had been a real exorcism. A real boy had lived though real terror. The story of his possession had never been told until the first edition of my book, *Possessed*, was published in 1993. Now, in this new edition, I have added Father Bowdern's diary, which has never been published before.

The original diary and one carbon copy went into sealed Catholic archives—one maintained by the Jesuits, the other by the Archdiocese of St. Louis. A third copy was given to the rector of the Catholic hospital where the exorcism ended. That third copy, like the other two, was expected to remain forever secret. But fate intervened.

When I first became interested in the exorcism, I did not know that the diary existed. All I knew was what I had seen in the newspaper item that had first aroused my curiosity: There was a living witness to the 1949 exorcism that had inspired the fictional book and movie. The item, in a gossip column in the *Washington Post*, said that a priest who had taken part in the exorcism had granted an interview to a reporter in Lincoln, Nebraska. Curious, I ordered a copy of the newspaper story. The priest who had given the interview, Father Walter Halloran, had provided a few tantalizing details about the exorcism. I wanted to see if he had any more information. But when I called the Nebraska university, where he had been teaching, he was no longer there. And no one would tell me where he had gone.

Using lore gleaned from six years as a student of Jesuits, I began making phone calls to Jesuits at universities and libraries throughout the United States. I finally found Father Halloran in a little Minnesota town, where he was the pastor of a church. After introducing myself on the phone and telling him why I called, I suddenly remembered that the day was Halloween. We both had a laugh together over that. We realized that we shared a similar sense of humor, and, somehow, that was all we needed. Soon we were talking as if we had known each other for a long time.

We were unable to get together for a while, but, until we met, we spoke frequently on the phone. In one conversation, Father Halloran casually mentioned that a Jesuit who assisted the exorcist had kept a diary. The news astonished me. I had never heard of an account of a modern exorcism. A diary kept by a Jesuit would be a trustworthy, eye-witness description of a mysterious rite long cloaked in superstition.

Could I see the diary? Father Halloran hesitated before he responded. The Roman Catholic Church routinely locked up its files on exorcisms. Perhaps I had pushed him too far. But never underestimate a Jesuit. "I think," he said, "that I can find a copy." A few days later I received a package from Father Halloran.

My hands were trembling when I tore open the package, which contained 24, single-spaced typewritten pages. I began reading: *Satan...diabolical...a huge red devil.* I was reading the words of a witness—one of fourteen witnesses, including nine Jesuits, who could "testify and verify different phenomena" about the exorcism. I later authenticated the diary through other sources, including a non-Jesuit source who provided me with the missing pages 25 and 26. I now had the most thorough and most reliable depiction of a modern exorcism written in modern times.

The odyssey of my copy of the diary is almost as incredible as the day-by-day narration of the exorcism itself. My copy had been locked in a room in a building about to be razed. By chance, these 24 pages of the diary were snatched from the doomed building. By further chance, the pages reached Father Halloran. And, because of a friendship launched by a Halloween phone call, the 24 pages reached me.

To tell here how the diary was hidden away in a locked room and how it was so fatefully found would be getting ahead of the story.

The story properly begins exactly as the diary begins, with what the diarist called the "Background of the case," the case of a boy possessed.

Chapter 1

"Is This You, Aunt Harriet?"

Robert Mannheim* was born in 1935 into a family struggling through the Great Depression. His father, Karl Mannheim, like many of the fathers in the Maryland suburb where the Mannheims lived, worked for the federal government. The pay was low, but the job was steady. Life kept tightening up as the Depression wore on, and soon Grandmother Wagner moved in. Three-generation households were not unusual then, for, as people often said, when times were hard, all you could depend upon was your family. That would be a lesson Robbie would hear again and again as he grew up.

In January 1949, when Robbie was still a few months away from turning fourteen, everyday life was as ordinary as it could be. He got up, had breakfast, went to school, came home, listened to favorite radio programs, did his homework, ate supper, and went to

---

*Robert Mannheim is not his real name. The author is also using pseudonyms for all members of the family, including Aunt Harriet and other relatives who will be introduced later.

bed. He was a slight boy, weighing about ninety-five pounds, with no obvious mental or physical problems. Not much for sports, he preferred playing board games around the kitchen table. As an only child, he had to depend upon the adults in the household for his playmates. One of these adults was his Aunt Harriet, Karl Mannheim's sister, who lived in St. Louis but visited the Mannheims frequently. When she stayed at Karl's house, Harriet responded to Robbie's interest in board games by introducing him to a new one—the Ouija board.

She taught him to place his fingers lightly on the planchette, a wooden platform that moved on little rollers across the polished wood surface of the Ouija board. Arrayed around the board were the letters of the alphabet, the numbers 0 to 9, and the words *Yes* and *No*. Robbie was fascinated by the Ouija board. He enjoyed the skittering movement of the planchette as it skimmed about, veering from one letter to the next, spelling out answers to questions that he or Aunt Harriet asked.

The Ouija board—its trademark name fused the French *oui* and the German *ja*—was a game, and something more. Because Aunt Harriet was a Spiritualist, she saw the Ouija board as a way to make contact between this world and the next. The planchette, she explained to Robbie, would sometimes move in response to answers given by spirits of the dead. They communicated by entering the consciousness of people at the board. The spirits, Aunt Harriet said, produced impulses that traveled through the medium to the planchette, which moved obediently to spell out words or point to *Yes* or *No*.

Aunt Harriet seems to have treated Robbie more like a special friend than as a nephew. She had an exotic quality, especially with her talk about Spiritualism. Between the visits of Aunt Harriet,

Robbie sometimes played at the Ouija board himself. He was used to finding solitary amusements.

Harriet devoted a great deal of time and energy to attempts to communicate with the spirits of the dead. She believed not only that life goes on after death but also that she could communicate with the spirits of people who had died. For years, Robbie's mother, Phyllis, had heard about Spiritualism from her sister-in-law. Phyllis would not call herself a Spiritualist, but she did believe in some of what Harriet professed. Robbie's father, Karl, did not give it much credence. Neither did Grandmother Wagner.

Aunt Harriet told Robbie and Phyllis that, lacking a Ouija board, spirits could try to get through to this world by rapping on walls. The phenomenon was well known to Spiritualists, who could cite many cases in which contact was established through rapping. By counting raps and responding with the same number, a living person could inaugurate a communication system and then develop a code. Rapping was slower and less efficient than the Ouija board, but it was another way for a spirit to get through.

The best form of communication with the spirit world, Aunt Harriet believed, was through a seance, in which believers joined hands with a medium, fusing their psychic energies. If the seance worked, a spirit took over the medium's entire body instead of just the fingers and hands. The record of Harriet's activities in Maryland does not include a seance. But, as subsequent events show, the Mannheim family was well aware of several methods for attempting to make contact with the dead.

Great forces now were beginning to focus on the Mannheims' home, a one-and-a-half-story frame house in Mount Rainier, Maryland, a suburb of Washington, D.C. Call them psychological forces, though this is a feeble designation for the overwhelming horror to come. Others, then or now, may want to call those forces diabolical or supernatural or paranormal. Whatever the origin, something powerful was about to invade Robbie's mind and possibly his soul.

One custodian of psychological forces at that time and place was Aunt Harriet. For a Spiritualist like her, attempts to deal with the dead were neither pagan nor dangerous. Most Spiritualists considered themselves good Christians, followers of Jesus Christ, who had proved, through his resurrection, the existence of life after death. Spiritualists, however, did not heed the biblical admonitions against consorting with spirits. Deuteronomy calls such trafficking "an abomination unto the Lord" and Leviticus says, "A man also or woman that hath a familiar spirit, or that is a wizard, shall surely be put to death: they shall stone them with stones: their blood shall be upon them."

The ominous biblical words show how deep in the human psyche is the fear of the dead. Yet, in the biblical story of Saul, even a king, once blessed by God, resorts to the use of a medium. King Saul, in disguise, goes to "a woman that hath a familiar spirit"—the witch of Endor. He asks her to bring up the prophet Samuel, who asks, "Why hast thou disquieted me, to bring me up?" Samuel, who can look into Saul's dark future, tells him that he will die in battle, which he soon does.

Many before and since Saul have sought that power—the ability to see the future. Saul's visit to the witch showed a belief that the dead, dwelling somewhere in the afterlife, could see future events and predict human behavior. The belief has persisted, as have fears about attempts to communicate with the dead. But the rewards sometimes seemed worth the risks: clairvoyance, power, and knowledge.

Attempts to communicate with the dead have traditionally been conducted through a medium. He or she summons up a spirit, who then takes over the medium. This is a form of possession. Spiritualists like Aunt Harriet did not look upon their beliefs as an acceptance of possession. But, whether using a seance or an Ouija board, Spiritualists did dabble in the same phenomenon that the Bible so vehemently denounced.

On Saturday, January 15, 1949, Karl and Phyllis Mannheim went out for the evening, leaving Robbie and Grandmother Wagner alone in the house. Not long after Karl and Phyllis left, Grandmother Wagner heard a dripping sound. She and Robbie checked every faucet in the neat, well-maintained house. They could not find the source of the dripping.

They went into each room, stopped and listened, straining to find the location of the persistent, rhythmic sound. They finally decided that the dripping came from Grandmother Wagner's bedroom under the sloping ceiling of the second floor. They entered and, while listening to the loud dripping, they saw a painting of Christ begin shaking, as if somebody were bumping the wall behind the painting.

By the time Karl and Phyllis Mannheim returned home, the sound of dripping had stopped. But another, stranger sound had begun: scratching, as if claws were scraping across wood. All four stood in Grandmother Wagner's bedroom and listened. Karl crouched down and looked under the bed. The scratching seemed to come from there. Karl smiled and said a mouse or rat had decided to come in from the winter cold to build a nest under Grandma's bed. The scratching finally stopped, and everyone went to bed, each with a private wonderment or fear.

About seven o'clock the following night, the scratching began again under Grandmother Wagner's bed. Again Karl Mannheim blamed a mouse or rat. He called in an exterminator, who pulled up a floorboard in search of signs of rodents. He found none, but he put down poison in case the rodent had only temporarily disappeared.

For the next several nights, the scratching continued, beginning about seven o'clock and fading away around midnight. Among family members there was little talk about the nightly noise. Outwardly, everyone agreed with Karl: A rat or mouse was making the noise, and eventually it would stop. The scratching was an annoyance, nothing more. Still, there was some desperation in his search. He tore up more floorboards and ripped down wall panels.

By later reports, no one at this time speculated much about the cause of the scratching. But Phyllis, at least, was beginning to think that the dripping and the scratchings were somehow connected with Aunt Harriet and her attempts to communicate with the dead.

On January 26, eleven days after the first scratching sounds occurred, Aunt Harriet died in St. Louis, where the Mannheim family had many relatives. Robbie, who seems to have been devastated by the death, went back to using the Ouija board. He spent hours at the board. His parents and grandmother were not interested in what questions he was asking and what answers he may have been reading as the planchette moved about the board. He almost certainly used the Ouija board to try to reach Aunt Harriet. Whatever his success, she did indeed remain part of the household, at least as a memory.

Around the time of Aunt Harriet's death, the scratching sounds in the grandmother's room stopped. Karl proclaimed that the noisy rodent had died or had gone away. But, upstairs in Robbie's room, new noises began, noises that at first he alone could hear. He described them as squeaking shoes. It was, he said, as if someone in squeaking shoes were walking along his bed. He did not seem to be frightened by the sound, which began just as he put on his pajamas and crawled into bed.

After six nights of squeaking shoes, Phyllis and Grandmother Wagner went into Robbie's room and lay with him on his bed. They all heard the sound of moving feet, but the feet seemed to be marching to the beat of drums. Up the bed, down the bed, up the bed, down—

Phyllis could stand it no longer. "Is this you, Aunt Harriet?" she suddenly asked.

No answer.

Phyllis waited a moment and said, "If you are Harriet, knock three times."

Something that felt like a wave of pressure pushed upon the three lying on the bed. The pressure seemed to pass through them and strike the floor beneath them. The sound of a knock reverberated from the floor. Another wave. Another knock. A third wave. A third knock.

Phyllis again waited, then said, "If you are Harriet, tell me positively by knocking four times."

A pressure wave, and then a knock. A wave. A knock. A wave. A knock...A wave and the fourth knock.

Now, below them, inside the mattress they lay on, they heard what seemed to be the scratching of a claw. It did not touch them, but they felt the sound undulating through the mattress. Afterward, comparing reactions, Phyllis and the grandmother remembered that, terrified, each had done the same thing. Each had tried to pretend that she did not hear the scratching. It was at that moment, they both later realized, that the mattress began to shake, gently at first, then violently.

When the shaking stopped, the edges of the bedcover flew out from under the mattress. As the women later recounted, the edges of the covers "stood up above the surface of the bed in a curled form as though held up with starch."

Wordlessly, Robbie, his mother, and his grandmother slipped out of the suddenly still bed and touched the stiffened coverlet. Its sides fell back, and the bed again looked normal. But the scratching on the mattress did not stop that night or the next night or the next. The scratching went on, night after night, for more than three weeks.

Nor were these alarming phenomena confined to the Mannheims' home. The desks at Robbie's school were moveable seat-desk units, with a single arm acting as a writing surface. Several times in January and February Robbie's desk lurched into the aisle and began skittering about, banging into other desks and causing schoolroom uproar. Although the teacher naturally assumed that Robbie's feet were propelling his wayward desk, he swore that he had not caused it to move. It moved by itself, he said. Later, describing the moving desk to his mother, Robbie said the desk glided around the floor like a planchette.

There is a vast, worldwide literature about events like these— bizarre, inexplicable happenings that people experience and attempt to describe. The accounts radiate out in concentric circles, with the frightened, stammering witnesses at the hub. Around the hub, in the first tight circle, are stunned relatives and friends, hearing and wondering, trusting but disbelieving. In the second circle, beyond those first auditors who know the witnesses, are the neighbors and the rumor mongers, telling what they heard or what they imagined they heard, garnishing the distant happening with erroneous details plucked from other stories or from their own inspirations. From that weak and ever widening circle usually comes the account that reaches the back pages of newspapers to be read with smirks by skeptics. Eventually, the accounts find their way into the magazines and books of the true believers, the zealots whose faith in the unexplained is not matched by a demand for facts.

But something different was to happen to the accounts of happenings in the Mannheim house. In the first circle would be not only the relatives and friends but also ministers, psychologists, and priests who would write down what they heard and saw. Through their testament, the events whirling about Robbie would be soberly recorded.

For the next few days, however, there would be only the hub. No outsider would be there to live the nights that began with dread. In the house, no one but Robbie and his family would be there to hear and see whatever it was that they believed they were hearing and seeing.

At home, Robbie was always on the scene just as something mysterious happened. A coat on a hanger seemed to fly out of a closet and across a room. A Bible seemed to rise from a bookcase and land at Robbie's feet. He was standing nearby when others saw an orange and a pear fly across a room. One day the kitchen table tipped over. Another day, the breadboard slid off the kitchen counter and clattered to the floor. One morning, Phyllis scolded Robbie for scattering his clothes all over the kitchen. Robbie swore that when he went to bed he had put the clothes on a chair in his bedroom.

One Sunday relatives came calling. They were all in the livingroom when the large stuffed chair that Robbie was sitting in seemed to rise slightly off the floor and then flip over. Robbie somersaulted onto the floor. Stunned, family members gathered around the chair. Robbie's father and uncle each sat in the heavy chair and tried to flip it over. Each man failed.

While the family members were still talking about the flipping chair, one of them pointed to a small table. A vase was slowly rising from the table. It seemed to hang in the air for a moment. Then it flew across the room and shattered against a wall.

Robbie's family at first tried to maintain a normal life. Robbie even joked about the funny things happening around him. One day, the family members piled into Karl Mannheim's car and set off for a visit to friends in Boonesboro, Maryland, about forty miles away. The ride was uneventful. The Mannheims, grateful for a respite from troubles at home, joined their friends in the livingroom. While the adults chatted, they saw something that they all later agreed they had seen: the rocking chair in which Robbie sat began spinning like a top. His feet were off the floor. It seemed impossible for the rocking chair to be whirling about. But they had seen it with their own eyes.

Something was happening to Robbie. But what? His frantic parents tried to explain the phenomena as mischief, tricks that he learned from some book on magic. Again and again, Robbie said, *I didn't do it! I didn't do it!*** But no one in school had believed him when he said that, and now it was happening at home and at the

---

**Here, as elsewhere in the book, quotations in italics are reconstructed from records. (See *Sources*.) Quotations in quotation marks are in the records verbatim or come from witnesses' reports.

friends' home. He said he was too embarrassed to go to school. His parents let him stay home while they tried to figure out what to do next.

The incidents of those weeks entered the memories of witnesses not as a narrative but as shards of a mosaic. When recounting the events later, the parents repeatedly said, "We tried everything." The sequence of their moves is not recorded. What is known is their desperation. Caught up in a maelstrom of frightening events, they turned to a physician, a psychologist, a psychiatrist, a psychic, and a minister.

The physician, the psychiatrist, and the psychologist left no known record of their findings—except for a remark from the psychiatrist. He "declared that he did not believe the phenomena." And he reported that he believed Robbie to be "normal." The physician also said he found nothing wrong with Robbie, though, in a remarkable understatement for Robbie's condition at the time, the doctor did say that Robbie appeared "somewhat high-strung." The psychic said that nothing could be done, implying, perhaps, that the ordeal had to play itself out.

The psychologist, who was on the faculty of the University of Maryland, practiced at the County Mental Hygiene Clinic. Robbie, according to one source, visited the clinic twice and failed to appear for a third appointment There is no available record of what happened at the clinic. In the typical examination sequence of the time, Robbie's intelligence quotient (IQ) would have been graded, his visual and auditory memory would have been tested, and he would have moved pieces of wood around and put pegs in holes while a stopwatch ticked in a test designed to measure the accuracy and speed of his hand movements.

He also probably would have had his mental health gauged by two other basic tests: word-association and responses to a series of illustrations. For each illustration he would have been asked to construct a simple story. This variation on the Rorschach ink blot test was considered a dependable way to gauge the health of a person's imagination.

A psychiatrist who has studied the practices of that day speculated on what kind of examination Robbie would have been given. "Specific questions would not be asked," she said. "It is doubtful, for example, that a psychologist in the clinic would have asked a question like, 'How long have you felt this way?' Practitioners of mental hygiene in those days tended to be satisfied with a patient's own description."

She guessed that Robbie would not say much about what had been going on around him. "Some patients," she said, "are good at disguising symptoms and keeping secrets from strangers, especially since the implication is that he would go to a hospital and be separated from his parents."

Psychiatric treatment at the time favored electric and insulin shock for the severe form of mental illness given the labels schizophrenia or dementia praecox or for what was vaguely described as depression. Frontal lobotomies were common. They were performed upon people who acted aggressively or showed symptoms of extreme paranoia.

Most likely, Robbie avoided treatment because no one could fathom what was happening to him. But the Lutheran minister to whom the Mannheims turned soon came up with his own theory.

He was the Reverend Luther Miles Schulze, the forty-three-year-old pastor of St. Stephen's Evangelical Lutheran Church, just over the Maryland line in Washington, D.C. Schulze talked to Robbie and his parents and listened politely to what they said had been happening in their home. Phyllis and Karl Mannheim told Schulze that they had turned to him because by now they were convinced that Robbie was the victim of an evil ghost. Phyllis wondered if it could be Aunt Harriet.

During several visits to the house Schulze saw furniture move about, apparently without being pushed by anyone. He saw dishes fly through the air, and he watched Robbie's bed shake. Schulze kept to himself a belief that Robbie somehow was causing these strange events. They were clever pranks, not mystic phenomena, Schulze thought. But they were real enough and terrifying enough to threaten the well being of a family he admired and had promised to help. So he called in another Lutheran minister and together they planned a religious approach to solving, or at least treating, the family's problem. He also had something else in mind, something that had nothing to do with religion.

Chapter 2

Hunting a Poltergeist

Reports of events in Robbie Mannheim's home do not make a coherent, consistent narrative. Viewpoints differ. Robbie himself, at this stage, is only a dim figure, the blurred center of events rapidly evolving from strange to horrifying. Details are often hazy and come from frantic parents and a terrified grandmother. Schulze's arrival adds new testimony to the day-by-day accounts of what was happening in the Mannheim home. Schulze was the first outsider to enter the family's ordeal and leave a record of what he saw. He came to answer a call for help, a call inspired by a belief that somehow he would wield religion as a weapon against whatever it was that was besieging the Mannheims' home.

At first, Robbie's parents told Schulze, they had thought that someone had been sleepwalking and inadvertently making the noises and somehow moving the objects. Another possibility, they said, was that someone was mischievously causing the phenomena. Either way, Robbie was the suspect. But now, they said, they were hearing and seeing things that could not have been caused by Robbie. There had been one particularly horrifying night.

The house had been quiet. Robbie was asleep in his room. Suddenly he began to scream. His parents and grandmother rushed to his bedroom. As he lay screaming on the bed, they watched a heavy dresser slide across the room to the door, blocking their exit. Then, one by one, full drawers opened and closed. And, they told Schulze, Robbie himself was changing. He was morose and kept to himself. One night, in his sleep, they heard him cursing them, using obscenities they did not dare repeat to the minister. They had not even thought Robbie knew any words like that. All their ideas about sleepwalking and pranks were forgotten.

Now, they said, they were convinced that some spirit—perhaps Aunt Harriet—had entered their house and might be attempting to enter Robbie. According to Schulze's account, at this point Robbie's mother and father were beginning to wonder about diabolical possession. They had then only a nebulous understanding of possession. And Schulze himself could add little.

As a Lutheran minister, he well knew that Martin Luther had considered all mental illnesses to be cases of diabolical possession. Enlightened Lutheran ministers like Schulze no longer believed that, of course. One of his first recommendations was for the family to seek psychiatric help; it was Schulze who recommended the visit to the County Mental Hygiene Clinic. But Schulze could not respond to the family's fears about possession.

Theologically, the Lutheran Church had no way to deal with diabolical possession. Luther had swept away many of the time-honored rituals of Catholicism, including exorcism, the casting out of demons. He believed that the rite of exorcism merely made a "display" of the devil. He preferred to confront the devil with "prayer and contempt."

Schulze seems not to have been intellectually or spiritually convinced of the possibility of possession. So he followed Luther's lead. "At first I tried prayer," Schulze later told an interviewer. "I prayed with the parents and the boy in their home and with the boy in my home. And there were prayers for the boy in church." He also urged the Mannheims to take Communion every Sunday. The closest Schulze got to exorcism, he said, was when he "ordered whatever it was disturbing him, in the name of the Father, Son, and Holy Spirit, to get out and let him alone."

By Schulze's account, the family did not take his advice to have Robbie examined by a psychiatrist. But the family told others that a psychiatrist had been consulted and had pronounced Robbie normal.

Schulze, working with another Lutheran minister, tried to aid the family by organizing prayer circles at the church. The circles were probably one of the ways that stories about Robbie began spreading around the community. His house became the haunted house and he became the haunted boy.

Mount Rainier lies along the northeast line of the District of Columbia, about six miles from the White House. But it could be a little town hundreds of miles from Washington. Its small frame and stucco houses are close together, and most of them have roofs that slope over front porches, putting the front doors in deep shadow. The backyards are small and fenced off. Along the tree-lined streets there is a sense of people wanting to live privately and quietly. Mount Rainier is the kind of place where the mayor knew all the longtime residents, most of the newcomers, and kept his eye on strangers. It was not long before many people knew something very odd was happening in the Mannheim house at 3210 Bunker Hill Road. (There is some dispute about Robbie's address. See discussion in Chapter Notes, Chapter 2, page 307.)

The ministers did not subscribe to the haunted house rumors. Nor did they agree with the parents' suspicion that evil was somehow connected with Robbie's experiences. What the ministers saw was a young boy and his family in torment. They were praying that God would relieve the Mannheims of that torment. Schulze was not comfortable with the idea of diabolical possession. To Schulze, the idea of possession of a person by Satan would have been a Roman Catholic belief. Since antiquity, Christian thought had held that the devil, as the leader of angels fallen from Paradise, was a powerful adversary. Among his wily powers, according to Christian theology, was the ability to possess a human being.

From Schulze's Protestant viewpoint, possession had to be a medieval relic, something that had been left to the Catholics when the Luther-led Reformation split the Christian world. But there were two other reservoirs of belief, both known to Schulze. Some conservative Protestants, including Lutherans, believed in a real devil, a being that could inflict evil. Schulze steered away from that fundamentalist view and turned toward another belief, an amalgam of the Spiritualism practiced by Aunt Harriet and one of Schulze's interests, parapsychology.

Spiritualism in the United States dates back to a case of rapping at a farmhouse in Hydesville, New York, in 1848. Two sisters, Kate Fox, twelve, and Margaretta Fox, fourteen, heard the rappings for several nights. Childishly, Kate one night snapped her fingers at the sound and, according to her later accounts, each of her snaps was echoed by a rap. She worked out a code with the rapper, who, she said, identified himself as a man who had been murdered in the house.

From sensational stories about the Fox sisters and their subsequent skills as mediums came a renewed belief in communication with the dead, and this inspired the founding of the Spiritualist Church in the United States. As a Spiritualist, according to the *Spiritualist Manual,* Aunt Harriet would have believed "in the communication between this and the spirit world by means of mediumship." This mediumship is a form of benign possession.

Spiritualists do not believe in diabolical possession, for they do not believe in evil spirits. "No being is naturally 'bad,'" says the *Manual*. But there are spirits who "have passed through this world and into the Spirit World in absolute ignorance of spiritual laws." Spiritualists also believe that no harm can come to a person acting as a medium.

So, if Aunt Harriet did introduce Robbie to Spiritualism, and if he did experiment as a medium, she acted as a well-meaning mentor, as someone who believed that she may have been helping his intellectual and spiritual growth. "As the master-musician improves the instrument he plays upon," says the *Manual*, "so, also a spirit controlling a human organism for the purpose of expressing wholesome thought, imparts a greater power, both to the brain and the spirit of the medium."

Schulze's knowledge of Spiritualism came not directly but via parapsychology, the study of events that do not appear to be explicable by conventional science. He shared with parapsychologists the belief that extra-sensory perception (ESP) existed in people, to varying degrees. ESP experiments, then as now, focused on three phenomena: telepathy, the ability to transmit thoughts from one mind to another without use of the normal senses; clairvoyance, the perception of events or things that are at great distances or otherwise concealed from sight; and psychokinesis, the movement or control of objects by the use of thought alone—a manifestation of mind over matter.

The difference between Spiritualism and parapsychology is a perceived difference between faith and science. Spiritualists intuitively accept ESP phenomena, along with the idea of mediums and communication with the dead; parapsychologists want to prove ESP and find a scientific explanation for it.

Schulze was particularly interested in psychokinesis, PK to parapsychologists. During his first meetings with Robbie's parents he heard about the moving objects, and he may have seen some examples of PK with his own eyes. But, Schulze reasoned, this was Robbie's own house. He could have been manufacturing the phenomena, consciously or unconsciously.

By the beginning of February, Karl and Phyllis Mannheim felt that they were near the breaking point. Night after night, Robbie thrashed around for hours, half-asleep or fully awake. When he finally did go to sleep, he screamed through nightmares or mumbled words and phrases, as if he were talking to someone. Something was torturing him. If this nameless agony kept up, his parents told Schulze, Robbie would go mad. Did Schulze have more to offer them than prayer?

Schulze hesitated to tell what was on his mind. He had been developing a theory. Without telling the Mannheims, he had started thinking of the events in the house as a phenomenon springing from Robbie himself. His theory seemingly agreed with the explanation that neighbors and friends of the Mannheims talked about among themselves: The strange happenings were the pranks of a boy entering adolescence.

The explanation is a familiar one. It appears again and again in reports of what are called poltergeists, from the German word "noisy ghost." Most cases contain two invariable elements: a teenager and noisy, inexplicable events in the vicinity of the teenager. Poltergeist reports usually are replete with references to noise—thumping, drumming, rapping, scratching, tapping, thudding—and the movement of objects. In thousands of recorded cases, going back through eight centuries, the details of the tales are amazingly consistent: beds stirring, plates flying, chairs moving, bedclothes ripping off the bed. Poltergeists, as the British poet Robert Graves once wrote, "show an appalling sameness of behaviour; humorless, pointless, uncoordinated."

The sounds in the Mannheim house resembled those reported in numerous others households where, for want of a better explanation or label, poltergeists were blamed. Many such events uncannily resemble what was happening around Robbie in January 1949. In 1862, for example, a Swiss lawyer began hearing, in a room in his home, "a repeated peculiar rapping of 10-12 blows, which came very quickly towards the end…I sought and found, with my ear to the wall, the precise location of the sounds, which, however, frequently moved. Thinking it must be a living creature, such as a rat, I hit the wall to frighten it away. Instead it more than once replied with the same sound, followed sometimes by one or two more powerful blows as if with a fist."

The record shows that three teenagers and an eleven-year-old lived in the lawyer's house. The family fled the house, leaving behind whatever it was that had harassed them. That, to Schulze, was a familiar pattern: Most so-called poltergeists did not accompany their victims from place to place. The phenomenon seemed to be grounded at a certain site occupied by the teenager, though Robbie had reported incidents at school. Schulze probably speculated that in a totally unfamiliar place Robbie would not be able to perform any tricks that implied a poltergeist was bothering him.

Schulze suggested that Robbie spend a night in Schulze's home. Robbie's parents agreed, if for no other reason than to get their son a full night's sleep. On Thursday, February 17, Karl Mannheim took his son to Schulze's home. There was some cautious talk about what had been happening in Robbie's house. "You're going to have a good night's sleep," Schulze told Robbie. "Nothing like that happens in this house."

As soon as Karl Mannheim left, Schulze, a friendly, sensitive man, sat down with Robbie. The minister tried to find an opening, a way to get Robbie to tell in his own words what his parents had been telling Schulze. When Robbie showed no sign of wanting to share any confidences with Schulze, the minister was wise enough to give up without antagonizing the boy. Finally, Schulze said it was time for bed.

Mrs. Schulze retired to a guestroom next to the master bedroom, where the minister and Robbie were to sleep. Schulze and Robbie put on their pajamas, said their prayers, and wished each other good night. They climbed into twin four-poster beds.

About midnight, Schulze was awakened by a sound. Robbie's bed was shaking. The minister reached out a hand and touched the bed. It was shaking, he said later, "like one of those motel vibrator beds, but much faster." Robbie was awake and motionless. "His limbs and head and body were perfectly still."

Schulze wanted to get himself and Robbie out of the room immediately. He rose from the bed and, speaking calmly, said that they both should get up and have some cocoa. He made the cocoa and took it into his study. Robbie politely thanked the minister for the cocoa but said little else. He was quiet and seemed undisturbed. He was probably so used to events like shaking beds and moving dressers that he no longer showed any exterior reaction. They finished their cocoa and returned to Schulze's bedroom.

Schulze directed Robbie to an armchair and suggested that he try to sleep in it rather than the bed. Schulze decided to keep a light on. Robbie sat in the chair. In moments the chair began to move. As Schulze described what happened next, Robbie "placed his knees under his chin with his feet on the edge of the chair. The chair backed up three inches against the wall. When it could move no farther in that direction it slowly tipped over…"

Schulze estimated that the chair took more than a minute to slowly tip over and topple Robbie gently to the floor. Robbie did not get out of the chair during the slow movement. He appeared to be in some kind of trance.

The minister had been standing in front of the chair. When Robbie slowly rose and stepped away, Schulze got into the chair and tried to tip it. The heavy armchair had "a very low center of gravity." He could not tip it.

Now Schulze decided that the safest place for Robbie was the floor. He put the boy between two blankets at the foot of one of the beds and climbed back into his bed. He left the light on.

About three o'clock Schulze awoke and saw Robbie and the blankets moving across the room. "The boy and the bedding moved as a unit slowly under the twin beds," Schulze recalled. "The four sides of the blankets, which had no folds, remained perfectly straight, with no wrinkles." Tired and dazed, Schulze could take no more. "Stop that!" he shouted, springing from the bed.

"I'm not doing it!" Robbie replied.

The boy and the blankets slid under a bed. Schulze stooped and saw Robbie bouncing up and down against the springs supporting the mattress. Stiff and seemingly again in a trance, Robbie did not flinch as his face hit the springs. Schulze pulled him from under the bed. Robbie's face was cut in several places.

If Schulze had thought that Robbie was faking, or even if he had thought that the boy was the victim of a poltergeist, he now had to consider the possibility that Robbie was possessed, that something was in control of this thirteen-year-old boy who looked so chillingly indifferent to his fate. Next day, Schulze took Robbie home. He had no explanation for what he had seen.

In the archives of poltergeist cases, there are stories of incidents far more sinister than flying plates and bouncing mattresses. Whatever the reason for the onslaughts, victims suffered. One well-documented case involves Eleonora Zugun, a twelve-year-old Romanian girl, who in 1925 complained that a demon named Dracu was harassing her. First came the usual rappings and moving objects. Then scratches and bite marks appeared on her face, arms, neck, and chest. She claimed that Dracu was pricking her with needles and biting her.

Whatever he may have known about parapsychology and the relatively benign legends of poltergeists, Schulze believed, after that terrifying February night, that he had been in the presence of some colossal force. It did not matter whether that force was a hallucination, an outburst of supernatural powers, evidence of parapsychological activity, or an eruption from some psychological fissure deep within Robbie. He was suffering unimaginable agony. Mute and unheeding, Robbie seemed to be plunging deeper into something Schulze could not fathom.

During the day, Robbie seemed normal, though tired and listless. At night, he knew no peace. The nightmares still tore his sleep. The scratchings in the mattress were continuing, night after night. Then, on Saturday, February 26, scratches began to appear on Robbie's body.

The scratches looked like the kind a cat makes, long and shallow, the marks of claws. They appeared on Robbie's arms, legs, and chest. Some of the scratches seemed to form letters of the alphabet, but the letters did not form words. Not yet.

Schulze now saw that whatever he had been trying to do was not strong enough to stop Robbie's agony. A force had been tormenting Robbie from the outside. Now the force seemed to be inside him, manifesting itself by emerging from his body in bloody lines. Possessing him. Schulze conceded defeat. As one of Robbie's parents remembered it, Schulze said quietly, "You have to see a Catholic priest. The Catholics know about things like this."

Chapter 3

"But Deliver Us from Evil"

At first Schulze believed he had seen the pranks of a poltergeist. But the scratches signified something more, something beyond his knowledge or experience. His remark that Catholics know "about things like this" was a dual admission. As a witness to Robbie's torment, he now may have suspected that an evil power was present. But, as a modern Lutheran, he had to concede a theological reality: Satan did not get much attention from mainstream Protestant churches. The Roman Catholic Church, however, believed Satan to be an integral part of Christian faith. From this stemmed the further belief that diabolical possession is real and exorcism can cure it.

Most Protestant denominations believed that possession and exorcism were legacies of the Middle Ages and had no place in a scientifically enlightened world. When Robbie's parents suggested that their son might be in the possession of a demon, they were turning to an idea that was older than Christianity, and all but abandoned by it. Diabolical possession was a belief of primitives. Christian missionaries confronted such notions in villages from Malaysia to Africa, from India and Nepal to Brazil and Trinidad.

But diabolical possession was not what a minister would expect to find a few miles outside of Washington, D.C., in 1949.

All Christianity once treated Satan as an actual being and believed that he could enter into a human being. All Christianity once had a ritual for driving Satan out of a human being. That ritual was exorcism, which was practiced rigorously and frequently from the birth of Christianity until deep into the Middle Ages. The source of Christian belief in exorcism was the New Testament's portrayals of Satan in a titanic struggle with Jesus. Under that theology, one way that Satan showed his power was by possessing people, and one way Jesus showed his power was by exorcising Satan.

Matthew, Mark, and Luke all describe exorcisms by Jesus. The victim of the best known biblical story of possession is a homeless, unclothed man in the country of the Gadarenes. Bound in chains because of the violent demon writhing in him, he drags himself before Jesus. When Jesus asks the demon his name, it replies, "My name is Legion: for we are many." Jesus orders the demons to leave the man, and they plunge into a herd of swine that "ran violently down a steep place into the sea, and perished in the waters."

In another exorcism, Jesus, while teaching in a synagogue in Capernaum, sees a man possessed with an unclean spirit, which he orders out of the man. Crying with a loud voice, the spirit vanishes. The Gospels also tell of Jesus casting seven devils out of Mary Magdalene and driving a devil out of the young daughter of a Greek woman. Jesus expels a demon from a young boy who was frothing and gnashing his teeth. After the exorcism, the boy appeared to be dead. "But Jesus took him by the hand, and lifted him up; and he arose." (Modern physicians believe the boy was suffering from epilepsy.)

The exorcisms by Jesus were ignored or glossed over by most Protestants, particularly Lutherans. Protestant theology explained them away as acts that showed Jesus accepting prevailing local beliefs. People in those days, said the modern theologians, believed in possession just as they believed that the sun circled the earth. Jesus' mission did not include correcting folk beliefs or misconceptions about the natural world.

Catholicism, while preserving dogmatic belief in possession, rarely acknowledged the existence of possession in the modern world. In Rome and in other places, a few priests who were designated as exorcists had devoted much of their lives to prayer and the study of diabolical possession. And, on rare occasions, they were called in by their ecclesiastical superiors for consultation on cases of possible possession. Every Catholic priest knew, theoretically, that one day he could be called upon to pit his soul against Satan. But in modern times no priest, particularly a young American parish priest, ever expected to be an exorcist.

Early one evening in late February, shortly after Schulze said that Catholics know about things like this, Karl Mannheim called the rectory of St. James, a Catholic church not far from the Mannheim home. He said he wanted to talk to a priest. The housekeeper brought Father E. Albert Hughes to the phone. Hughes talked to Mannheim for a short time and told him to drop by the rectory the next morning.

Protestants did not often meet priests in those days. By long Catholic tradition, Catholics did not enter Protestant churches. Catholics who carried the tradition to extremes would not even set foot in a Protestant church to attend a friend's funeral or wedding. Inter-faith marriages were rare for Catholics, and those who did marry outside their faith almost invariably met great resistance from priests and family.

The Mannheims were desperate, Lutherans in search of help from a Catholic priest, a father and mother trying to save their son from something they could describe but not understand. They took Robbie to the rectory, where all three met Father Hughes for the first time. The Mannheims undoubtedly felt uncomfortable talking to Father Hughes, and the feeling was just as undoubtedly mutual.

Hughes, a brash, handsome twenty-nine-year-old, had not met many Protestants and had little knowledge of possession or exorcism. He was not an intellectual. He believed in his faith, and he dutifully taught and practiced its tenets, but he did not give much thought to profound matters. Many of Hughes' parishioners, particularly the older ones, likened him to the easygoing, wisecracking priest played by Bing Crosby in the movie "Going My Way." A woman of his parish would later say of him, "He was young and spoiled—real Irish, you know, shot a lot of blarney. He had no understanding of common people, of real life. Yet he thought he knew it all."

As Hughes recalled the visit years later, the boy, disliking the visit to the rectory, berated the priest with foul language. By Hughes' recollection, the room turned very cold as the boy, apparently demonstrating his power, caused the phone on Hughes' desk to move. Whatever actually happened, Hughes was frightened, felt he was in the presence of evil, thought that Robbie was possessed, and wondered if an exorcism was warranted.

Hughes promised to pray for Robbie and gave the Mannheims a bottle of holy water and blessed candles. Holy water is ordinary water, blessed by a priest with a prayer. The water-blessing prayer, which dates to the Fourth Century, exorcises any demons that might be in the water. The candles, made of beeswax and never of tallow, were from a stock also specially blessed and placed on the altar, where they were lighted for Mass and other ceremonies.

Back home, Phyllis Mannheim opened the bottle of holy water and went around the house, sprinkling every room. She then placed the bottle on a dresser. She lit the candles and placed them in Robbie's room.

Next morning Phyllis called Hughes. *The bottle was picked up by something and smashed. When I lit one of the candles the flames shot up to the ceiling and I had to put it out for fear the house would be set on fire.*

What happened next is not quite clear. Hughes apparently told her to try again. She called back. He heard a crash. *The telephone table just broke into a hundred pieces.*

Hughes apparently decided to go to the house and talk to Robbie to gain a sense of what was happening to the boy. The confusion about the sequence of Hughes' acts may well stem from the priest's own immediate confusion. What soon happened to Hughes so affected his mind and memory that for a long while he was unable to give a coherent account of his dealings with Robbie.

In one version given by Hughes, he heard Robbie speak Latin, although the boy had never learned the language. According to Hughes, Robbie said, *"O sacerdós Christi, tu scis me esse diabólum. Cur me derógas?"*—"O priest of Christ, you know that I am the devil. Why do you keep bothering me?"

Such fluent Latin would have stunned Hughes and started him thinking about possession. Whatever the details, if Hughes believed the possibility of possession, he would have opened his *Rituale Romanum,* the official book of Catholic rituals, known in English as *The Roman Ritual.* Based on rituals that go back as far as the first century, and first published in 1614, it had changed little since then. Every priest has one, though rarely does he have to turn to it and look up "Exorcism of the Possessed." The book devoted fifty-eight pages to exorcism. The pages in this section, as in the others in the *Ritual* of that era, were alternately in English and Latin. "Exorcism of the Possessed" began with twenty-one detailed instructions. The third instruction to a prospective exorcist said:

> Especially, he should not believe too readily that a person is possessed by an evil spirit; but he ought to ascertain the signs by which a person possessed can be distinguished from one who is suffering from melancholy or some other illness. Signs of possession are the following: ability to speak with some facility in a strange tongue or to understand it when spoken by another; the faculty of divulging future and hidden events; display of powers which are beyond the subject's age and natural conditions; and various other indications which, when taken together as a whole, pile up the evidence.

The ability to speak in an unknown language traditionally was that kind of evidence. The rules in the *Ritual* said that the evidence was to be taken to what the instructions call "the Ordinary," the ecclesiastical term for the person who has, of his own right and not by deputation, immediate jurisdiction in church matters. The Ordinary weighs the evidence and then decides whether to allow an exorcism. He also chooses the exorcist. For Hughes, the Ordinary was the Archbishop of Washington, the Most Reverend Patrick A. O'Boyle.

O'Boyle was a protegè of the most powerful Catholic prelate in America, Francis Cardinal Spellman, Archbishop of New York. O'Boyle, born in 1896 of Irish immigrant parents, was ten years old when his father died. His mother took on a job typical of Irish Catholic widows. She became a housekeeper for priests. O'Boyle grew up wanting to be like them, and he entered the seminary as soon as he was old enough.

When he was ordained, he was assigned to the Archdiocese of New York and taught for a time at a child-care institution on Staten Island. Spellman, then a bishop, spotted O'Boyle as an energetic young priest. In 1939, when Spellman became Archbishop of New York—the nation's most important archdiocese—he took O'Boyle under his wing. After the outbreak of World War II, Spellman was appointed U.S. military vicar by the pope. Spellman made O'Boyle director of Catholic War Relief and kept him on a career path as an administrator.

In May 1947, when the Archbishop of Baltimore and Washington died, the Vatican divided the jurisdiction, creating the Archdiocese of Baltimore and the Archdiocese of Washington. O'Boyle, then in New York as the executive director of Catholic Charities, was made archbishop of the new Archdiocese of Washington. It was the first time that a monsignor—the ecclesiastical title that O'Boyle held—had been appointed an archbishop in America without having previously served as a bishop. On January 14, 1948, Spellman consecrated O'Boyle archbishop in St. Patrick's Cathedral, New York, and a few days later O'Boyle went to Washington to take up his new post.

So, in February 1949, when Hughes was thinking of going to O'Boyle to discuss a possible exorcism, the Ordinary was an archbishop who had had no pastoral experience, no specialized theological training, and whose career had been invested much more in administration than in arcane matters like diabolical possession. By Hughes' account, he went first to one of O'Boyle's aides, the chancellor of the archdiocese, who told Hughes to go slowly. The impetuous Hughes replied, *I've spent two weeks on it, and that's slow enough.* The chancellor relented and made an appointment for Hughes to see O'Boyle.

Anything connected with any Hughes-O'Boyle meeting is in the secret archives of the archdiocese and may be read and distributed only by the sitting archbishop. But churchmen seeking information on exorcisms have been able to learn something about the case from O'Boyle's files. These indicate that O'Boyle took little interest in what Hughes presented to him. O'Boyle was the kind of prelate who once saw a young priest in shirtsleeves and immediately gave orders that all priests in his archdiocese must wear black fedoras, black suits, and roman collars no matter where they were or what they were doing. He was not the kind of prelate who would pay much heed to the first of *The Roman Ritual's* instructions on exorcism:

> A priest—one who is expressly and in special wise authorized by the Ordinary—when he intends to perform an exorcism over persons tormented by the devil, must be properly distinguished for his piety, prudence, and integrity of life. He should fulfil this devout undertaking in all constancy and humility, being utterly immune to any striving for human aggrandizement, and, relying not on his own, but on the divine power. Moreover, he ought

to be of mature years, and revered not alone for his office but for his moral qualities.

Father Hughes, young, rash, and not given to projecting an aura of holiness, was an unlikely candidate for exorcist. Nor is there any indication that either he or O'Boyle followed the next instruction:

> In order to exercise his ministry rightly, he should resort to a great deal more study of the matter...by examining approved authors and cases from experience...

An unpublished, third-person account of Hughes' appointment simply says, "[T]he Archbishop...authorized Father [Hughes] to begin the exorcism. Father [Hughes] understood that this should be done by a very holy man because the devil is wont to expose the sins of the priest; so the Father went to Baltimore and made a general confession." It is not unusual to go to another jurisdiction to make a general confession, which differs from an ordinary confession. Hughes would have deeply examined his life and found his weaknesses and confessed them to a priest designated to hear other priests' confessions. A general confession prior to exorcism, as one priest puts it, is like the vigil a knight kept on the eve of battle.

Hughes held to a theological theory that said Satan, during an exorcism, could not exploit or even cite sins that have been forgiven in confession. So, if Hughes made a successful confession, he was at least assured that Satan would not taunt him about his past sins. But Hughes did little else to prepare himself for the ordeal of exorcism.

It seems incredible that O'Boyle did not give the assignment to any one of dozens of theologians right at hand at Washington's

Catholic University or Trinity College. He also could have called upon the theological or psychological faculties of Georgetown University, a Jesuit institution.

Hughes would have had only a cursory knowledge of demonology, the formal branch of Catholic theology regarding Satan and his demons. Demonology, a subject usually linked with angelology in theology courses, was not given much time or attention. Young seminarians were expected to learn how to be priests, not exorcists. They were being prepared to work as curates or assistant pastors in parishes. The seminary courses focused on those tenets of Catholic theology that prospective priests needed most to learn. As priests, they would be dealing with problems of faith and morals brought to them by ordinary Catholics. Instructors in the seminary rightfully believed there was little chance that a priest, especially a new priest like Hughes, would be confronted with a need to perform an exorcism.

But here was Hughes and here was O'Boyle and here was Robbie. On a winter's night in 1949 they were all involved in an exorcism. O'Boyle reportedly told Hughes not to write anything down about the exorcism and never to talk about it. He seems not to have given the young priest any other instructions.

Robbie, meanwhile, was getting worse. He was no longer going to school or doing much of anything else. The scratches came now every night. What little sleep he got was a troubled, writhing sleep of exhaustion. He seemed often to be in a trance or under a spell and at times appeared to be in need of psychiatric treatment.

The rules for exorcism said, "If it can be done conveniently, the possessed person should be led to church or to some other sacred and worthy place, were the exorcism will be held, away from the crowd. But if the person is ill, or for any valid reason, the exorcism may take place in a private home."

Hughes decided that Robbie belonged in a hospital, under restraints. Hughes may have been desperate. He had no one to confide in, nowhere to turn. A member of the parish, then in grade school, remembers "an old, white-haired, wispy sort of priest" wandering around the parish at that time. But Hughes, in his own terse and evasive account, makes no mention of consulting another priest.

The same young parishioner, then an altar boy, has another memory of Hughes: "One morning he came in and he looked awful. His face was mottled. It was like hives. He was exhausted, disheveled. He seemed caught up in something."

Robbie was admitted to Georgetown Hospital, part of the Jesuit-run Georgetown University-Georgetown University Medical School complex in Washington. Hughes seems to have done this on his own initiative, secretly, and without an attending physician. One report says that a psychiatrist arranged the admission and, when Robbie turned balky, summoned Hughes. Another report says that the hospital was well aware that an exorcism would take place. This seems more likely, since it was a Catholic hospital, and it had the atmosphere of one. Nuns, most of whom were nurses, glided along the corridors in white habits and white bonnets. Crucifixes hung on the walls, and Mass was said daily in the chapel.

On some day between Sunday February 27 and Sunday, March 6, Robbie was taken to Georgetown Hospital and admitted under an assumed name. The mother superior of nuns issued strict orders that no record was to be kept on the exorcism. On Hughes' orders, straps were attached to the bed and passed across the bedclothes covering Robbie's slight body. (The instructions for exorcism say the demoniac may be placed "in fetters if there is any danger.") Robbie lay on his back, his eyes closed. At this point there is little to go on but second-and third-hand reports. One says that Hughes entered wearing a doctor's surgical gown over his surplice and cassock and that Robbie, in a powerful voice, ordered Hughes to remove a cross that was there, but could not be seen. Another story—traced back to a priest who frequently visited the hospital— has a tray, carried into the room by a nun, sailing out of her hands and smashing against a wall.

A third report, made years later, describes the scene in these words: "There were crucifixes on the wall and nuns were the nurses. And the hospital bed rammed all the way across the room, all by itself. Scratch marks would suddenly appear on his chest while nuns were looking on. They couldn't keep the bed still." Another report, based on one of Hughes' own accounts, says that Robbie burst into curses in a strange language—later said to be Aramaic, a Semitic tongue spoken in biblical times. (A later, well-documented record on Robbie's case does not mention any such language competence.)

Hughes, following the rules, would have said Mass that day and offered special prayers for success. Over his black cassock he wore a starched white surplice. On his head, probably set straight rather than at its usual rakish angle, was his black biretta. Around his neck was a purple stole whose broad ends hung down the surplice. He walked into the room carrying a gleaming gold aspersorium half full of holy water. He began by sprinkling the room with holy water. He put the aspersorium on a table and approached the bed. Robbie still lay with his eyes closed. A nun and perhaps an orderly were probably in the room.

Hughes knelt at the side of the bed, *The Roman Ritual* in his hands. He began to recite the Litany of the Saints—the "Who's Who of Heaven," as pious jokesters like Hughes used to call it: "Holy Mother of God...St. Michael, St. Gabriel...All ye holy angels and archangels...All ye holy virgins and widows, All ye holy men and women, saints of God..." He asked God for delivery "from all evil, from all sin, from Thy wrath, from sudden and unlooked death, from the snares of the Devil." He would have said this in Latin, as he would have said the prayer that began with *"Ne reminiscaris, Domine..."* "Remember not, O Lord, our offenses, nor those of our parents: neither take retribution on our sins..." Finally, preparing for the actual prayers of exorcism, Hughes began saying the Our Father. *"Pater Noster..."*

The instructions told the exorcist to say the prayer "inaudibly" until he came to the phrase *"Et ne nos indúcas in tentatiónem"*— "And lead us not into temptation." At that point, the other persons in the room—probably a nurse and an orderly—were to end the prayer, audibly, with Hughes: *"Sed líbera nos a malo"*— "But deliver us from evil." Hughes was then to say a psalm and begin the first of the exorcism prayers.

One of Robbie's arms moved almost imperceptibly under the strap. He slipped his hand out of restraint. No one noticed when he reached his hand down the side of the bed and somehow worked a piece of the bedspring loose...

Hughes screamed and struggled to his feet, his left arm hanging limp. Blood was staining the surplice and stole. Robbie had slashed Hughes' arm from shoulder to wrist. To close the wound required more than one hundred stitches.

In his account of the exorcism, Hughes does not mention this incident. He did not continue the exorcism. He disappeared from

St. James soon after being wounded and reportedly suffered a breakdown. A long while later some of his former parishioners saw him preaching at Catholic churches elsewhere in the archdiocese. On the altar, he could raise only one hand when, during the most sacred moment of Mass, he held the consecrated host aloft. People who saw him then said he seemed haunted and withdrawn, as if he were forever looking inward.

Chapter 4

The Scratches Said St. Louis

After Robbie slashed Father Hughes, the boy was quickly discharged from the hospital, which hushed up the incident so well that few people on the medical staff knew anything had happened. In Mount Rainier, parishioners at St. James were told that their priest had met with an accident and would be away for some time. But rumors swept the parish. *That Mannheim boy! Stabbed Father Hughes! They say he barely escaped with his life.* People claimed they heard maniacal cries and saw lights radiating around the house. Robbie again became the hub of fear and turmoil. Neighbors who at first had joked about the haunted house and its bewitched boy now shunned the Mannheims. Police got anonymous calls asking them to investigate the goings-on at the Mannheim house.

There are some indications that the Mannheims quietly moved about this time, to a similar house about half a mile away. But no change of address would end the ordeal. After the slashing, Robbie seemed to plunge deeper into his spells, as his mother and father called them. Phyllis Mannheim was more convinced than ever that her son was in the grip of something evil, something not of this world. The Reverend Mr. Schulze had at first scoffed at the idea of demonic possession. But he had become convinced enough to call in a priest. And Father Hughes had been convinced enough to start an exorcism. Now he had given up, and Phyllis thought about doing the same. "They were ready to raise the white flag," says a priest who was later involved with the possession.

But Phyllis needed only to look at her son to know that she had to see this through, no matter what it was. He was, the doctors had said, the only child she would ever bear.

She and Karl talked about making another move, a temporary one. She was a native of St. Louis, Missouri, where both she and Karl had kin. They could take Robbie to the home of relatives there. Perhaps in a new setting, far from Mount Rainier, Robbie would be able to shake off whatever it was that seemed to have him in its power.

Robbie's parents were still discussing the plan about St. Louis when something happened that convinced them to go. One night, while Robbie was getting ready for bed, he looked in the bathroom mirror and screamed. His mother rushed into the bathroom. Robbie's pajama top hung open. He was trembling. Scrawled across his thin chest were scratches that spelled out in blood a single word: *Louis*.

Phyllis Mannheim tried to be calm. She took Robbie in her arms, felt his pounding heart next to hers. She led him into his bedroom. *We'll go to St. Louis*, she told him. *We'll go to St. Louis*. She began speaking rapidly, telling him she would start working on it right away. But it would take time. Karl Mannheim had to arrange time off from work. There were relatives to call, train tickets to buy…Robbie doubled up in pain and let out a moan. He pulled down his pajama pants. On his hip his mother saw blood ooze through his skin. It was as if scratches were emerging from him, as if something were clawing at him from the inside. The glistening scratches formed a word: *Saturday.*

Phyllis Mannheim was too stunned to sense that Robbie's body was acting like a Ouija board. She asked, *How long?* As he screamed and grimaced again, she realized, to her horror, that her question would cause him pain, forcing forth another answer in blood. Now on his chest it came: scratches that she read as meaning they would stay there: *3½ weeks.*

Schulze later wrote that he and his own physician "saw no words," but they both did see "nerve reaction rashes which had the appearance of scratches." Recalling what was said by the family at that time, Schulze wrote, "Now he has visions of the devil and goes into a trance and speaks in a strange language, they tell me. I am insisting that the family return here to their home and put the boy into a hospital under the care of a physician who is sympathetic to the case. My physician is sympathetic. Theirs went to the mental hygiene clinic only after insistence and persisted in trying to treat the boy with Barbitol [a barbiturate used primarily to sedate people]."

Robbie's mother disregarded Schulze's advice. She said later that she felt compelled to obey the messages. Reason would say that she should have resisted, since the force that was causing Robbie's torment had seemingly produced the awful bleeding messages. But earthly logic had long since departed from this family. Robbie's body had given them signs, and they would follow those signs.

On Saturday, March 5, Robbie, Phyllis, and Karl Mannheim went to Union Station in Washington, where they boarded an overnight train for St. Louis. Watching the scenery roll by, Phyllis Mannheim had an opportunity to look back over the past seven turbulent weeks and try to sort out what she had seen and experienced.

Aunt Harriet had been alive when it all began on January 15, when the scratching started. When she died on January 26, there seemed to have been a change: It was almost as if something were growing and getting closer to Robbie. Now it was inside him. Robbie's mother could not describe what she felt—the presence, the stalking. She had not written anything about what was happening. She had no way to compare one day with the next. But there was no doubt that things were changing. The scratchings that had been on a wall in January now were appearing on her son's body.

Had she been imagining all this? Phyllis began counting how many people she knew who had seen what she and Karl had seen: relatives, friends, ministers, a priest, nurses, nuns. And the teachers and kids at school. And the neighbors. Those friendly neighbors who had offered to help. Some had heard the rumors, and they had hinted that they believed Robbie had been playing tricks. Others had seen objects moving, apparently on their own. Phyllis completed her count with them. Fourteen. There were now fourteen people who had witnessed events for which there was no earthly explanation.

What was going on in Robbie's mind? Where had he got the strength—and the cunning—to slip his small hand down to the bedspring and work loose a crude weapon? Was he feeling rage when he slashed Father Hughes? What was driving this frail boy? And where was he being driven?

Deep in our folklore is an old phrase that we utter, not realizing what we say: *What on earth possessed him to do that?* Possession: the idea that some force could invade a soul and overpower it. We have buried that primitive fright under layers of logic and science. In our world, in Phyllis Mannheim's world, possession is the stuff of nightmares. But in other cultures, possession is an everyday reality, a belief shared by everyone in the community.

Phyllis and Karl Mannheim had no cultural belief in possession and, with the violent ending of the attempt at Georgetown Hospital, no faith in exorcism. They were parents who, while living in a world too sophisticated for possession, saw, across the chasm, a son writhing in a strange world where possession existed. How to reach him, how to save him became their quest. It was a quest without guides, but not without lore. To bring back Robbie they would have to venture into domains of superstition and the supernatural. They would be going where few had gone in modern times.

Religion divided the Mannheims' kin in St. Louis. Some were Catholic and some were Lutheran. All the relatives loved Robbie and sympathized with the Mannheims. Everyone offered help. When they arrived in St. Louis, Phyllis and Karl Mannheim faced a choice that reflected the conflict between Catholic and non-Catholic approaches to possession. In the wake of the devastating experience with Father Hughes, they decided to turn again to a Lutheran minister—and, incredibly, to a new form of Ouija board.

On Monday, March 7, at the St. Louis home of Lutheran relatives, Robbie's aunt and uncle gathered two or three other relatives around a porcelain kitchen table. One of them wrote the alphabet on a sheet of paper and held a pencil over it. They all sat in absolute silence, seeking what they called an alphabetical medium. The table moved, and the person holding the pencil underlined a letter. Another person at the table wrote the letter on another sheet of paper. The table moved again, and again the pencil-holder underlined a letter and the other person wrote it down next to the first.

And so it went—table motion, then underlined letter…table motion, then underlined letter—until the people at the table got their message. It was from Aunt Harriet: She was the spirit causing the unexplained phenomena. It was not the devil.

The relatives next went to a bedroom to watch Aunt Harriet prove that she was hovering around. While they stood there, a heavy bed moved about three feet. No one was near it.

Robbie had been off in a corner reading a comic book. Suddenly, he screamed and doubled up in pain. Phyllis, sensing what had happened, opened his shirt and saw the now familiar scratches oozing fresh blood. Coming so immediately after the moving-table message, the words, she thought, probably pertained to Aunt Harriet. Usually, those who saw the messages in blood later reported where on Robbie's body the writing appeared and what the words spelled out. But no information about this particular message was reported.

Robbie went to bed, and after a round of "Good night, Robbie," his relatives left him alone. Soon they heard noises in the bedroom and rushed in. The bed was shaking violently. Robbie lay quite still. Phyllis stepped close to the bed and bent to listen. She could hear the scratching, up and down the mattress, as if some beast were inside trying to get out. Some relatives approached the bed and stood near her. They, too, later said they heard the scratching. All night long people went in and out of the bedroom to watch the bed shaking and listen to the scratching. Robbie slept fitfully, but when he was awake he was strangely calm.

Next day, Tuesday, March 8, the Mannheims moved to the home of other relatives—-Robbie's Catholic Aunt Catherine, who was married to Karl Mannheim's brother, George. Like Karl, George had been brought up Catholic but was not a practicing Catholic. He had married in a Catholic church to satisfy his wife's family. As a condition for this "mixed marriage," as the Catholic Church referred to it, George Mannheim had agreed that he and Catherine would raise their children as Catholics. They had two sons and a daughter. Billy was younger than Robbie. Marty was about Robbie's age. Elizabeth attended St. Louis University, a Jesuit institution.

Like all of the Mannheims' St. Louis relatives, George and Catherine had heard every detail of Robbie's ordeal. They knew also that Phyllis' side of the family had called on a local Lutheran minister to help. His arrival and departure had been much swifter than the Reverend Mr. Schulze's. In a reprise of what had happened back in Maryland, the Lutheran minister in St. Louis suspected diabolical possession and urged that a Catholic priest see Robbie. After that recommendation, the minister hastily departed.

Karl and Phyllis—especially Phyllis—resisted the idea of calling in another priest. Phyllis still clung to the belief, eerily verified by the moving-table seance, that Aunt Harriet, for some unknown reason, was haunting Robbie. Phyllis would rather have a ghostly aunt possessing her son than a demon in league with Satan. And the slashing of Father Hughes had unnerved her. Robbie might scream and writhe, beds might move, and vases might fly. But there had been no violence until the Catholic exorcism had started. That was the association in Phyllis' mind: exorcism and violence.

All day Tuesday Robbie seemed content enough. When his cousin Marty came home from school, the two boys played. Suppertime passed without incident. Later, among themselves, the four adults congratulated each other on pulling Robbie out of what had been plaguing him. Phyllis began thinking of the *3½ weeks* message, and decided that Robbie, who had missed so many days of school already, should be enrolled in Marty's school.

She called Robbie over and told him her decision. Robbie looked at her coldly, grimaced for an instant, and opened his shirt. The scratches said: *No School.* At another time, when she mentioned school, Robbie held up his wrists. Scratches outlined a red *NO* on each wrist. Then he lifted his trousers. On each leg was a large *N.* She shuddered. This was not Robbie. There was some new power within him. She said later that she felt she was reading an order from someone. She was afraid. There would be no more talk of school.

On Tuesday night, Robbie went to bed with Marty. The adults filed in and out of the bedroom for a round of uneasy good nights. The boys seemed fine. They looked the way they had looked on other visits, two cousins sleeping over, ready to horse around as soon as the parents left. A few minutes later, sounds started coming from the bedroom.

To Phyllis and Karl, the sounds were maddeningly familiar. To George and Catherine, they were frighteningly new. All four rushed into the bedroom. Scratching sounds seemed to come from everywhere, but they apparently originated in the mattress. As everyone watched, the mattress flopped up and down furiously. Then it started to move forward, pressing toward the corner posters at the bottom of the bed. Both boys lay on their backs, perfectly still.

Now it was the turn of Marty's parents to know fear. Their own son lay inside this vibrating, scratching menace that had seized his bedroom. Their own home had been invaded. Something had to be done about it. Catherine felt a deep need for a priest.

Elizabeth Mannheim, after being told what had happened in Marty's bedroom, suggested that she talk to one of her Jesuit teachers at St. Louis University. Maybe he would know what to do. To Robbie's parents, especially Phyllis, a priest meant more violence, more madness. But they could not object. This was not their home. And what if Catherine were right? What if Marty now was in danger? They agreed to let Elizabeth speak to a Jesuit.

Chapter 5

A Priestly Blessing

Next day, Elizabeth approached her favorite teacher, Father Raymond J. Bishop, S.J., the forty-three-year-old head of the Department of Education and a superb teacher of prospective teachers. Bishop was a good listener, and he always had time for his students. He also had a quality that he shared with many other members of the Society of Jesus: He was a priest who was devout but did not act pious.

Bishop saw the concern on Elizabeth's face and immediately juggled his schedule to meet with her. Like nearly all Jesuits, Bishop had spent his career teaching boys and men. St. Louis University had been an all-male institution until it began admitting women after the war. Co-education was still somewhat of a novelty on the campus in 1949, as was the giving of advice to women students on personal matters. Bishop braced himself for the meeting.

He felt a sense of relief when she began by telling him it was something about her young cousin from out of town. Then she told Bishop what had happened in the two St. Louis area homes that Robbie had visited—the moving furniture, the scratches on Robbie's body, the feeling of menace. Mostly she told of what she had seen in her own home and how her little brother had been caught up in what had first puzzled and then terrified the two households.

Bishop would later say that he had sensed from the beginning that Robbie was threatened with possession. But he did not share his suspicions with Elizabeth. He kept his priestly instinct to himself, while he thought about what possession was and how it could be proved. If Robbie were possessed, there were certain signs that he would have to see for himself. He needed to find out more about Robbie. But before he did that, he decided to talk to other Jesuits. He told Elizabeth he would get back to her as soon as possible.

Bishop then sought out Father Laurence J. Kenny, S.J., a man renowned for his warmth and wisdom. Kenny, who was in his nineties, had only recently retired as a professor of history. He was the confessor to many of the priests in the Jesuit community at the university. He had been around long enough to have seen and heard a wider range of human vice and virtue than anyone else in the community. (He later recalled meeting a Lutheran minister who came to the university on behalf of Robbie. As Bishop told it, Elizabeth had first come to him. Both events may have happened. The family, with Catholic and Lutheran branches, was using both churches in search of relief.)

After hearing what Elizabeth had told Bishop, Kenny, too, suspected that this was a case of possession. He urged a meeting with Father Paul Reinert, S.J., president of the university.

There is a surface sameness about Jesuits in their black cassocks. All of them get the same long and rigorous training. Most of them live out their careers in the same province, as a Jesuit administrative region is called. Those who are around the same age have had the same teachers, have been to the same seminaries and universities, have read the same textbooks, have heard the same stories, and have told the same jokes. Their discipline creates a climate of sameness. They are controlled by rules and regulations as strict as those of a military organization, which, in fact, was the model for the Society of Jesus. But within that black-robed society are individuals as diverse as soldiers of the French Foreign Legion. A Jesuit typically is very much an individual, opinionated and bristling with proudly honed quirks.

Each of the three priests conferring over Robbie spoke from different experience and from a different facet of the Jesuit ethic. Bishop, bright and logical, knew that he had let his intuition eclipse his reason. He was allowing the medieval belief in possession to arise at a modern university. But he sensed something deeply wrong and needed counsel. Kenny, old and wise, believed that whatever it was that had prowled the world in the Middle Ages could still lurk in twentieth-century shadows. Reinert, taking his university through a crucial time, did not need an added burden. He was a scholar in the harness of a reluctant administrator. "There is something insidious," he once said, "about the effect of administration on a man's mentality." He had taken a vow of obedience, however, and since he had been ordered to be a university president, he had become one.

Reinert was proud of his university, and dedicated to it. He did not want Bishop to plunge headlong into what could be an embarrassing episode for St. Louis University. He believed that the university, intellectual center of the Missouri Province, was playing an important role in an effort on the part of many American Jesuits to take the Society of Jesus—and American Catholicism—into a new era. Reinert's campus housed the controversial Institute of Social Order, a liberal think tank founded by American Jesuits against the counsel of critics in Rome and within their own U.S. ranks. Jesuits of the university community had been on the front lines in the war over desegregating St. Louis.

The Institute of Social Order had pioneered Jesuit efforts to end segregation in the city. Jesuits had run four black parishes, as well as all-black schools, employment bureaus, summer camps, and a retreat house. Passions had flared over the issue, and Reinert's predecessor had angrily expelled the most vociferous Jesuit from the community. But in 1944, the university became the first educational institution in Missouri to integrate. Three years later, the Most Reverend Joseph E. Ritter, Archbishop of St. Louis, desegregated the archdiocese.

Jesuits are used to operating outside the Catholic hierarchy of pope-to-bishop-to-pastor. The Jesuit hierarchy is made up of Jesuits. Each province operates under a Father Provincial, who reports to the Superior General in Rome, and he is under the authority of the Pope. Historically, Jesuits have often clashed with the Vatican, and in those conflicts the power of the black-robed Superior General had won him the epithet of the Black Pope.

In 1949, the Jesuits and the Vatican were at peace. But, as always, the Jesuits were a group apart. When Jesuits wrote to each other about Jesuit matters, they often referred to the Society as *Ours*, as in, say, a historical reference—"When Ours first went to St. Louis…" Many American Jesuits had more faith in themselves than in the central authority of Rome, more interest in this world than any that might lie beyond. When a Jesuit of the Institute wrote an article, his subject was more often about social justice than about spiritual devotions. American Catholicism is formed around the parish, an ecclesiastical neighborhood that often coincides with the secular neighborhood. Each pastor is under the supervision of a bishop or, in metropolitan areas, an archbishop. Jesuit communities at such institutions as St. Louis University, are under dual control. The Father Provincial governs the Jesuits and their activities in his province; the bishop or archbishop governs some of the spiritual activities of the Jesuit priests. Without his permission, they cannot say Mass, perform marriages, dispense Holy Communion, or even preside over the funeral and burial of a Catholic under his jurisdiction.

This presented Reinert with another problem. If Father Bishop's strange story turned out to be a possible case of diabolical possession, then Reinert's university would have to deal with Ritter's archdiocese on the question of performing an exorcism. Just as Father Hughes had had to get Archbishop O'Boyle's permission to perform an exorcism, Father Bishop would have to get the consent of Archbishop Ritter. Relations between the university and the archdiocese were fine. Ritter, like Reinert, fostered modern religious thinking, and obviously they saw eye-to-eye on the morality of desegregation. But how, Reinert thought, could he hand over this medieval enigma to Ritter? What effect would an exorcism have on the Jesuits' relationship with Ritter? What would the non-Catholic public think about a university that had resurrected such superstition?

Not long before, the Society of Jesus had changed the tasks of the presidents of Jesuit universities, who had also been rectors, responsible for the spiritual well being of both the university and the Jesuit community. Now another Jesuit was rector, and Reinert had no direct responsibility for solving what was essentially a spiritual problem. But he did talk to Bishop.

Bishop later reported that he spoke to Kenny and Rinert. He did not mention speaking to the rector. One fact is certain, however: in that initial discussion of Elizabeth's appeal for help, the Jesuit community decided that Jesuits were duty-bound to solve the problem. The rector could have simply ordered Bishop to tell Elizabeth, a practicing Catholic, to go to a priest in her own parish. But, by doing that, the rector would have been rebuffing Elizabeth and ignoring the spiritual responsibilities felt by Bishop and Kenny. And, if Elizabeth did seek counsel from a parish priest, he would have to go to Ritter to receive permission to perform an exorcism—and Ritter would discover that the Jesuits of St. Louis University had been pusillanimous.

Anyone who had ever learned Latin from a Jesuit teacher has heard that word. Imparting a lesson in etymology and ethics simultaneously, Jesuit teachers point out that *pusillus* meant "very small" and *animus* meant "soul." Cowardice is not just a matter of ignoble fear; cowardice shrinks the soul. This is not the Jesuit way.

Bishop did not record exactly what Reinert said. But he obviously did not want to plunge into anything blindly. He advised Bishop: *Go to the house, give it a priestly blessing, and see for yourself what's going on. Then we'll decide what to do next.*

Elizabeth had chosen well. Bishop was open and responsive to her, as he was to all his students. "He was a very kind person," said a Jesuit who knew him well. "He was a sensitive man." He was also a man who had been serving people for most of his life. Born of German immigrants in Glencoe, Minnesota, he attended a parochial school in his hometown, then went on to a secular high school. He wanted to be a teacher, so he enrolled in the Normal Training Department of Glencoe Public High School. After a year's training, he spent a year teaching in rural Minnesota schools. He then entered the University of Minnesota to become a pharmacist. There he decided to change his life and become a Jesuit.

His training, like that of every Jesuit, followed traditions that trace back to the founding of the Society of Jesus in 1540 by Ignatius of Loyola, a Basque nobleman and soldier. While convalescing from a battle wound, Ignatius read a book on the lives of the saints and was inspired to hang up his sword and begin a life dedicated to God. He founded a religious order unlike any that had gone before. Members of the Society of Jesus were not to be contemplative monks. They were to be soldiers of Christ, men "ready to live in any part of the world where there was hope of God's greater glory and the good of souls."

Bishop entered the Society in 1927 and took up a spiritual system of discipline and studies—*Ratio Studiorum*—little changed since the sixteenth century. After a few months of probation, he began a two-year novitiate devoted to prayer and meditation, interspersed with humbling menial chores. Moving in silence through a tightly scheduled day, he was paced by bells. There were, as a Jesuit of that era wrote, "bells for rising, bells for meditation, bells for Mass, bells for breakfast, bells for classes…" At the end of the novitiate, he took vows of obedience, chastity, and poverty. He could put *S.J.* after his name and a biretta on his head. For the next eleven years he was known as a scholastic, a Jesuit on his way to priesthood.

For Bishop, the silence and the bell-measured days continued at St. Stanislaus Seminary in the farmlands of Florissant, Missouri, on the outskirts of St. Louis. There he studied Greek and Latin for two years, then three years of philosophy. All classes were in Latin, as were the debates staged to test both a scholastic's knowledge and his ability to think and speak on his feet. Scholastics lived a life of study, isolation, and humiliation. They were given a list of twenty-five *culpas*, or faults—among them, "obeying with reluctance," "want of punctuality," and "speaking to others harshly, peremptorily, or sarcastically." Anyone who succumbed to a fault had to admit to it publicly.

In his seventh year, a scholastic is given an assignment that interrupts his seminary studies. Usually he is assigned to teach in a Jesuit high school for two or three years. Bishop's assignment was the high school operated by St. Louis University. Next came four years of theology. At the end of the third year, the Jesuit is ordained a priest and is a scholastic no more. He is at last addressed as *Father*, rather than *Mister*. By the time he is ordained, he has been in the Society for thirteen years. Then begins a year of tertianship, meaning the third trial period (the first being the brief probation and the second the novitiate). At least part of a tertianship is usually devoted to priestly, rather than scholarly, work.

All of these fourteen or fifteen years add up to what the Society calls the "formation" of a Jesuit. When Bishop's formation ended, he was assigned to Rockhurst College in Kansas City, where he was to become the dean of the College of Arts and Sciences. But his career was abruptly changed by the sudden illness of the director of the Department of Education at St. Louis University. Bishop was ordered to St. Louis to assist the ill director. When he died, Bishop took over. He had been head of the department for about seven years when Elizabeth asked to talk to him about Robbie.

After conferring with Reinert, Bishop called Elizabeth and told her he would like to see Robbie as soon as possible. That evening, Wednesday, March 9, a member of the family picked Bishop up at the university and took him home. The car pulled up in front of a substantial, two-story brick house set back behind a front yard lawn on a quiet street in a suburb a few miles northwest of St. Louis. Elizabeth introduced Bishop to her parents and then ushered him into another room to meet with Robbie's parents. Dealing again with a priest, Karl and Phyllis Mannheim were at first shy and awkward. As far as they were concerned, this quiet-spoken, kindly Father Bishop was just another priest like Father Hughes. They would not have realized that there was a profound difference between Father Hughes, a young parish priest on his own, and Father Bishop, a priest who could draw upon the resources of the Society of Jesus.

The Mannheims soon warmed to Bishop and went over what had been happening to them and to their son since January 15. Bishop questioned them gently, probing for inconsistencies in their stories, getting details, taking notes. *Where was Robbie when the fruit flew in the kitchen? About that incident with the chair: You then sat in the chair yourself, Mr. Mannheim? And you say, Mrs. Mannheim, that you have listed fourteen witnesses? And what exactly did each one see?* Bishop was trying to keep his interview unemotional and non-religious. It was an exercise in logic and reasoning, a search for facts.

The Mannheims told him about the Ouija board, the kitchen-table seance, the death of Aunt Harriet. They said they had talked to a psychiatrist in St. Louis, but, like the psychiatrist in Maryland, he had been of no help. The parents were curiously reticent in talking about their experience with Father Hughes. For some reason known only to themselves, they told Bishop that Hughes had not met Robbie in person. They also said that they understood that Hughes had taken steps toward performing an exorcism but had not done so. They may not have wished to tell Bishop about the slashing of Hughes at Georgetown Hospital. Whatever the reason, Bishop did not learn of the abortive hospital exorcism.

Bishop next talked to Robbie and found him to be like many of the freshmen whom Bishop, as a scholastic, had taught in St. Louis University High School: quiet, not very athletic, bored by books, but ready to learn. Not the kind of boy who makes trouble for his parents. Yet, the Mannheims had told him that Robbie had turned unruly, had threatened to run away, and seemed to be on the verge of violence. It was as if something were trying to seize him, they told Bishop. They had only scant knowledge of the phenomenon called possession, but what they said alerted Bishop. He was greatly disturbed by what he was hearing, but he tried not to show it.

Bishop went from room to room, blessing each one by softly murmuring prayers in Latin and making the sign of the Cross with his upraised right hand. Bishop had brought with him holy water blessed in the name of St. Ignatius, who is said to have performed an exorcism. Bishop sprinkled the holy water as he gave his blessing. In the bedroom that Robbie was using, Bishop gave what he later called "a special blessing," which he repeated over Robbie's bed.

The "priestly blessing" that Reinert had advised was a low-level exorcism against what theologians call infestation, the mildest form of diabolical activity. The phenomena that the Mannheims had reported to Bishop—scratchings in the wall and floor, noises, flying objects—may have indicated that demons were stalking sites around Robbie. Such a diabolical presence, according to long-held belief, could be countered by a mild form of exorcism, the exorcism of a place.

Bishop, following that old Christian tradition, was trying to rid a place of unearthly powers. "Places—churches, houses, towns, countryside—may be strained and influenced by a variety of causes, and frequently by more than one of them at a time," a Catholic treatise on exorcism explains. A site, says the treatise, could be infested by ghosts; by magicians dabbling in the occult; by repeated sinful activities (such as at the site of ancient fertility-cult rites); by "place memories" of sin or violence; by poltergeists. These causes are not necessarily demonic and are not subject to exorcism. But, just in case demonic interference is involved, "it is sound general principle to conduct an exorcism in general."

In 1599, a Jesuit, Martin Del Rio, had set down descriptions of eighteen kinds of demons or demonic apparitions. The sixteenth kind included "spectres which in certain times and places or homes are wont to occasion various commotions and annoyances," spirits that might disturb a sleeper's slumber "with clattering of pots and hurling of stones, and, having pulled away his mattress, turned him out of his bed." This description, so typical of the behavior of a poltergeist, also covers the kind of annoyances endured by an apparent victim during the infestation stage of possession.

Bishop would have known that by now it no longer seemed to matter where Robbie was; he was plagued wherever he went. Chances were that "the case," as Bishop later called it, already had progressed from infestation to the next stage, obsession. In that stage, according to a theological definition published in 1906, "the demon never makes him [the victim] lose consciousness but nevertheless torments him in such a manner that his [the demon's] action is manifest."

The scratchings and thumpings in Robbie's house, back in Maryland, would have been signs of the infestation stage. The scratches on Robbie's body, which Bishop had not yet seen for himself, indicated obsession. What had not yet appeared were indications of the third stage: actual possession, defined by the same 1906 source as a state produced when a demon makes the victim "lose consciousness and then seems to play in his body the part of the soul: he uses, at least to all appearances, his eyes to see with, his ears to listen with, his mouth to speak with…It is he [the victim] who suffers as if from a burn if his skin is touched with an object which has been blessed."

Bishop had also brought a relic, which he attached, with a safety pin, to a corner of the pillow on Robbie's bed. The cloth pouch contained a tiny bit of material, enclosed in a small glass case. The fragment, too old and infinitesimal to be readily identified, was a second-class relic of St. Margaret Mary. A second-class relic is a remnant of something reputedly touched by a saint—a shred of clothing, a sliver of wood. A first-class relic is from the saint's body; usually it is a chip of bone or a lock of hair.

Jesuits were especially devoted to St. Margaret Mary Alacoque, a seventeenth-century French nun, because her spiritual adviser was a Jesuit. He encouraged her when, against initial opposition within the Church, she started what became worldwide devotions to the Sacred Heart of Jesus. In pinning her relic to Robbie's pillow, Bishop was invoking the intercession of a woman who had claimed to have experienced a moment of mystical union with Jesus. She said that Jesus had appeared before her, placed her heart inside his own, "and made me see that mine was like a tiny atom which was consumed in that ardent furnace. Then he drew it out like a burning heart-shaped flame, and put it back in the spot from which he had taken it." Catholic immigrants brought the practice of revering the Sacred Heart to the United States. Devotion focused on an image found in countless U.S. Catholic churches and homes: Jesus looking out from a painting or lithograph and revealing his flaming, bleeding heart, wreathed in a crown of thorns. Undoubtedly, Bishop had grown up seeing that image in his own home.

When it was time for Robbie to go to bed, the boy went upstairs. A few minutes later, Bishop went into Robbie's bedroom and bid him good night. Bishop then returned to the first floor for a few more words with Robbie's parents and uncle and aunt before he would be driven back to—.

Suddenly, they all heard something. They stopped talking and listened. The noises—thumpings, bangings—came from the second floor. Then Robbie screamed, and they all rushed to the stairs.

Chapter 6

The Nights of the Priests

At Robbie's bedroom door, the others stood aside for Father Bishop. He saw Robbie's mattress moving back and forth. "The boy lay perfectly still," Bishop later reported, "and did not exert any physical effort. The movement in one direction did not exceed more than three inches, the action was intermittent and completely subsided after a period of approximately fifteen minutes."

Bishop took out the little bottle of holy water blessed in St. Ignatius' name and sprinkled it on the bed in the form of the sign of the cross. "The movement ceased quite abruptly," Bishop wrote in his imperturbable, third-person style, "but began again when Father stepped out of the room."

Robbie cried out—"a sharp pain seemed to have struck R. on his stomach," as Bishop described it. Mrs. Mannheim rushed to the bed and pulled back the covers. She lifted Robbie's pajama top enough "to show ziz-zag scratches in bold red lines on the boy's abdomen." Bishop precisely noted that "during the fifteen minutes the boy was not out of the view of six observers"—Father Bishop, Robbie's parents, uncle and aunt, and, presumably, cousin Elizabeth.

The mattress soon stopped shaking, and everyone left the room. Robbie looked as if he were about to drop off to sleep. It was fifteen minutes after eleven.

The next day, Thursday, March 10, Father Bishop began talking to a close friend, Father William S. Bowdern, S.J. Robbie's cries echoed in Bishop's mind as he recounted what he had seen and heard. Bowdern, puffing on the inevitable Camel, listened intently. This was not some Jesuit discussion about the fine points of Augustinian theology. This was about a boy, a thirteen-year-old boy in some kind of spiritual trouble, and Bowdern was immediately interested. He spent far more time dealing with troubled people than with theology.

Unlike the overwhelming majority of Jesuits in the community, Bowdern did not teach. He was pastor of St. Francis Xavier Church, named after a 16th-Century Jesuit who was one of the six men in Ignatius' original Society of Jesus. St. Francis Xavier Church was better known as Xavier or the College Church. Although built and run primarily to serve the students and faculty of the university, Xavier was also a parish church that served the large Catholic community around the university. The church itself, modeled after a cathedral in Ireland, was built of native limestone trimmed with Bedford stone. It has a strong, imposing Gothic air with a great pillared nave and soaring fan vaulting. Architectural critics have called it a fine example of nineteenth-century Revival English Gothic.

As pastor, Bowdern answered to the rector of the university and to Archbishop Ritter, who, as Ordinary of the archdiocese, was the superior of all priests in his jurisdiction. But in reality Bowdern had a great deal of autonomy. Though a member of the Jesuit community, he was not part of the university faculty, and he belonged more to his parishioners than to the Jesuit community. It was said of him that he had not missed a wake in St. Louis for the past ten years.

While Jesuits of the community lived in a communal house and ate their meals at the refectory table, Bowdern lived, like any pastor, in a rectory, a small wooden house nestled between the church and a Jesuit residence called Verhagen Hall.

Bowdern was the administrator of a busy church, with a full schedule of baptisms, weddings, sick calls, funerals, and wakes. He was accessible to anyone who knocked on the rectory door, and he never seemed to tire of listening to the people who came to him with their fears and misdeeds. One or two new Jesuit priests were assigned to him as assistant pastors, usually for a few months at a time. They were young, had just been ordained, and were on their one-year tertianship, a respite of spiritual service before they got their first major academic or scholarly assignments.

Bowdern, fifty-two and a native of St. Louis, had joined the Society of Jesus at the age of seventeen, after completing high school at St. Louis University Academy (later called St. Louis University High School). He was short, stocky, black-haired and square-jawed with a reputation for cool, decisive action. He smoked Camels incessantly.

After ordination he was made principal of the high school at St. Mary's College in Kansas, where he had taught during his scholastic years. He moved on to St. Louis University High School, where he became principal. He then was appointed rector of Campion Jesuit High in Prairie du Chien, Wisconsin. In 1942 he began a four-year tour as a U.S. Army chaplain, serving in both the

European and China-Burma-India theaters. Soon after getting out of the army in 1946 he became pastor of the College Church.

Bowdern was a professed Jesuit, a distinction not readily understood outside the Society. The process begins near the end of the period of philosophical training, when Jesuit scholastics are given a grueling comprehensive oral examination, in Latin. Those who score higher than six out of ten are put in what was known as the long course. The others are assigned to the short course.

Although both sets of scholastics study for the same length of time, the "short" and "long" indicate the intensity and depth of the course of study each has been assigned. A Jesuit who successfully passes the first oral examination and a later one in theology is professed, provided his moral character also is deemed to be sufficiently distinguished. He takes a fourth vow: obedience to the pope. Several times in their history the Jesuits have had problems with the Vatican, and this fourth vow is a gesture underlining Jesuit acceptance of papal authority.

Professed Jesuits are qualified for posts of authority, such as Father Provincial (the head of a province) or the president of a university. Usually, only professed Jesuits can teach philosophy and theology. Jesuits who are not professed are known as "spiritual coadjutors." In everyday practice, Jesuits do not distinguish each other as professed or coadjutor. But the designation is in their personnel records and it had an effect on careers. As one Jesuit explained it, "Instead of being the vehicle of the Society accepting you, you vow to obey the Pope and never make a move to diminish the Society. You accept the Society."

So Bowdern, as a professed Jesuit, did not outrank his friend Bishop, who was not professed. But, as a rector, he had been on a different career track. To many of the younger Jesuits in the community, Bowdern was more mentor than colleague. Although Bishop and Bowdern had forged a friendship in the St. Louis Jesuit community, their relationship on this day in March was complex. Bishop wanted, and got, from Bowdern the advice of a friend. He also got counsel from a man who, as one Jesuit described him, was "totally fearless."

Bishop did not later report on his conversation with Bowdern, and it is risky to speculate on what they discussed. Jesuits, with their Ours view of the Society, are not easily perceived or analyzed by an outsider. But it is reasonable to assume that Bishop saw himself as a teacher who had been drawn into something that was beyond his knowledge or experience. It would make sense to hand "the case," as he referred to it, over to someone who would bring more experience to bear—Bowdern the pastor, Bowdern the Army chaplain. Given the complexities that Jesuits can weave around moral issues, there may have been another reason: Bishop considered Bowdern to be a holy man. To Jesuits, there is a meaningful distinction between pious and holy. Piety can be seen or acted out; holiness is internal, soulful, and, if need be, tough.

A Jesuit who knew them both believed that, of the two, Bishop was the more pious—a word avoided by most Jesuits, who are notoriously hard-bitten about their religion. Jesuits rigorously defend their faith, relying more on reason than revelation. Bishop, with his second-class relic and St. Ignatius holy water, seemed to have acted in a pious way, if piety is an overabundance of faith. It smacked of credulity, which, to a Jesuit, was an intellectual offense.

A less pious Jesuit would have asked probing questions, investigated the family background, and would have hesitated before so quickly crossing the threshold of reason and entering the realm of mystery. And yet Bishop had witnessed something that seemed beyond reason. He would later write that he had seen the mattress shake, had seen the zigzag scratches appearing on Robbie's body. Bishop soon did start asking questions and looking into the background of the case. But his initial instinct had been to react piously, and as a result he had crossed the threshold.

After his first entry into Robbie's world, Bishop may not have wanted to rely on his own sense of piety. He may have wanted a witness he could trust, a priestly witness. And he had a good candidate in his friend Bowdern, a staunch, seasoned priest who had seen the face of war, a Jesuit whom other Jesuits called a holy man.

By the time the two priests had finished talking on that Thursday evening, Robbie was in bed, after an uneventful day. A short time later, the mattress started shaking again. Sounds of scratching filled the room and beat a rhythm like that of tramping feet. It was as if something were marching toward Robbie. The safety pin on his pillow opened by itself and the relic arced to the floor, as if it had been tossed there.

On Friday, Elizabeth told Bishop what had happened the night before. Bishop said he would return to the house that night with Father Bowdern. Elizabeth arranged for her father to pick up Bishop and Bowdern, who did not drive, at the College Church about ten o'clock.

Bowdern was nearing the end of an exhausting novena, nine days of special devotions at the College Church. Each day there were prayer services at noon, in the afternoon, at suppertime, and at nine o'clock in the evening. Bowdern officiated, giving a homily at each service. He was not a great preacher. He tended to repeat words for emphasis. But his homilies, drawn from everyday life, were always well received. The major service, complete with choir, was at nine o'clock on Friday night. The church was packed for the end of the novena, in honor of the church's patron saint, Francis Xavier.

Bowdern was a devout man, and his three years as pastor at the College Church had made him aware of the value of relics, holy water, votive candles, and other accouterments of faith. They were not the stuff of reasoned theological arguments over good and evil; they were legacies from the days of the medieval church. But Bowdern knew that relics and holy water often gave comfort and invoked calm and even healing. So, when he set off for the house where Robbie was staying, he took with him two relics. One was a first-class relic of St. Francis Xavier, a symbol of the kind of traditional Catholicism that disconcerted those Jesuits who wanted their religion to become more appealing to modern Catholics.

Xavier, a missionary in India and Japan, died in 1552 on a desolate island off Canton (Guangzhou), China, and was buried there. Two months later, his grave and coffin were opened. Accounts of the time say his body had not decayed, a familiar assertion about potential candidates for sainthood. The body was taken to Goa, the capital of the Portuguese enclave in India, and enshrined in a church. The Jesuit Superior General ordered the right arm of the corpse to be severed at the elbow and brought to Rome, where it was placed in the altar of a church.

What Father Bowdern was taking to the house was a piece of bone from Xavier's right arm. The relic rested in velvet lining, behind glass, in a gold reliquary that looked like a tiny monstrance. Bowdern also brought a crucifix that had been hollowed out to house two first-class relics. One was that of St. Peter Canisius, a sixteenth-century Jesuit theologian who founded half a dozen colleges and was a zealous Counter-Reformation writer and preacher. The other relic was from a collective group of saints known as the

North American Martyrs, six Jesuits and two lay assistants killed by Indians in French America during the seventeenth century.

When the two priests were ushered into the house, it was some time after ten o'clock. Bishop introduced Bowdern, who told Robbie's parents that he was also going to give a priestly blessing. Like Bishop, Bowdern was able to draw upon years of experience in dealing with boys Robbie's age. He chatted with Robbie, probing gently about what had been happening. Then Robbie went upstairs to get ready for bed. He was occupying his cousin Marty's room. Marty was sleeping in another room. Robbie's parents said goodnight to him about eleven o'clock. A few minutes later he yelled for help.

The priests, Robbie's parents, Elizabeth and her parents all dashed up the stairs and into Robbie's room. He was sitting up, his face pale. On other nights when something happened, he had been passive and seemingly unaware of what went on around him. Tonight he looked like a scared kid.

Robbie said that he had felt some kind of force in the room. The safety pin on the relic of St. Margaret Mary had opened, and the relic had risen from the pillow, sailed across the room, and struck a mirror. "It sounded like a pebble hitting," he said. The mirror did not break.

He held up his left arm. On the outer forearm were two scratches in the form of a cross. Father Bishop leaned closer to examine the scratches and asked if they hurt. "The pain," Bishop later wrote, "was similar to that produced by a scratch of a thorn. The cross remained evident for approximately forty-five minutes."

Father Bowdern, inwardly jolted by what he had seen, calmly read the novena prayer of St. Francis Xavier and blessed Robbie by moving the Xavier reliquary over him in the sign of the cross. Only

Bowdern and Bishop realized that a fragment from a bone in a saint's forearm was being used to bless a boy who had just manifested a bloody cross on his own forearm.

Bowdern pinned the crucifix reliquary under Robbie's pillow, next to the relic of St. Margaret Mary. This time there was no shaking of the mattress, no scratching, no tramping of feet.

Everyone bade Robbie good night again and went downstairs, where Bishop began collecting facts. He decided to rely on what he had been trained for: rational thinking and judgment. He started by making up a dossier on the boy and his family. Headed *Case Study,* it begins with Robbie's name, address, birth, and religion. It continues:

> *Maternal Grandmother*—practicing Catholic until
> the age of fourteen years.
> *Paternal Grandfather*—Baptized Catholic but no
> practice.
> *Father*—Baptized Catholic but no instruction or
> practice.
> *Mother*—Baptized Lutheran.

Upstairs, all was still. Downstairs, Bishop was getting this information, along with accounts of events going back to January. Bowdern would ask an occasional question but he left most of the interviewing to Bishop. The priests were about to leave when from upstairs came a loud crashing sound.

Again everyone converged on Robbie's room. Robbie said he had been dozing when a bottle of holy water, left by Father Bishop on Wednesday, flew from a table, about two feet from Robbie's bed, and landed six feet away, in a corner of the room. Although it hit the floor hard, it did not break.

Bowdern, without a word, took his rosary out of his pocket and placed it around Robbie's neck. He stood on one side of the bed and motioned Bishop to the other side. Together, they began to recite the rosary. Robbie, as a Lutheran, would have recognized one of the prayers. "Our Father, Who art in heaven," the priests began. But they ended the prayer with "deliver us from evil" and did not add the "For Thine is the power" phrase used by Protestants. He did not notice, and, in fact, almost no one ever did, that the "deliver us from evil" phrase of the Our Father was a mild form of exorcism.

Then, "Hail, Mary, full of grace...blessed is the fruit of thy womb, Jesus...pray for us sinners..." To Robbie, these were strange words coming from these strangers in their black suits and round white collars. And the words were repeated again and again as Father Bishop's fingers moved over the black beads like the ones around Robbie's neck. He looked down and touched them...Robbie calmed down as the prayers droned on, until the tenth Our Father and the fiftieth Hail Mary marked the end of the rosary. Then Bowdern, in a spontaneous homily, told Robbie about three children around his age who had seen something that other people had not seen.

Bowdern's story was about Our Lady of Fatima, a vision that appeared to three children who were tending sheep near Fatima, Portugual in 1917. Bowdern told Robbie that the beautiful woman in the vision was the mother of Jesus—the Mary in the Hail Mary prayers that the priests had just said. She called herself Our Lady of the Rosary and told children to say the rosary, which the priests had just done. Bowdern talked a little about Our Lady of Fatima. Prayers said to her, he said, reached Jesus, and he responded to the prayers.

His words calmed Robbie, who sleepily said good night. Each priest blessed Robbie one more time and then, about twelve-thirty, the priests were driven back to the campus. The long night had finally ended.

But, about five minutes after Elizabeth's father left with the priests, the exhausted people downstairs—Elizabeth, her mother, Robbie's mother and father—heard a heavy scraping noise in Robbie's room. They dragged themselves up the stairs one more time and turned toward Robbie's room. They found their way into the room blocked by a heavy bookcase, whose back was to the door. The bookcase had been on the other side of the bed. Phyllis Mannheim peered around the bookcase. Her son still lay there, again looking confused and frightened. A stool that had been in front of a dressing table now stood near the bottom of the bed.

She pushed her way into the room and lay on the bed, comforting Robbie. Robbie's aunt and Elizabeth managed to move the bookcase to its place alongside the bed. They put the stool back in front of the dressing table. Then everyone but Phyllis left. She remained on the bed with Robbie.

They were still trying to sleep when both of them, Phyllis said later, sensed a force entering the room. The stool near the dressing table fell over. Robbie felt something stir under his pillow, then felt the crucifix containing the relics slowly moving along his body and down to the foot of the bed. He reached for the relic of St. Margaret Mary. The safety pin was there, but the relic was gone. He did not speak. Neither did his mother. They waited, knowing before it happened what they would next hear and feel.

Then it came, the scratching and the shaking of the mattress, gently at first, and then more and more violent. The scratching, louder and louder, at higher and higher pitch, engulfed them. The mattress quaked violently, moving in a mad, frenzied rhythm.

For some reason, Phyllis Mannheim at that moment thought of Aunt Harriet.

She got out of the bed, taking Robbie with her. The room, to their eyes and ears, was still a bedlam of scratchings and thumpings. The others, on the ground floor, heard the sounds but this time they did not ascend the stairs. They waited, hearing the door open and shut and hearing Phyllis and Robbie on the stairs.

They had never seen Phyllis looking like this. She was so shaken that she seemed to be on the verge of hysteria. She was speaking, not in sentences but in gasps of words. What she said and did next is not recorded. The record is scant about the subsequent events on that long, terrifying night. "The five people in the home," says Father Bishop's diary, "then decided to ask questions of the spirit."

Phyllis Mannheim was leading them back to the beginning, to the tap-tap-tap attempts to get in touch with Harriet, to the feeling that somehow Harriet, not an unknown demon, was *doing this to us.*

Phyllis gathered them—these Catholics of her husband's family—and told them, *Harriet is at the bottom of this. We have to contact her. It's about the money.*

Phyllis went back over Harriet's last days. It was a tale they all knew. Harriet had been lingering between life and death for some time. On the night of January 25 she told her family—husband John, sons Danny and Mark, daughter Alice—to go to bed and let her die while everyone slept. Harriet died sometime between two and two-thirty on the morning of January 26.

Don't you see? The mattress, the scratching. Listen. They listened. The noise upstairs had stopped. *Don't you see. Look at the time. Just before three.* Phyllis tried to get them to understand why she was thinking about Aunt Harriet. *She knew when she was going to die. And she came back to tell us something, and she's trying to reach us at the exact same time of morning that she died.*

They began to ask questions, with Phyllis directing the impromptu seance. The previous session had been on March 7 around the kitchen table at the home of the Lutheran branch of the family. This one, at Phyllis' direction, was, incredibly, in the bedroom, amid the scratchings and the thumping mattress.

Elizabeth and her parents hung back, believing, as Catholics, that their souls would be endangered by any attempt to raise the spirits of the dead. Although Robbie was obviously the hub or the target of the turmoil in the bedroom, he was not part of the questioning of Harriet. Phyllis Mannheim seems to have been instinctively shielding Robbie while she went after Harriet.

The only account of this scene comes from Father Bishop's diary. The details were given to him in fragments as he questioned each of the adults, trying to keep his focus on Robbie and what was happening to the boy. Here, and elsewhere in the diary, Bishop detaches himself and sets down only what he saw and heard or what witnesses he spoke to saw and heard. He has only one mission: the rescue of Robbie from whatever it is that is stalking him.

Bishop's account of how this long night ended is frustrating, for it raises questions to which answers are no longer available. No one connected with that night spoke of the incident about Harriet's money. And, in his diligence to get at the facts about Robbie, Father Bishop did not follow up on this fascinating, though ancillary, event.

"The five people in the home then decided to ask questions of the spirit," Bishop wrote. Imagine that group gathered in the bedroom. On one side of the bed, where a rosary had been said only hours before, stood Karl Mannheim's brother George, married to Catherine, a Catholic. Next to them stood Elizabeth, the college student, wan and bewildered by what had come to her home, by what role she had played in bringing in a priest. Here she was standing in her brother Marty's bedroom, watching the mattress shake, hearing the scratching begin again. Marty had been drawn into this…this…whatever it was…on the first night. Now he was in another room, sleeping peacefully, she hoped. She was taking this all in. In a few hours she would be seeking out Father Bishop to tell him what had happened after he and Father Bowdern left.

On the other side of the bed stood Phyllis and Karl Mannheim, part of the Lutheran branch. They had known Harriet the Spiritualist, the Ouija board believer. Now, alongside this quaking bed they were going to turn to Harriet again.

The questions asked in the tempest of the bedroom focused on money that Aunt Harriet had hidden in a metal box shortly before she died. Bishop's account does not name the questioners. But it seems extremely likely that the questions were asked by Phyllis and by Karl Mannheim, trying to reach his dead sister.

The interview with Aunt Harriet consisted of a shouted question, such as, *Where is the money?* In response, the bed shook and thumped. Someone would shout, "Harriet, stop!" The shaking would stop momentarily "as though [Harriet] were listening for a question." Then the question would be repeated or elaborated on—*Is it in this house?*—and the bed would shake. Then someone, most likely Phyllis, would interpret the shakes—*She says "No"*. The bed would stop shaking if Harriet agreed with the interpretation or continue shaking if Harriet disagreed.

Through this bizarre dialogue, Phyllis believed, she and Karl were able to learn that Aunt Harriet had hidden a map in the attic of her home, and only Karl would be able to find it. This map would lead him to the metal box containing the money, but the money was destined for Harriet's daughter Alice.

Did Karl slip off, find the map, and then the money? Only the family knows, and no one in the family then or now wanted to talk about Aunt Harriet's hidden legacy. Probate Court records indicate that she did not leave a will. So there is no public record to show whether she even had an estate to leave.

To Robbie and his case, the question of Aunt Harriet's metal box (and whether or not it was found) is important only because it shows she was continually involved in his life after her death. For Robbie and his parents, she became a stubborn, possibly malevolent memory that somehow came forth as a thumping, scratching presence. The reasonable mind wants to see the thumping and the scratching as hallucinations. But to Robbie and his family, what they saw and heard was real. They believed their senses, though they did not understand the motive for what they experienced. Was Aunt Harriet causing this? Was she a restless spirit from the afterlife? Did that make her a manifestation of evil? Did something happen between her and Robbie, something so darkly secret that it now haunted him?

Later that Saturday, Elizabeth told Bishop what had happened after he and Bowdern had left. The questions were plaguing her and the rest of the family. She was sure that something was pursuing Robbie, wherever he went. It had started in Maryland, and now, it seemed, it was getting worse each night. Bowdern, with the novena ended, could now devote more time to the mystery that Bishop had brought to him.

Both men knew that diabolical possession was a possibility that they had to face. Bishop's report makes it seems likely that at this point they knew little, if anything, about the abortive exorcism attempted by Father Hughes in February. To them, the case was new. They began looking at it rigorously. If they were to ask Archbishop Ritter for permission to perform an exorcism, they needed more than accounts of flying relics and moving bookcases.

They agreed that Robbie could have caused all of the incidents that had occurred so far in St. Louis, including the moving of the bookcase, which they estimated to weigh about fifty pounds, across a polished wooden floor. They also agreed that they had to treat as hearsay the parents' reports of occurrences in Maryland. Phyllis Mannheim's list of fourteen witnesses was interesting but was also hearsay.

Robbie himself was an enigma. Bowdern and Bishop compared him to the teenage boys they had taught. He was in many ways a typical boy: not too studious, given to comic books rather than classics. A bit spoiled, perhaps, as an only child might be expected to be. A good boy, obedient, respectful toward his parents and elders. But he was so calm, so detached. He seemed simultaneously aware of, and oblivious to, what was happening around him. Given what he had been through since January, he could easily be mentally ill. Or, if not seriously ill, on the verge of a breakdown caused by his nights of shattered sleep.

Just as Father Hughes had turned to the *Roman Ritual* in February, Bowdern and Bishop now did the same. The section on exorcism had twenty-one rules and observations about possession and exorcism. One rule urged a study of cases of possession and warned that a prospective exorcist "should not believe too readily that a person is possessed by an evil spirit," for the victim might be suffering from a mental illness. Like Hughes, they checked the signs of diabolical possession. They had not heard him speak in a strange tongue or divulge future and hidden events or display any extraordinary powers. *What have we got?* the Jesuits asked each other. *Maybe not enough.* There was a kind of "display of powers"—the seemingly random movement of everything from fruit and chairs to relics and crucifixes. But this could have been nothing more than the display of a boy's conscious or subconscious mischief. That kind of phenomenon was classic poltergeist behavior, inevitably centering around a teenager. *Disturbing? Yes. Perplexing? Yes. But diabolical? Maybe.* The two Jesuits, especially Bowdern, began a crash course in possession. "Billy Bowdern went right to the books," a Jesuit remembered. He searched through the theological works in the university library, tracing the evolution of Church dogma on evil, the devil, exorcism, and possession. Bowdern would have found the Jesuit Del Rio's specters that "are wont to occasion various commotions and annoyances." *Interesting.* Del Rio, without noting it, was merging the folkloric tradition of the poltergeist with diabolical possession. Such historic models of ill-defined demons strengthened the thinking of Bishop and Bowdern. The family's chronicling of the case, so carefully recorded by Bishop, showed a classic progression from infestation, the poltergeist-like siege around Robbie in Maryland, to obsession—menaced, scratched, but not yet taken over. Next came possession itself. *Maybe we can stop it here.*

Bishop and Bowdern decided to ask Archbishop Ritter to find and appoint an exorcist to perform the rite before a demon entered Robbie.

Chapter 7

The Archbishop Gets the Case

Neither Father Bowdern nor Father Bishop wanted to be Robbie's exorcist. In their hasty research—between Saturday, March 11, and Tuesday, March 15—they learned enough about exorcists to decide that neither of them was the priest for the task. Two cases, one in seventeenth-century France and one in twentieth-century America, would have convinced them.

The French case began as an epidemic of possessions among nuns in an Ursuline convent in Loudun, a town in western France, where a lecherous priest had just been burned at the stake for witchcraft. During the frenzy that accompanied his trial and execution, tales of possession flourished in the convent. Eventually, seventeen nuns and some of their students, most of them young noblewomen, claimed to be possessed. Exorcists flocked to Loudun. Then, in December 1634, with great reluctance, a Jesuit provincial bowed to the wishes of Church officials and dispatched four Jesuits to Loudun as reinforcements.

Bowdern and Bishop would doubtlessly have heard of the Loudun case. It was one of the most famous in the Jesuit annals, though little known to the general public. (Aldous Huxley's best seller, *The Devils of Loudun*, had not yet been published.) Documentation about the case was extensive and readily available to any serious researcher.

Though witchcraft and demons still prowled Christian minds in seventeenth-century France, Europe had emerged from the Middle Ages and was on the verge of the Age of Enlightenment. Many Catholics were questioning the probability of possession, and Jesuits were among the leading doubters, especially about the epidemic at Loudun.

One reason for their doubts was the failure of any of the reputed demoniacs to show any of the traditional signs of possession. None of the young women demonstrated an ability to speak or understand a previously unknown language. None of them levitated or exhibited superhuman strength, though they could perform prodigious feats of contortion. Sometimes "they passed the left foot over the shoulder to the cheek. They also passed their feet over the head until the big toes touched the nose. Others again were able to stretch their legs so far to the left and right that they sat on the ground, without any space being visible between their bodies and the floor."

Many Jesuits believed that the belching, snorting, writhing nuns were merely hysterics consciously or unconsciously feigning possession. But one of the Jesuits sent to Loudun, thirty-four-old Father Jean-Joseph Surin, believed. He concentrated on exorcising what seemed to be the worst case, the prioress of the convent, Sister Jeanne des Anges. Before Surin's arrival, she had resisted extraordinary attempts to expel the seven devils she claimed were inhabiting various parts of her body. (She said that the one in her belly had been successfully exorcised with the aid of an enema of holy water.)

The prioress was closely observed by both believing and skeptical witnesses. Like Robbie, she exhibited scratches that erupted on her body. A bloody cross appeared on her forehead and stayed there for three weeks. Another day, during her regular exorcism session in the convent chapel, she was squirming around "like a tumbler" when she screamed the word *Joseph*. At that moment, a witness wrote, she held up her left arm, and "I saw a color rise, a little ruddy, and run for the length of an inch along her vein, and in that a great many red specks, which made a distinct word; and it was the same she spake, 'Joseph.'" The name persistently appeared even after she was rid of her demons, and for nearly thirty years she went about France displaying this brand from her possession.

Her cure, according to Surin, occurred after he prayed that the demons move from the prioress to him. Noble as Surin's motive may have been, he was ignoring theological warnings that possession and exorcism were not to be trifled with. His experiences, eloquently described in his writings, led later theologians to believe that Surin, a somewhat mystical priest, had been tricked into praying for the demons to transfer to him. The theologians came to the conclusion that the victim of possession was only a lure; Satan's desired victim was the exorcist himself. A modern Jesuit theologian, appraising Surin's fate, wrote that possession and obsession are "hazards, which we are powerless to control," and "we must never desire them."

Surin soon found himself possessed, and his description of that state has provided modern theologians and psychiatrists with insights into the effects of possession. For Bowdern and Bishop, the well-documented Loudun possessions would have answered questions. *What did it mean to be possessed? What might it be like for Robbie?* Here was Surin's answer, in a letter to a Jesuit friend:

"I find it almost impossible to explain what happens to me during this time, how this alien spirit is united to mine, without depriving me of consciousness or of inner freedom, and yet constituting a second 'me,' as though I had two souls...I feel as if I had been pierced by the pricks of despair in that alien soul which seems to be mine...I even feel that the cries uttered by my mouth come from both souls at once; and I find it hard to determine whether they are the product of joy or frenzy."

He felt himself turning into a devil. He could not stand being near the wafers of Holy Communion. When he tried to make the sign of the cross, "the other soul turns my hand aside, or takes the finger between the teeth and savagely bites it." Surin's demons, whether of hell or his own tortured mind, tormented him for twenty-five years. Only shortly before his death did he feel at peace. Two other Loudun exorcists died soon after their work there, and other priests attributed the deaths to the revenge of the exorcised demons.

Bishop and Bowdern did not believe either of them could be a Surin, not because they feared such a fate as his or the other Loudun exorcists' but because they were men of the twentieth century, not of the seventeenth. They believed deeply in their faith and the teachings of their church. Included in those teachings were the exorcisms performed by Jesus, and in those teachings were the words of Church Fathers and numerous saints, all attesting to possession and exorcism. But, to a priest in 1949, exorcism was an extraordinarily rare duty, because possession was no longer, as it once had been, a matter of everyday experience.

From the early centuries of Christianity, through the Middle Ages, and into the seventeenth century, possession had been so common in Europe that the Church needed an abundance of exorcists, most of them laymen. The role of exorcist was recognized as a minor order that could be held by a non-priest. (Other minor orders included acolytes, who helped priests at church services; porters, charged with guarding church entrances; and lectors, who read the Scriptures and other passages during worship.) In the twentieth century, priests had altar boys and janitors, and the worshipers were literate and could do their own reading. Acolytes, porters, lectors—and exorcists—were vestiges of another age of faith.

Though empowered as exorcists, Bishop and Bowdern, like virtually all American priests, had never been called to use the power. Now questions about it had come to their doorstep. *And this Father Hughes in Maryland. Yes, well, he may have applied for permission…But nothing happened.* As far as Bishop and Bowdern knew, Father Hughes had not actually performed an exorcism. All they had to go on was what Robbie's parents had told them. Phyllis and Karl Mannheim may not have fully understood what had happened at Georgetown Hospital in February. Whatever they did know, they were not sharing their knowledge with these new priests.

Bishop and Bowdern struggled with the problem. Robbie was a boy in torment—perhaps about to become possessed and suffer as Surin did. *But was Robbie just mentally ill? Where were the signs? A young American boy in need of an exorcism? How can it be?* Exorcisms were of the Old World. *Never in America…*

Then Bowdern found a pamphlet describing an exorcism in Earling, Iowa, in 1928. The woman who was possessed, unidentified in the pamphlet, was later known only as Mary. She was a forty-year-old countrywoman who, since girlhood on an Iowa farm had been periodically plagued by demonic voices. Physicians and psychiatrists who examined her pronounced her mentally and physically well. The decision to exorcise her came slowly and with some reluctance. Dubious Church authorities were not anxious to allow it, but Mary's pastor, Father Joseph Steiger, pressed the case and finally won permission.

In August 1928 Mary was taken to a convent in secrecy. A sixty-year-old Franciscan friar, Father Theophilus Riesinger, a friend of Steiger, was appointed the exorcist. On the day the exorcism was to begin, Riesinger ordered Mary strapped to the bed and held down by the biggest nuns in the convent. He donned a surplice over his brown, rope-girded robe, slipped a purple stole around his neck, and walked to the side of Mary's bed. As he made the sign of the cross over her, according to the pamphlet

> with lightning speed the possessed dislodged herself from the bed and from the hands of her guards; and her body, carried through the air, landed high above the door of the room and clung to the wall with a tenacious grip. Real force had to be applied to her feet to bring her down from her high position on the wall.

She let out a scream that sounded like "a pack of wild beasts." Out of her mouth during the long exorcism came froth and spit and vomit "that would fill a pitcher, yes, even a pail full of the most obnoxious stench…"

Her body, the pamphlet said,

> became so horribly disfigured that the regular contour of her body vanished. Her pale, deathlike and emaciated head…became as red as glowing embers. Her eyes protruded out of their sockets, her lips swelled up to proportions equalling the size of

hands, and her thin emaciated body was bloated to such enormous size that the pastor and some of the sisters drew back out of fright, thinking that the woman would be torn to pieces and burst asunder.

The exorcism went on, day after day. Mary was fed intravenously much of the time. Riesinger took on "the appearance of a walking corpse, a figure which at any moment might collapse." He addressed the devils in English, German, and Latin, and received replies in each language. One demon identified himself as Judas Iscariot. Another voice said he was Mary's father and that he had summoned the demons by cursing her for refusing to submit sexually to him.

About nine o'clock on December 23 "with a sudden burst of lightning speed, the possessed woman broke from the grip of her protectors and stood erect before them. Only her heels were touching the bed." Riesinger blessed her and the stiffness of her body gave way and she fell, exhausted, upon the bed. "Then a piercing sound filled the room causing all to tremble vehemently." Voices called out, "Beelzebub…Judas…Hell." An awful stench permeated the room and Mary cried out, "My Jesus, mercy! Praised be Jesus Christ!"

The account of Mary's possession and exorcism made for fascinating reading. But a woman rising to the ceiling? Vomit by the pailful from someone being fed intravenously? There was an embarrassing absurdity about the pamphlet, which was full of pious phrases and credulous claims.

Jesuits and Franciscans had long been rivals. (A Franciscan pope, Clement XIV, dissolved the Society of Jesus in 1773. It was restored in 1814.) Neither Bishop nor Bowdern could picture himself in the sandals of that Franciscan Riesinger, craning his neck to see a demoniac sailing upward. Riesinger had died, apparently of natural causes, in 1941. If he had been alive, Bowdern and Bishop probably would not have consulted him. His kind of wild testimony they did not need.

There is no record available on the correspondence and discussions between the Jesuit community and Archbishop Ritter over Robbie's case. What is known is that Bowdern got the permission of his superior to write a letter to Ritter asking that an exorcism be authorized and an exorcist be chosen. Bowdern had decided that he was not qualified to be an exorcist, especially since he did not feel that he was a holy man. Instead, he would present the case to the archbishop. He briefly described what Bishop and he had seen and what the family had reported.

While Bowdern and Bishop were planning the presentation of the case, they stayed away from Robbie's house. His parents told the priests that the mattress shaking and the scratching continued on Sunday, Monday, and Tuesday. A stool, the parents said, had sailed from one side of Robbie's bed to the other, and the relic of St. Margaret Mary had flown up from the pillow to which it had been re-pinned. Bishop duly noted the reports in his diary.

Anticipating authorization from Ritter, Bowdern began to think about recruiting an exorcist. He believed the person should be a theologian, preferably a Jesuit. Discreet inquiry was made among theologians in the community and in the province. Two were actually asked. Both politely turned Bowdern down. Bowdern never said why the theologians rejected him. Bishop makes no mention in his diary of Bowdern's recruitment attempt. But another Jesuit remembered, "The ones who refused said they didn't have the strength. It was not a case of skepticism. They just didn't feel capable."

Bowdern apparently made the formal request to Archbishop Ritter on either Monday, March 14, or the following day. Ritter, according to a priest who has examined the archives, did not delegate the Jesuits' request to one of his monsignors. Unlike O'Boyle in Washington, Ritter did his own research and would make up his mind without any assistance. His first reaction was to withhold permission. A modern prelate who was building a reputation in the modern wing of the Church, he dreaded the backlash that could come from publicity over an exorcism. It could set back the Church and make him look ridiculous among his fellow American prelates, who saw him as a leader who could take the Church into a new, ecumenical era.

Ritter was fifty-four years old and the archbishop of Indianapolis in 1947 when Pope Pius XII named him archbishop of St. Louis. A year later he ordered the desegregation of all the churches and schools in the archdiocese. When diehard Catholic segregationists threatened to defy him, Ritter said he would excommunicate anyone who tried to impede him. The surprised opponents backed off, and segregation went smoothly, as it had at St. Louis University three years before. Ritter's fast action against segregation typified his aggressive approach to moral issues. He was already a well-known U.S. churchman. He would be made a cardinal in 1961, and at the Vatican Council in 1962 he would lead the progressive faction, which included a number of Jesuits.

Ritter did not like what Bowdern brought him. He was not comfortable about exposing his archdiocese to the kind of ridicule that had come in the wake of the exorcism in Iowa in 1928. He knew that other U.S. bishops or archbishops had rejected petitions for exorcisms, forcing the reputed demoniac to move to another diocese and try again. Or wind up in a mental hospital. He could

do that, but he did not like passing the buck. When he replaced the
regal Cardinal John J. Glennon as archbishop of St. Louis, Ritter
had been compared to Harry Truman, a Missourian who talked
straight and said of his Presidency, the buck stops here. Ritter ran
his archdiocese the way Truman ran his White House.

For Ritter looking beyond his archdiocese to his own reputation, for Reiter concerned about his university, for Bishop and
Bowdern searching for a modern route to an ancient phenomenon—for all the clergy now drawn into Robbie's case, the issue was
not about exorcism. It was about evil.

The fundamental work of all these men was the advancement of
good and the defeat of evil. If evil were stalking Robbie, moving
along the classic infestation-obsession-possession path, then these
men had no real choice. They could not turn away from Robbie, for
if they did they would be turning away from their avowed life's work.

Possession is the bondage of evil. Primitive and advanced cultures
of every era have believed in it. And every culture that believed in
possession had found means to relieve it. For Catholics, that means
was the rite of exorcism. Ritter now held the key to this exorcism.

As a matter of faith, he had to believe in the existence of evil.
Belief in the devil, according to some modern theologians, was not
a dogma that Catholics had to accept. The Bible, particularly the
New Testament, states that the devil exists. He is an actor in biblical scenes that proclaim his existence in the Gospels of Matthew,
Mark, Luke, and John, and in the writings of Paul. Since Catholics
accept the Bible as divinely inspired, according to the traditional
theological argument, the devil must be accepted along with other
biblical teachings. Modernists held that the devil was metaphorical,
and metaphors are not articles of faith.

If Ritter did not believe in the existence of the devil, he could, in conscience, reject the request and suggest that Robbie find his cure through psychiatry. But Archbishop Ritter, as a Catholic prelate, at least had to profess a belief in the existence of the devil. What he had to endorse in Robbie's case was another matter: the *presence* of the devil.

Theologians have long pondered the question of the devil's presence within a human being, starting with the assumption that God put restrictions on the work of the devil. "If the devil could do everything he wanted," wrote St. Augustine, "there would not remain a single living human being on earth." But, even with God restraining the devil, the Bible says, he "is prowling like a roaring lion looking for someone to devour."

Ordinarily, the devil of the Scriptures does no more than tempt, luring people into acts of evil. He focuses on the weak body while the God-fearing soul fights him off. As the Apostle Paul wrote about this belief, "For I delight in the law of God after the inward man. But I see another law in my members, warring against the law of my mind, and bringing me into captivity to the law of sin which is in my members…So then with the mind I myself serve the law of God; but with the flesh the law of sin."

This dual view of the human condition—a feebly moral body and an embattled soul—frames the concept of diabolical possession, the devil's ultimate assault on the body. Possession, wrote a Catholic theologian, "consists in the presence of the devil within the human body, over which the devil has total and despotic control. The victim becomes a blind instrument of the devil…[S]ince the possessed person is not aware of his or her actions during a diabolical seizure—and much less able to exercise any control—the victim of possession is not responsible for his or her actions, however outrageous, wicked or perverse."

Ritter had no conclusive way to prove that Robbie was possessed or in imminent danger of being possessed. The boy showed none of the traditional signs cited in the *Roman Ritual.* So Ritter faced a dilemma: If Robbie were suffering from mental illness rather than diabolical possession, evil was not involved. An exorcism would do no good and could even worsen his condition. But if this were diabolical possession, then evil, a terrible form of evil, was present and Ritter had to order a priest to risk his soul to save Robbie's.

If evil was acknowledged, Ritter could not dismiss the petition. He was duty-bound to challenge the evil and struggle against it. However, he would fight as a general; the exorcist would fight in the trenches.

There is a basic theological hypothesis about evil: Don't go near it. On a catechism level, Catholic children are warned to stay away from "occasions of sin"; adults received sophisticated versions of the same advice.

An exorcist has to touch evil, breathe it, focus on it. A priest perceives himself as living and working on the side of God. To work against the devil, an exorcist enters the deep, clutching shadow of evil. When he appears, the demons turn their evil on him. The exorcist priest, though he sees himself as an agent of good aided by an almighty God, simultaneously sees himself as a mere human being pitted against a powerful enemy with long experience in perpetrating evil.

If an exorcist wavered with doubt or fear when he ventured into the shadows of evil, he risked his own destruction and perhaps that of the person he had been called on to save. The unofficial, but quietly promulgated, reason given for Father Hughes' failed exorcism was that he had suffered a momentary "lapse of concentration." Ritter may have known this, through discreet inquiries to his fellow archbishop in Washington. Or he may have sensed it through his own experience with young priests. If he did authorize an exorcism, he did not want one that ended with a physically or spiritually maimed priest. He wanted a successful exorcism, and he knew that success depended upon the priest he selected.

Like Bowdern and Bishop, Ritter looked up what the *Roman Ritual* said about the qualities that an exorcist must have:

> A priest...when he intends to perform an exorcism over persons tormented by the devil, must be properly distinguished for his piety, prudence, and integrity of life. He should fulfill this devout undertaking in all constancy and humility, being utterly immune to any striving for human aggrandizement, and relying, not on his own but on divine power. Moreover, he ought to be of mature years, and revered not alone for his office but for his moral qualities.

Piety, prudence, and integrity of life. Ritter knew many priests who could qualify (and some who could not). Like Bowdern, Ritter had probably thought first of calling on a theologian. He could reach out to the faculty at any seminary, whether run by Jesuits or by the archdiocese. He could select a priest in his own chancery. He could ask another bishop or archbishop to provide him with an exorcist. Instead, Ritter chose Father Bowdern.

It has become Jesuit lore that when Ritter told Bowdern he was to be the exorcist, Bowdern said, "Nothing doing," and the archbishop said, "You've got it."

Chapter 8

"I Cast Thee Out"

Archbishop Ritter gave Father Bowdern one order: You must promise never to discuss this exorcism with anyone. Bowdern readily agreed. But, because he had found it "very difficult to find any authentic literature on cases of possession," he decided on his own that Father Bishop should keep "a minute account each day of the happenings each preceding day and night." One reason for such a diary, he said, was that it "would be most helpful to anyone placed in a similar position as an exorcist in any future case."

Late in the afternoon of Wednesday, March 16, Bowdern sent a message to Walter Halloran, a twenty-six-year-old scholastic who was studying at St. Louis University for his master's degree in history. Halloran had been a Jesuit for eight years and had known Bowdern ever since Halloran went off to Campion Jesuit High, where Bowdern was rector. Over the years, four Halloran brothers had gone to Campion, an isolated boarding school where, as Walter Halloran remembered, "We were off by ourselves—just the Jesuits and the kids. Billy Bowdern ran a good school. He was very professional that way. He just took for granted that you were there to learn, and if you didn't you were in trouble. You were to be a Christian gentleman."

While Halloran was attending Campion, he decided to become a Jesuit. Bowdern had been one of his models. Although Bowdern was twice Halloran's age, a camaraderie had developed between them, and, after Halloran's ordination five years hence, they would become close friends. And, like his model Bowdern, Halloran would become an Army chaplain in combat.

"Walt," Bowdern said, "I'll be needing you to drive me someplace tonight. Can you do it?"

Halloran had frequently driven Bowdern on parish errands and sick calls, and he agreed to pick him up that night. He liked driving for Bowdern, and, besides, a Jesuit scholastic was expected to do what a Jesuit priest asked.

Halloran brought the parish car around to the rectory about nine o'clock. Bowdern gave him the address. Halloran checked a map and began heading northwest. He was concentrating on finding street signs and did not pay much attention to what Bishop and Bowdern were talking about in low voices. He had noticed that both priests were wearing cassocks and carrying surplices, and he did wonder what kind of sick call needed two priests in surplices.

When Halloran pulled up in front of the house, Bowdern leaned over the front seat and said, "Come on in with us." His invitation surprised the young scholastic. Before he could ask a question, Bowdern, standing on the sidewalk before the dark lawn, calmly told Halloran, "I'll be doing an exorcism. I want you to hold the boy down in case it's needed." (This suggests that Bowdern may have known about the attack on Father Hughes, though he never mentioned the attack to anyone, possibly to allay apprehensions.)

Halloran was stunned. He knew what an exorcism was, but only as a theological abstraction, something that happened in the Bible, not in a St. Louis suburb. But this was no time to ask questions. Bowdern and Bishop were already walking up the front porch steps. Halloran followed, wondering but not worrying. He trusted Bowdern, but wondered what he meant about holding down a boy. If things got rough, well, Halloran had played some football and was an athlete in fine shape.

Bowdern introduced Halloran to Robbie, his parents, aunt, uncle, and Elizabeth, whom Halloran vaguely recognized as someone he had seen on campus. They crowded into the living room. Bowdern smiled at Robbie and began talking, easily, confidently, speaking at times directly to Robbie and sometimes to the adults. He said that he was going to give him a new kind of help. He encouraged his listeners to ask questions, but they asked few. He had calmed them, readied them for something they knew nothing about. "These are special prayers, special prayers for a situation like this," he finally said. "And I think, I think we may as well start."

Robbie said good night, went upstairs, and got ready for bed. His mother waited a few minutes and then went up to Robbie's bedroom. She stepped to the top of the stairwell and called down to say, "Robbie is all set now."

Bowdern went upstairs alone and spent a short time with Robbie. As Bishop reported this later, Bowdern helped Robbie "to examine his conscience and make an act of contrition." There is no eyewitness report on this meeting between priest and boy, but it can easily be imagined. *Robbie, you know what your conscience is, right?* And then Robbie, in his halting, polite way, trying to get around the word and giving up. He was sleepy. *It's what's inside you, the part of you that tells you what's right and wrong. Okay?*

Bowdern drew upon his years as teacher and counselor of adolescent boys to probe Robbie's heart, to see if a conscious hoax were at the bottom of all this. *Now what I'd like you to do, Robbie, is look at that conscience of yours and make sure that there isn't anything you want to tell me. Anything you tell me, Robbie, will be just between you and me. I promised God a long time ago that I wouldn't ever tell anyone any secrets told to me.* Robbie might have mentioned a couple of fibs, a few times when he talked back to his mother. He said nothing to make Bowdern feel that this was a boy with a bad conscience. *Now I'm going to ask you to say after me what Catholics call an act of contrition. All that means is that it's a way of saying to God that you're sorry for what you've done and you won't do it again.*

Bowdern began the act of contrition, phrase by phrase, pausing for Robbie to repeat the words. "Forgive me, Father, for I have sinned…" Bowdern was convinced that he was dealing with a boy who was troubled and was not feigning that trouble. The quiet session with Robbie did not provide Bowdern with any new evidence that the boy was possessed. But the priest now believed, in his own conscience, that he was doing right by performing an exorcism. He told Robbie that he would be right back and would be bringing his friends with him.

Downstairs, Bowdern ducked into his stiffly starched surplice. Bishop did the same. Each took a purple stole from his pocket, unrolled it, kissed it, and placed it around his neck. Then each put on his biretta. Halloran wore the scholastic's formal attire: black suit, Roman collar, and black, shirtlike vest. Bowdern and Bishop each carried a *Roman Ritual,* a book of more than four hundred pages, gilt-edged and bound in black. Bowdern also carried a small bottle of holy water.

Bowdern had carefully studied the *Ritual's* twenty-one specific instructions. They seemed logical enough to him, though he may have smiled at the warning not to "digress into senseless prattle." This he was not wont to do under any circumstances. Another instruction suggested that he move Robbie to a church or to "some other sacred and worthy place." He decided against this suggestion, believing that Robbie would be more comfortable in familiar surroundings.

Bowdern accepted the advice to stick to the words in the *Ritual* and not attempt any extemporaneous statements of his own. This was not a place for homilies. And he would not argue with the demons or try to make any bargains with them. "For oftentimes," said the *Ritual*, "they give deceptive answers and make it difficult to understand them, so that the exorcist might tire and give up, or so it might appear that the afflicted one is in no wise possessed by the devil."

The *Ritual* had a ritual of exorcism for place and a ritual for people. Although the *Ritual* had a specific sequence of prayers for each of the rites, the exorcist had some freedom. Unlike sacraments, for which there were strict formulas, decisions about the rite of exorcism depended upon the exorcist, since only he, in combat with the demon, could know the best strategy.

The prayers of exorcism for people who were possessed included suggestions for Gospel readings, psalms, and other prayers. All readings were in Latin. The three principal exorcism prayers were identified by the Latin words that began them: *"Praecípio"*—"I command," a summoning of the "unclean spirit." Another began: *"Exorcízo te"*—"I cast thee out." The third began: *"Adjúro te"*—"I adjure thee."

The Catholic Church viewed an exorcism as a direct confrontation between Satan and Christ, with the priest summoning up the power of Christ through the prayers. Father Bowdern had said

Mass, had made his general confession to Father Kenny, and had spent much of the day in prayer. He had also begun to fast, which was recommended in the *Ritual*. Bishop, as Bowdern's assistant, probably followed Bowdern's lead.

Bowdern fussed for a moment with his stole, nodded to Bishop and Halloran, and started up the stairs.

They walked into the room, Bowdern leading the way. Behind them came Robbie's mother, aunt, and uncle. Bowdern made the sign of the cross and sprinkled holy water on the bed. Then he knelt at one side of the bed. Bishop knelt opposite him. The family members knelt alongside the priests. Halloran did not know what to do. Bowdern motioned for Halloran to kneel at the foot of the bed. Halloran's eyes were on the level of the mattress. He was peering through the metal bars at Robbie.

Bowdern led them in a series of prayers of faith, hope, love, and contrition. Robbie, lying in the bed, joined in. Then Bowdern began the Litany of the Saints: "*K'ýrie, eléison*"—Lord have mercy on us.

Bishop and Halloran answered, "*Christe, eléison*"—Christ have mercy on us. And the rhythm began: invocation by Bowdern, response by Bishop and Halloran:

"*Christe, audi nos*"—Christ hear us.

"*Christe, exáudi nos*"—Christ graciously hear us.

"*Sancta Maria, ora pro nobis*"—Holy Mary, pray for us.

"*Ora pro nobis*"—Pray for us.

"*Sancta Virgo vírginum…*"—Holy Virgin of virgins…

"*Ora pro nobis.*"

"*Sancte Míchael—*"

"*Ora pro nobis.*"

"*Sancte Gábriel—*"

The mattress began to move. Halloran saw it go up and down before his eyes. He turned his head, shifting his wide-eyed gaze to Bowdern.

"It's no problem, Walt," Bowdern said softly. "Just go ahead and pray." And he resumed the litany, his voice strengthening as he summoned up the saints. They were grouped by types. First came Michael, Gabriel, Raphael—the archangels, the only angels with names. Then all the holy innocents and virgins, then the saintly widows and the martyrs, and the holy priests, and the monks and hermits, and the founders of religious orders—Anthony, Benedict, Bernard, Dominic, Francis, and Ignatius. The litany produced an image of phalanxes of saints coming to the aid of the boy, who, eyes closed, lay on the mattress, which seemed to be moving to the rhythm of the litany.

Then the litany shifted from a reciting of names to a reciting of pleas to God:

"Ab omni malo, libera nos, Dómine"—From all evil, O Lord, deliver us.

"Ab omni peccáto…"—From all sin…"

It continued in Latin. Robbie listened to the drone and the hum of the words that sounded as if they came from another world, another time. He did not know the meaning of the words, but he sensed their comfort and the way they were wrapping themselves around him, around this room…

The Latin went on, with Bowdern saying something and Bishop and Halloran saying something in response. What the strange words meant were:

"O Lord, deliver us."

"From thy wrath—"

"O Lord, deliver us."

"From sudden and unprovided death—"

"O Lord, deliver us."

"From the snares of the devil—"

"O Lord, deliver us."

"From anger, and hatred, and every evil will—"

"O Lord, deliver us."

"From the spirit of fornication—"

"O Lord, deliver us."

"From lightning and tempest—"

"O Lord, deliver us."

"From the scourge of earthquakes—"

"O Lord, deliver us."

"From plague, famine, and war—"

"O Lord, deliver us."

"From everlasting death—"

"O Lord, deliver us."

The Latin litany now coursed through the articles of Catholic faith, from the mystery of Christ's incarnation to the day of judgment. Robbie could sense a shift in the words. The priest who was leading this long prayer was saying longer phrases now. And the other priest and the young one in black were changing what they were saying.

"...*Ut inimícos sanctae Ecclésiae humiliáre dignéris*"—That thou wouldst vouchsafe to humble the enemies of holy Church—

"*Te rogámus, audi nos*"—We beseech thee, hear us.

"...*Ut ómnibus benefactóribus nostris sempitérna bona retríbuas*"—That thou wouldst render eternal blessings to all our benefactors—

"*Te rogámus, audi nos.*"

"Ut animas nostras, fratrum, propinquórum et benefactórum nos-trórum ab aetérna damnatióne erípias"—That thou will deliver our souls and the souls of our brethren, relatives, and benefactors from eternal damnation—

"Te rogámus, audi nos."

And then they were back to the beginning, to the words that had started the litany:

"Kýrie, eléison."

"Christe, eléison."

"Kýrie, eléison."

Bowdern paused, turned a page, and began intoning more Latin. *"Ne reminiscáris...*He was saying, "Remember not, O Lord, our offenses, nor those of our parents: neither take retribution on our sins." Then, whispering the words, Bowdern began the Our Father. *"Pater noster..."* He raised his voice near the end:

"Et ne nos indúcas in tentatiónem"—And lead us not into temptation—

And Bishop and Halloran answered, *"Sed líbera nos a malo*—But deliver us from evil.

Although Robbie and his mother and aunt and uncle did not know the Latin words, they knew how the Our Father ended, and there it was, the point of all this: Deliver us from evil.

Bowdern paused again, and everyone shifted, easing stiffening knees. This was getting awfully long. The mattress kept shaking. Last night, Phyllis Mannheim remembered, the shaking had continued for two hours. She wondered why all these prayers had not stopped the mattress.

Bowdern began the Fifty-third Psalm, still speaking in Latin. He was saying:

"Save me, O God, by thy name, and further my cause by thy power. O God, hear my prayer; give ear to the words of my mouth. For proud men have risen against me, and men of violence have sought my life…Gladly will I sacrifice unto thee. I will praise thy name, O Lord, for it is good. In every need He hath delivered me, and mine eye hath seen the confusion of my foe. Glory be to the Father, and to the Son, and to the Holy Ghost, as it was in the beginning, is now, and ever shall be, world without end. Amen. Preserve thy servant—"

Bishop's voice suddenly cut in. *"Deus meus, sperántem in te"*— Who places his trust in thee, my God.

The rhythm changed and Bowdern and Bishop, reading from their copies of the *Ritual*, began speaking alternately. *"Esto ei, Dómine, turris fortitúdinís,"* Bowdern said. Then Bishop answered in Latin, and what they were saying was:

"Be unto him, O Lord, a fortress of strength."

"In the face of the enemy."

"Let the enemy have no power over him."

"And the son of evil do nothing to harm him."

"Send him, Lord, aid from on high."

"And from Sion [Zion] watch over him."

"O Lord, hear my prayer."

"And let my cry come unto thee."

"The Lord be with you."

"And with thy spirit."

Bowdern paused again. He now spoke slowly, and in his Latin words there was a sense of potency and import. In this prelude to the actual words of exorcism, he established two theological points: the existence of Satan, the angel who had fallen, with his legion of followers; the coming of Jesus, the Redeemer and Son of God, to free the world from Satan's grasp. Bowdern said in Latin:

"O God, Whose nature it is ever to show mercy and to spare, receive our petition, that this thy servant, bound by the fetters of sin, may by thy sweet forgiveness be pardoned.

"O Holy Lord, almighty Father, eternal God and Father of our Lord Jesus Christ, Who didst one time consign that fugitive and fallen tyrant to everlasting hell fire, Who didst send thy Sole-Begotten into the world to crush the spirit of evil with his bellowing, do thou speedily give heed and hasten to snatch from ruination and from the noonday demon a human being, created in thine image and likeness.

"Strike terror, O Lord, into the beast that lays waste thy vineyard. Grant confidence to thy servants to fight most manfully against that reprobate dragon, lest he dare despise them who put their trust in thee, and lest he say with Pharaoh who once declared: 'I know not God, neither will I let Israel go!'

"Let thy powerful right hand prevail upon him to depart from thy servant, Robert." Here Bowdern made the sign of the cross over Robbie. The mattress had ceased moving. Robbie was staring at the ceiling light. His hands were clutching the coverlet.

"So that he may no longer hold captive him whom it has pleased thee to make in thine image and to redeem through thy Son." Bowdern's voice rose. "Thou Who livest and reignest in the unity of the Holy Spirit, God, forever and forevermore."

Bishop said firmly, "Amen."

Bowdern stood and moved closer to the bed. *"PRAECÍPIO TIBI!"* he shouted: I COMMAND THEE.

Robbie screamed.

Bowdern continued, in thundering Latin. *"Praecipio tibi, quicúmque es, spíritus immúnde, et ómnibus sóciis tuis…"*—I command thee, unclean spirit, whosoever thou art, along with all thine associates who have taken possession of this servant of God, that, by the mysteries of the Incarnation, Passion, Resurrection, and Ascension of our Lord Jesus Christ—

Robbie screamed again. His mother stood, but something held her back. The scream was a scream of pain, not fear. Robbie stirred and threw back the coverlet and blankets. His pajama top was open. Across his stomach were three long red welts.

"—by the descent of the Holy Spirit, by the coming of our Lord—"

Robbie squirmed and screamed again. At this next mention of *Dóminus* new welts appeared on his stomach. And now the room filled with a new rhythm: each *Dóminus* (Lord) or *Deus* (God) seemed to produce new welts and scratches. It was as if something deep within Robbie was trying to cut its way out. He squirmed out of his pajamas, and the scratches kept appearing, lacing his body with bloody stripes in long, clean lines.

`"—unto judgment, thou shalt tell me by some sign or other thy name and the day and the hour of thy departure."

"I command thee, moreover, to obey me to the letter, I who, though unworthy, am a minister of God—"

Deus! More scratchings. (Bishop would precisely describe them as "marks raised up above the surface of the skin, similar to an engraving.)

"—neither shalt thou be emboldened to harm in any way this creature of God"—

Deus! Now little lines of glistening blood appeared on Robbie's legs, his thighs, stomach, and back. He writhed in pain. A scratch zigzagged across his throat. Red marks arose on his face, which twisted in pain.

Bowdern rarely looked up from the pages of the *Ritual.* He began the exorcism prayer again. *"Praecipio tibi, quicúmque es, spíritus immúnde—"*

Something now rippled on Robbie's right leg. As Bowdern again commanded the demon to identify himself, red welts formed an image on the leg. It was, the witnesses later said, an image of the devil. "The arms were held above his head," Bishop recorded, "and seemed to be webbed, giving the hideous appearance of a bat."

Bowdern read on—"I who am a minister of God—"

Deus! Across Robbie's chest the letters H E L L appeared in marks that looked and felt to the touch like the scratches of thorns. The word was arranged so that it faced him, like a word scrawled on a page, when the screaming boy looked down on his chest. There was blood enough for Bishop to daub at it with his handkerchief.

"—dicas mihi nomen tuum, diem, et horam éxitus tui, cum áliquo signo"—Thou shalt tell me by some sign or other thy name and the day and the hour of thy departure.

At that moment came what seemed to be the sign: The letters G O appeared on Robbie's stomach. An X that looked like a brand appeared on his right leg. Bishop wondered. Did this mean the devil would leave at ten the next morning? Or did it mean the devil would stay for ten more days? G O was on Robbie's lower abdomen, with what looked like a third letter directly above his sparse pubic hair. Perhaps this meant that the devil would leave by way of urine or excrement, Bishop thought. This was a traditional exit route, according to medieval accounts of exorcism.

Robbie relaxed and appeared to sleep. Bishop methodically counted the marks on the boy's body. He lost count after twenty-five because some marks webbed into clusters of rakings and welts.

Bowdern had several calming prayers to choose from between the first *Praecipio,* which he had repeated, and the next, furious prayer of exorcism. Among the prayers he now read aloud was one to St. Michael the Archangel, revered by Christians, since at least the fourth century, as a warrior angel who triumphed over Lucifer.

"Princeps gloriosíssime caeléstis milítiae, sanctee Michaéle Archángele—"

"O Most illustrious prince of the heavenly hosts, holy Michael the Archangel, from thy heavenly throne defend us in the battle against the princes and powers, against the rulers of this world's darkness. Come to the assistance of humankind, whom God has created in His own image and likeness, and whom He has purchased at a great price from Satan's tyranny…Intercede for us to the God of peace, that He would crush Satan under our feet…Lay hold of the dragon, the ancient serpent, no other than the demon, Satan, and cast him bound into the abyss, so that he may no longer seduce mankind.

"In the name of Jesus Christ, our Lord and God—"

Robbie stirred in his sleep. Eyes tightly closed, mumbling words, he began to punch the backboard of the bed. He grabbed his pillow and punched it several times.

Phyllis Mannheim, slumped in a corner of the room, could not believe what she was seeing. Never before, she told Bishop later, had she seen Robbie turn violent. Here, as at Georgetown Hospital, the rite of exorcism seemed to trigger outbursts of fury from Robbie.

Bowdern leaned over the thrashing body and sprinkled holy water. Robbie awakened with a start. Bishop took the boy's pulse. It was normal. The priests asked him what he had been dreaming.

He said he had been fighting a huge red devil. It felt slimy and was extremely powerful. The devil was fighting to keep Robbie from passing through iron gates at the top of a pit that was about two hundred feet deep and very hot. There were other, lesser devils around. But Robbie's opponent was the big red devil, and Robbie had started to feel so strong that he thought he could beat the devil.

Bowdern and Bishop exchanged glances. Although Robbie could not have understood the combative Latin words of the prayer to Michael, he seemed to have acted out the message in his dream.

Bowdern decided to resume the exorcism, beginning now the most powerful prayer.

"Exorcízo te, immundíssime spíritus, omnis incúrsio adversárii, omne phantásma, omnis légio"—I cast thee out, thou unclean spirit, along with the least encroachment of the wicked enemy, and every phantom and diabolical legion.

"In nómine Dómini nostri Jesu Christi"—In the name of our Lord Jesus Christ—

Bowdern leaned so close over Robbie that he could see his eyes moving under his tightly closed eyelids. Bowdern made the sign of the cross over Robbie, who was breathing deeply. His arms began moving rapidly. He seemed to be fighting again at the edge of the pit.

Still leaning over the boy, Bowdern, his voice hoarse but still commanding, said, *"eradicáre, et effugáre ab hoc plásmate Dei."*—Depart and vanish from this creature of God. Bowdern again made the sign of the cross over Robbie and resumed speaking: *"Ipse tibi ímperat, qui te de supérnis caelórum in inferióra terrae demérgi praecépit"*—For it is He Who commands thee, He Who ordered thee cast down from the heights of heaven into the nethermost pit of the earth.

The prayer rolled on as Robbie continued to thrash around on the bed.

"He it is Who commands thee, Who once ordered the sea and the wind and the storm to obey. Hence, pay heed, Satan, and tremble, thou enemy of the faith, thou foe of the human race! For thou art the carrier of death and the robber of life; thou art the shirker of justice and the root of all evil, the fomenter of vice, the seducer of men, the traitor of the nations, the instigator of envy, the font of avarice, the source of discord, the exciter of sorrows! Why tarriest though resisting, when thou knowest that Christ the Lord—"

At *Christum Dóminum,* Robbie thrashed more violently. Bowdern signaled to Halloran to come around the bed and hold Robbie down. Halloran, a strapping athlete, could not hold down the ninety-five pound boy. Robbie's uncle grabbed one shoulder while Halloran held the other. Robbie shouted at them, demanding they let him go. He struggled against them.

Bowdern kept up the steady beat of the prayer. *"Christum Dóminum vias tuas pérdere?"*—that Christ the Lord doth bring thy plans to naught?

More words, more struggling, then, as Bowdern said, *"Recéde ergo in nómine Patris."* He moved his right thumb on Robbie's brow, tracing the sign of the cross three times—one for God the Father, one for God the Son, one for God the Holy Spirit. "Wherefore, get thee gone in the name of the Father, and of the Son, and of the Holy Spirit. Make way for God the Holy Spirit through this sign of the holy Cross of our Lord Jesus Christ. Who liveth and reigneth with the Father and the selfsame Holy Spirit, God, forever and ever."

Bishop, his voice a whisper, said, "Amen."

"Dómine, exáudi oratiónem meam," Bowdern said, sounding greatly weary—O Lord, hear my prayer.

"Et clamor meus ad te véniat," Bishop responded—And let my cry come unto thee.

"Dóminus vobíscum," Bowdern said—The Lord be with you.

"Et cum spíritu tuo," Bishop responded—And with thy spirit."

Bowdern took a deep breath, said, *"Orémus"*—Let us pray." And he started another prayer. He continued to speak in Latin. What he said was:

"O God, Creator and Defender of the human race, Who hast formed man in thine image, look down with pity upon this thy servant, Robert, for he has fallen a prey to the craftiness of an evil spirit. The ancient adversary, the archenemy of the earth, enshrouds him in shuddering fear. He renders his mental faculties befuddled; he keeps him bewildered by making him sore afraid; he holds him in a state of perturbation, as he strikes terror within him."

Bowdern glanced from the book to the boy, where the words of the prayer were manifest. Robbie flailed his arms, pivoted his head, and, eyes still shut, spat in Halloran's face, turned and spat in his uncle's face. He worked an arm free—as he had managed to do at Georgetown Hospital—and lashed out at the men trying to hold him. They grabbed his arm and again pinned him down.

"Drive out, O Lord, the power of the devil, and banish his artifices and frauds. Let him, the wicked tempter, be routed afar. By the sign"—Bowdern traced a cross on Robbie's forehead and

Robbie spat in the priest's face—"of thy name let thy servant be protected and safeguarded in both body and soul."

Holding his left hand to his face as a shield, Bowdern made three crosses on the H E L L on Robbie's blotchy chest while saying, "Keep watch over his reason, rule thou over his emotions, bring cheer into his heart."

Bowdern stood up and stepped back, continuing, "Let there vanish from his soul the temptations of the mighty adversary. O Lord, as we call upon thy holy name, graciously grant that the evil spirit, who hitherto terrorized over us, may now himself fly terror-stricken and may he depart vanquished. Thus let this servant of thine offer thee with steadfast heart and sincere mind the meed that is thy due.

"Through Jesus Christ"—more spitting, more grappling—"thy Son, our Lord, Who liveth and reigneth with thee in the unity of the Holy Spirit, God for all ages."

Bishop uttered, "Amen."

It was well past midnight now. Everyone except Robbie was worn out. Bowdern particularly was exhausted. But his voice did not falter. There were two more long prayers. Perhaps if he did not hesitate, perhaps if he pressed on, the demon would leave. Perhaps it would not be like Loudun, where it had gone on day after day, week after week, month after month…

He gathered his strength, in an almost biblical way. He was emerging from his fatigue, feeling new power. He spoke now in what he thought was his mightiest voice. *"ADJURO TE!"* And what he said was:

"I adjure thee, thou ancient serpent, by the Judge of the living and the dead, by thy own Creator, by the Creator of the world, by Him Who has the power to consign thee to hell, that thou speedily depart in trembling, along with thy raving followers, from this servant of God, Robert, who seeks refuge in the bosom of the Church. I adjure thee once more"—another cross on the brow—"not by my own weakness but by the might of the Holy Spirit, begone from this servant of God, Robert, whom the Almighty has made in His image.

"Yield, therefore, yield, not to myself but to the minister of Christ! For it is the power of Christ that compels thee, Who brought thee under the subjection of His Cross. Quake before His arm, for it is He Who silenced the groans of hell, and brought forth the souls unto light. Be afraid of the body of man"—a cross on that H E L L across Robbie's heaving chest—"be in dread of the image of God." Then a cross traced on the brow. "Make no resistance, neither delay in leaving this person, for it has pleased Christ to take up His dwelling in man.

"Let it not occur to thee to despise my command, because thou dost recognize in me a poor sinner. It is God Himself Who commands thee." By inserting † before a particular word, the *Ritual* instructed the exorcist as to each moment at which he was to make a sign of the cross. At the † next to "thee," Bowdern sliced his steady hand through the air. Spit dripped from his face and hit his hand. Now, with each evocation, he made the sign of the cross in the air, amid the shouts and the breathing, and the weeping of Robbie's mother, and the spittle, the incredible amounts of spittle.

Again and again Bowdern's right hand knifed through the air as he said, in Latin, "The majesty of Christ commands † thee! God the Father commands † thee! The Holy Spirit commands † thee! The mystery of the Cross commands † thee! The faith of the holy apostles Peter and Paul and the other saints commands † thee! The blood of the martyrs commands † thee! The constancy of the confessors commands † thee! The devout intercession of all holy men and women commands † thee! The power of the mysteries of Christian faith commands † thee!

"Go out, then, thou transgressor, go out, thou seducer full of deceit and perfidy, thou horrible creature, make way, thou monster, make way for Christ, in whom thou has found nothing of thy works. For He has stripped thee of thy might and laid waste thy kingdom; He has overcome thee and put thee in chains, and has blown up thy war materials. He has cast thee out into exterior darkness, where ruination is being made ready for thee and thine abettors.

"But to what purpose dost thou resist in thy insolence? To what purposes dost thou brazenly refuse? Thou art guilty before the almighty God, Whose laws thou hast transgressed. Thou art guilty before His Son, our Lord Jesus Christ, Whom thou didst presume to tempt, Whom thou wast emboldened to nail to the Cross. Thou art guilty before the human race, for through thy blandishments thou didst proffer it the poisoned cup of death.

"I adjure thee, therefore, thou profligate dragon, in the name of the spotless † Lamb, Who walked upon the asp and the basilisk and tread underfoot the lion and the dragon, depart from this man"—Bowdern made a cross on Robbie's brow—"depart from the Church of God"—Bowdern turned and blessed the others in the room. "Quake and fly afar, as we call upon the name of the Lord, before Whom hell trembles, to Whom the heavenly Virtues and Powers and Dominations are subject, Whom the Cherubim and Seraphim praise with unending voice as they sing: Holy, holy, holy, Lord God of Sabaoth [Hebrew for *armies* or *hosts*]! The Word made flesh commands † thee. He Who was born of a Virgin commands † thee. Jesus † of Nazareth commands thee.

"For when thou didst mock at His disciples, He did shatter and humble thy pride, and did order thee out of a certain man; and when He had cast thee forth, thou didst not even dare except by His leave to enter into a herd of swine. And now as I adjure thee in His † name, vanish from this man whom He has created. It is hard for thee to want to resist. † It is hard for thee to kick against the goad. † For the longer thou dost delay thy departure, the heavier thy punishment shall be; since it is not men thou dost contemn, but rather Him, the Ruler over the living and the dead, Who shall come to judge the living and the dead and the world by fire."

Bishop said, "Amen," and Robbie heard again the two priests alternate the familiar Latin epilogue to prayer:

"Dómine, exáudi oratiónem meam."

"Et clamor meus ad te véniat."

"Dóminus vobíscum."

"Et cum spíritu tuo."

Again Bowdern said, *"Orémus"* and began another prayer in Latin.

"O God of heaven and God of earth, God of the angels and God of the archangels, God of the prophets and God of the apostles, God of martyrs and God of virgins, thou hast the power to bestow life after death and rest after toil; for there is no God beside thee, nor could there be a true God apart from thee, the Creator of heaven and earth, Who art truly the King of Whose kingdom there shall be no end. Hence I humbly implore thy sublime Majesty, that thou wouldst vouchsafe to deliver this thy servant from the unclean spirits. Through Christ our Lord."

"Amen," Bishop repeated.

Bowdern paused and looked down on a living, writhing nightmare. On the soaking, crumpled sheets, Robbie grimaced in his sleep, twisting and spitting. He was as strong now as he had been hours ago. Halloran and Robbie's uncle still held the boy but they were weakening. Sweat and spit splotched their faces and stained their clothing. Phyllis Mannheim and her sister-in-law huddled together near the head of the bed, Phyllis beyond sobbing. The women were transfixed with terror and grief. Bowdern looked over to Bishop, whose face also glistened with sweat and spit. There was a fleck of blood on his surplice, where it had touched Robbie's body. Bowdern caught Bishop's eye and nodded. Yes, there was more. The night would go on.

Bowdern held the *Ritual* in his left hand, a finger in his place, and with his right hand picked up the bottle of holy water. He took a step forward and poured water onto Robbie's head. He awoke, startled, looked around, sat up, and sank back onto the damp pillow. He said that where he had been was very, very hot. He weakly asked for water. Phyllis went into the nearby bathroom to get him a glass of water. By the time she came back he was asleep again and, strangely strong, struggling once more.

Several times during the night, at the end of a prayer, Bowdern repeated the pouring of the holy water on Robbie. Bowdern and Bishop both felt that while Robbie was awake he was calmer. A couple of times the water did not awaken him, and Bishop or Bowdern slapped him lightly on the face to rouse him.

Finally came the last prayer of exorcism.

"I cast thee out," Bowdern began, "every unclean spirit, every phantom, every encroachment of Satan, in the name of Jesus Christ † of Nazareth, Who, after John baptized Him, was led into the desert and vanquished thee in thy citadel. Cease thy attack on man, whom He has made for His honor and glory out of the slime of the earth. Tremble before wretched man, not in the condition of human frailty but in the likeness of almighty God. Yield then to

God, † for it is He Who in Pharaoh and his army did drown thee and thy malice through His servant, Moses, in the depths of the sea. Yield to God, † Who, by the singing of holy canticles on the part of David, His faithful servant, banished thee from the heart of King Saul.

"Yield to God, † Who condemned thee in the traitor, Judas Iscariot. For He menaces thee with a divine † scourge, before Whose countenance thou didst tremble and cry out, saying, 'What have we to do with thee, Jesus, Son of the Most High? Hast thou come hither before the time to torture us?' He threatens thee with everlasting fire, Who at the end of time will say to the wicked: 'Depart from me, ye cursed, into everlasting fire which has been prepared for the devil and his angels.'

"For thee, O evil one, and for thy followers there will be worms which never perish. For thee and for thine angels is made ready an unquenchable fire, because thou art the prince of accursed murder, thou the author of lechery, thou the leader in sacrilege, thou the model of vileness, thou the teacher of heretics, thou the inventor of every obscenity. Depart then, † O evil one, depart, † accursed one, depart with all thy falsity, for God has desired that man be His temple. But why dost thou linger here yet longer? Give honor to God the Father † Almighty, before Whom every knee bows. Give place to the Lord Jesus † Christ, Who shed for men His most precious blood. Give place to the Holy † Spirit…"

Bowdern suddenly raised his voice to a shout. *"Discéde ergo nunc"*—Begone, now! He raised his hand one last time, cutting the air savagely in a great, final sign of the cross. "Begone, thou seducer! Thy place is in solitude, thy dwelling in the serpent. Humble thyself, and fall prostrate! This matter brooks no delay. For behold, the Lord, the Ruler comes quickly, and fire will burn before Him, and it will go on ahead and set flames round about His enemies.

"Man thou canst betray, but God thou canst not mock. It is He that drives thee out, from Whose eyes nothing is hidden. By him art thou cast forth, to Whose might all things are subject, By Him art thou expelled, Who hath prepared unending hell for thee and thine angels, from Whose mouth there shall come forth a pointed sword, Who shall come to judge the living and the dead and the world by fire."

Bishop said, "Amen."

The room was suddenly calm. Robbie was in what seemed to be real sleep, free of nightmare. Bowdern fell to his knees and prayed silently for a moment, his head touching the soaked sheet. It was nearly five a.m.

Then, with his eyes tightly closed, Robbie sat up and began singing. "Way down upon the Swanee River, far, far away" he sang, his voice squeaky and extraordinarily loud. He swung his arms in wide, sweeping gestures out of sync with the music. He cackled, the words crowding upon one another and, his arms still flailing in a frenzied attempt at keeping time, he swung into "Ole Man River, dat Ole Man River, he mus' know sumpin'—." His eyes opened several times during the wild recital, he seemed to smile, and he resumed singing, garbling the shouted words, screeching the music.

Bowdern, though spent, began praying again. The *Ritual* recommended several prayers—excerpts from the Gospels, psalms, the Athanasian Creed, which added its words of dogma to all the other words of faith and menace that paced that long night into morning. Bishop, usually methodical but on this night stunned and weary, did not record what prayers were said.

He ended his record with this note: "About 7:30 AM, R began a natural sleep and continued quite peacefully until 1:00 PM of the 17th. Then he ate an ordinary meal and participated in a game of monopoly."

Chapter 9

"He's going! He's going!"

Father Bowdern believed deep in his soul that he was in combat with Satan. And, as that long and terrible night lengthened into morning, he had felt weighed down by a heavy burden. His only weapons were his faith and the *Ritual,* with its prayers and instructions. His only strategy was to soldier on, doing again and again what he had done last night and through the dawn and into the morning. He thought he knew his limits, and, because he was an honest man, he did not know whether he could hold out for all the nights this combat would need. But he would try. He was not a man who gave up easily. He was, said a friend, a man who never did anything to "make things easy for himself."

The *Ritual* said that some kinds of evil spirits could not be driven out, except by prayer and fasting. Bowdern profoundly believed in prayer. As for fasting, he said to Halloran, "We're supposed to fast. But I've got a lot of work to do. I don't think I can do it on bread and water." A typical fast for a Jesuit priest was a breakfast of a soft-boiled egg and dry toast, a cheese sandwich for lunch, a regular dinner but without meat. The fasting Jesuit could not eat between meals, but he could drink whenever or whatever he wanted.

So it would be prayer that sustained Bowdern, prayer and faith. The *Ritual* advised the exorcist to keep in mind what Jesus said when the apostles failed to exorcise a child. Jesus said he succeeded because he believed and they did not: "For verily I say unto you, If ye have faith as a grain of mustard seed, ye shall say unto this mountain. Remove hence to yonder place; and it shall remove; and nothing shall be impossible unto you."

Bowdern told Bishop and Halloran he had no idea how long this would last. The exorcism could consume their days and nights indefinitely, but at the same time each man had to carry out his regular duties. And, because of Archbishop Ritter's demand for secrecy, none of them could use the exorcism as an excuse for being sleepy, which they all were on this Thursday, St. Patrick's Day, and the second day of the exorcism.

Halloran faced the most trouble. Like Bowdern and Bishop, Halloran began his day at 5 a.m. But, as a Jesuit scholastic, he had far less freedom than the two priests and lived more of an institutional life. Among his superiors was a priest, known as Father Minister, who kept the scholastics on track. Although Halloran had some independence as a student, his non-study hours were rigidly controlled. There was no way that he could stay out all night without extraordinary permission.

Somehow, though, the two priests covered for him. All Jesuits, scholastics and priests, lived in individual rooms known as cells. Halloran's was on the floor of a residence hall reserved for scholastics. He managed to get back to his cell, shave, shower, and make it to his classes without alerting the Prefect of Discipline. Bowdern had a full day of pastoral work to perform, and Bishop had his schedule of classes.

Bowdern telephoned Robbie's family during the day, heard about the afternoon Monopoly game, and also learned that Robbie's father was arriving back from Maryland. He was trying to keep his job and had gone home. Phyllis told Karl what had happened on Wednesday night and he said he would fly to St. Louis and arrive in time for Thursday's session.

About 9:30 p.m., Halloran pulled up in front of the house and followed the priests inside. Phyllis met them at the door. Karl and his brother, she said, were upstairs, holding Robbie down. The Jesuits could hear noises coming from the bedroom.

Phyllis said that Robbie had spent an uneventful day and seemed unaffected by the events of the night and morning. They had all eaten supper, and there was talk of another Monopoly game. Then, around nine o'clock, Robbie had suddenly become drowsy. Sleep came on him so quickly that he had dozed off while getting undressed for bed. He had hardly crawled into bed before he began thrashing and shouting, in his sleep. The horrors of last night had begun again.

Bowdern and Bishop put on their surplices and stoles and went upstairs. Halloran followed. In the bedroom, Karl and his brother George were at the head of the bed, leaning heavily on Robbie, who was struggling in their hold.

Bowdern splashed holy water in Robbie's face and slapped him sharply several times. The boy sat up and looked around, then fell back asleep and began squirming and screaming. The *Ritual* had warned about this. Sometimes the demons put the demoniac into an unnatural sleep to keep the victim from being aware of the exorcism.

Bowdern motioned for Halloran to join the other two men holding Robbie down. It did not seem possible that such a slight boy could be mustering such strength. A sign of possession, Bowdern thought.

He opened the *Ritual* and began reciting the first of the prayers. Robbie reacted violently. His eyes closed, he turned toward his father and spat in his face. Then he spat on his Uncle George and on Halloran. Bowdern moved closer, speaking loudly and authoritatively over Robbie's shouts. The boy, eyes still tightly shut, managed to slip away from the three men gripping him and, with a swift move, reached out, grabbed Bowdern's stole, and tore it easily.

Father Bishop, who had just sprinkled holy water on Robbie's face, caught a jet of spit full in the face. Phyllis moved forward to stroke Robbie's brow with a cloth. He turned his closed eyes toward her and, swerving around the cloth, unerringly spat in her face.

He twisted his head. Halloran ducked, but Robbie caught him square in the face. "He was an utter marksman at a distance of four or five feet," Halloran later marveled. "His eyes were closed and he'd spit right in your face."

Bowdern never wavered. He kept reading the prayers and Bishop and Halloran kept responding on cue. Robbie's Aunt Catherine began reciting the rosary. While she tolled the beads, others joined her. *Hail Mary, full of grace...* and *Our Father Who art in heaven...*

Occasionally, Robbie emerged from his nightmare sleep. He looked startled when his parents asked him why he was spitting and fighting. Exhausted and awake, he remembered nothing about his actions. All he knew was that he had been asleep. During these moments of puzzled wakefulness, Bishop checked Robbie's pulse. It was normal, just as it had been the night before. Bishop also looked Robbie over for scratches and welts. There were none.

Then Robbie would fall back into what Bishop dubbed "the deep tantrum sleep" and the spitting and the shouting would begin again. A few times Robbie screamed threats at the people who were holding him. And, at such words as *Dóminus* and *Deus,* he arched his slim body off the bed or thrashed about wildly. Once in a while he would hum a tune or pitch his voice high and, offkey, start singing "Way down upon the Swanee River…"

Bowdern kept reading and, when he had finished the prayers of exorcism, he led rosaries, staying at the bedside until, at about one-thirty in the morning, Robbie fell into what seemed to be a normal sleep. When Bowdern was certain that Robbie was asleep for the night, he led the way downstairs.

Bishop went around with his notebook, asking questions of everyone who was in the room and jotting down their observations, along with his own. Then the priests and Halloran said good night and drove back to the university.

Bowdern, after a few hours' sleep, arose, said his regular daily Mass at Xavier, and looking haggard and worried, tried to concentrate on being a pastor for the rest of the day. But his mind was on his war with Satan over a little boy who did not seem to know about the war. That Friday afternoon he heard from Robbie's parents. They said that Robbie had what they called a "spell" shortly after lunch. Karl Mannheim held Robbie tightly in his arms while Phyllis the non-Catholic and her Catholic sister-in-law recited the rosary. Robbie stopped his struggling in about an hour and seemed to return to normal.

Bowdern, Bishop, and Halloran returned to the house at seven o'clock. The three chatted and played a game with Robbie. (Bishop did not note what the game was, and Halloran, asked about it forty years later, did not remember it.) Robbie seemed to enjoy the company, but shortly after eight he said he was getting sleepy. He went up the stairs and got ready for bed. As soon as he got into bed, the priests and Halloran gathered again in his room.

Bowdern led the other Jesuits in the rosary, and Robbie, haltingly, joined in. When the last of the fifty Hail Marys and ten Our Fathers had been recited, Bowdern mentioned Our Lady of Fatima, a story that Robbie had enjoyed when Bowdern first told it to him. Then the priest began reciting a prayer specifically to Our Lady of Fatima. Robbie seemed calm and had remained awake. Bowdern took his place at one side of the bed, Bishop at the other. Halloran knelt again before the bars at the bottom of the bed. Bowdern opened the *Ritual* to the section on exorcism and began the first prescribed prayer, the Litany of the Saints.

"*K'yrie, eléison,*" Bowdern said.

Bishop and Halloran answered, "*Christe, eléison.*" And once more the rhythm of the litany sounded in the bedroom—Bowdern reciting a Latin phrase, Bishop and Halloran responding.

Christe, audi nos."

Christe, exáudi nos."

"*Sancta Maria, ora pro nobis.*"

"*Ora pro nobis.*"

"*Sancta Virgo vírginum—*"

"*Ora pro nobis.*"

"*Sancte Míchael—*"

"*Ora pro nobis.*"

"*Sancte Gábriel—*"

The mattress began to shake.

Bowdern interrupted the litany, marked his place in the *Ritual* with a finger, took up the bottle of holy water from a table next to the bed, and sprinkled the bed with water. The mattress stopped shaking.

Bowdern opened the *Ritual* again and the three Jesuits resumed the chant of the litany:

"*Sancte Ráphael.*"

"*Ora pro nobis.*"

"*Omne sancti Angeli et Archángeli.*"

"*Ora pro—*"

Robbie erupted, arms and legs flailing. He tore at the blanket and sheet and pummeled the pillow. Halloran moved to the head of the bed and grabbed the boy. His father and uncle rushed in and joined Halloran. All three of the men were holding Robbie down. Yet he twisted and arched his body. "The contortions," Bishop later recorded, "revealed physical strength beyond the natural power of R."

Robbie jerked his head out of grasping hands and started spitting. Although his eyes were closed, he never missed. Father Bishop ducked—in vain—and sprinkled holy water. Robbie writhed under the droplets, as if in pain. "He fought and screamed in a diabolical, high-pitched voice," Bishop's diary says.

Bowdern stopped reading and, following one of the instructions in the *Ritual,* tried to touch Robbie with a relic. Robbie spat on it and swiftly pivoted and spat on Bishop's upraised hand. Next, Bowdern reached under his surplice and removed from a pocket inside his cassock a small gold box called a pyx. In it was a round wafer, a consecrated host. This was what Catholics revered as the Blessed Sacrament, the body and blood of Christ.

Robbie's feet were moving rhythmically, as if he were marching off to some new battle at the edge of the pit. Bowdern held the pyx near the sole of a foot. That leg stopped moving while the other kept marching through Robbie's nightmare.

Suddenly, Robbie was conscious. He said his arms were sore, and he looked at his father and uncle and Halloran. He seemed to know that they had made his arms sore by clutching them. But he said nothing. Then, just as suddenly as he had awakened, he closed his eyes, fell back on the pillow, and began thrashing and screaming.

Bowdern continued the prayers. Between screams Robbie sometimes tried to repeat the words. He seemed to calm down and, for an instant, the men released him. In that instant, says Bishop's diary, "R stood up in bed and fought all those around him. He shouted, jumped, and swung his fists. His face was devilish, and he snapped his teeth in fury. He snapped at the Priest's hand in the blessings. He bit those who held him."

Pressed down on the mattress, Robbie resumed struggling and spitting while the prayers droned on. For hours he fluctuated between frenzy and calm. Then, about midnight, during a period of calm, his exhausted holders released him.

In an instant he was on his feet, standing in the middle of the bed. He dropped to his knees and began salaaming, bending at the waist and touching his head to the mattress. After several silent salaams he began to chant, "Our Lady of Fatima, pray for us" and then switched to saying the words to the "Hail Mary." While everyone else in the room gathered around the bed, spellbound, Robbie put the pillow in front of his knees and began beating a rhythm that sounded like the clop-clop-clop of trotting horses. He abruptly stood again and, to Bishop's eye, "began his strong fight for the eviction of the devil." Bishop continues, "His gyrations were in all directions. He pulled off the upper part of his underwear, and held his arms high above himself in supplication. Then he made as though he were trying to vomit from his stomach. His gestures moved upwards, close to his body. He seemed to try to lift the devil from his stomach to his throat."

Robbie asked someone to open the window. The cold night winds whipped into the bedroom.

"He's going! He's going!" Robbie cried in a sweet, victorious voice. "There he goes!"

Robbie fell back on the bed, his body limp, as if drained of its strange surge of strength.

Everyone in the room knelt by the bed. Bowdern led a prayer of thanksgiving. Phyllis Mannheim wept for joy. Robbie, his face beatific, told of his triumph. He said he had seen a huge black cloud that had darkened his vision. Upon the cloud had appeared a cowled figure in a black robe. And the figure had walked away, growing smaller and smaller until he vanished.

Robbie got out of bed, put on his bathrobe, and, smiling happily, walked downstairs with the three Jesuits. He talked with them for a few minutes and then said goodbye to them at the front door. It was about 1:30 a.m.

At 3:15 a.m., the phone rang at the College Church rectory. Dreading what he was going to hear, Father Bowdern picked up the phone. *It's Robbie.* He was clutching his stomach in pain and shouting, "He's coming back! He's coming back!"

Bowdern got dressed rapidly and, careful not to awaken anyone else, rounded up Bishop and Halloran. "I had just gotten into bed," Halloran remembers, "and he came in and said, 'We're going to go again.'"

Lights were blazing in one house on the dark street when Halloran pulled up. The three Jesuits silently filed into the house, went up the stairs, and Bowdern began the prayers of exorcism again. It was as if nothing had happened. There was Robbie writhing on the bed. There were his uncle and father holding him down. More prayers, more screams, more spit. And finally, at 7:30 a.m., Robbie fell into what looked like a natural sleep.

Bowdern, Bishop, and Halloran got back into the car and drove off in silence. Bowdern clutched his *Ritual.* Sometimes, the instructions said, the demons "leave the body practically free from every molestation, so that the victim believes himself completely delivered. Yet the exorcist may not desist until he sees signs of deliverance." *But what are those the signs? Robbie had shouted, "He's going!" and "There he goes! Weren't those signs? What are the signs?* For the first time, Bowdern felt despair, the most dreadful sin, for it drained the soul of hope.

Chapter 10

The Sign of the X

Father Bowdern, eyes puffy from lack of sleep, walked into the sacristy of St. Francis Xavier Church and stepped over to the lavabo, where he washed and dried his hands before vesting for Mass. He turned to the nearby vesting table, a broad, waist-high wooden cabinet. Lent had begun, and so he pulled out the wide drawer containing the outer purple vestments. He placed them on the flat surface and reached into another drawer for the other vestments.

He kissed the hem of the amice, a white, oblong piece of linen, placed it across his shoulders, crossed it on his chest, passed its long linen straps around the waist of his cassock, and tied them. He ducked into the alb, a white tunic that reached to his feet, then encircled it with a long white cincture that he knotted at the waist. On his left arm he draped a purple maniple that had a cross embroidered on both sides. Around his neck he placed a purple stole that was wider and longer than the one used during the exorcism. Finally, he picked up the chasuble, a sleeveless mantle, lowered his head, and donned the last purple vestment. Embroidered on the part of the chasuble that covered his back was a large cross.

Fully vested, he put on his biretta. A waiting altar boy opened the heavy wooden door leading to the sanctuary and Father

Bowdern followed the boy out. People stirred in the pews beyond the altar rail. The parishioners who made up the small Saturday congregation stood as Bowdern handed his biretta to the altar boy, ascended the steps to the altar, bowed to kiss the cool marble altar stone, and touched his right thumb to his forehead and his chest in the sign of the cross. He turned and moved his hand in a sign of the cross that blessed the congregation.

He felt peace and strength here in this church. The despair had vanished. He descended the stairs and, turning toward the tabernacle, which held the Blessed Sacrament, he said, *"Introibo ad altaré Dei"*—I will go onto the altar of God.

The altar boy responded, *"Ad Deum qui laetificat juventutem meam"*—To God who giveth joy to my youth.

And this was the way it was most of the time. Latin in the hush of a church, Mass as the service he gave to people. Being a Jesuit in the deepest spiritual tradition, the tradition of Ignatius.

The dozens of stained-glass windows around the church reveal much about the Jesuit view of the world. Windows in the transepts portray the three social orders affected by the teachings of Christ: the state, the Church, and the family. The human relationship to the material world is symbolized by images of the three basic human occupations: farming, transport, and commerce. Another window depicts the Jesuit martyrs of North America, whose relics Bowdern had taken to Robbie. Nearby were windows showing scenes from the lives of Jesuit saints with unabashedly parallel scenes from biblical stories.

In the great soaring apse, lancet windows draw the eye upward from the main altar. The windows portray, in gold-haloed splendor, the three persons of the Holy Trinity. Around them cluster hosts of angels and a rainbow, the ageless symbol of hope.

Saturday followed the pattern of the other days. Robbie played, read comic books, listened to the radio, got under people's feet, acting like a normal thirteen-year-old boy. With darkness would come the darkening of mood, and at the edge of sleep would come the horror. Bowdern decided to try to push the dark period into an earlier hour, to spare Robbie, his family, and his visitors a nightlong siege. Perhaps if Robbie got to bed around eight o'clock, the ordeal would end at eleven or midnight instead of being prolonged into the morning.

Bowdern, Bishop, and Halloran arrived precisely at seven o'clock that evening and spent most of an hour trying to lull the household into a calm before another storm. At eight o'clock Robbie went to bed and in a few minutes Bowdern led the others into the room.

Robbie, Bowdern realized, had not shown any signs of violence until the exorcism began three nights before. *Would every exorcism usher in violence? If exorcism touched off this violence, what would end it?*

Bowdern knew that ultimately he was the prize the demon sought. That he did not fear. What he loathed was arousing the beast within Robbie and seeing him in torment. Bowdern was beginning to accept that the exorcism of Robbie would torture them both but that ultimately good would prevail. He must focus only on that. He must not despair again. He must not flinch at the fury he unleashed with his words of prayer. He began.

Robbie shouted and writhed against Halloran's hold. Bowdern sensed that tonight would be worse than the night before. He kept reading, Bishop kept responding, Halloran kept responding between grunts.

Bowdern began the *Praecípio*—"I command thee, unclean spirit"—and watched over the top of the *Ritual* as Robbie snapped his teeth and barked like a dog. "…thou shalt tell me by some sign"—

Bowdern was speaking in a language that Robbie could not understand. Yet at those Latin words seeking a sign, Robbie gave a sign: He urinated. The urine streamed from him and spread a stain across the blanket covering him. The stench was overwhelming. Bowdern commanded that the demon give his name. And again Robbie urinated. Bowdern asked the hour of the demon's departure. And the urine came from him again.

His pajamas and the bed were soaked, and still the urine came. He awoke suddenly, doubled up in pain, and cried out that the urine was burning him. As he spoke, he half-choked on the words because, he managed to say, his throat was burning too. He said he felt on fire in his throat and penis.

At times, the instructions in the *Ritual* had warned, "the evil spirits place whatever obstacles they can in the way, so that the patient may not submit to exorcism." Bowdern was tempted to shout and curse the demon. But he resisted, heeding the warning about directly engaging the demon.

He finished the *Praecípio* and moved on to the opening of the Gospel of St. John—"In the beginning was the Word, and the Word was with God, and the Word was God." As he prayed, he stepped forward, and made the sign of the cross on Robbie's brow, lips, and chest.

The urinating stopped and the words went on. "*Omnípotens Dómine, Verbum Dei Patris, Christe Jesu, Deus et Dóminus univérsae creatúrae"*—O Almighty Lord, Word of God the Father, Christ Jesus, God and Lord of all creation! The prayer continued: "...in fear and trembling I suppliantly call upon thy holy name: grant unto me, thy most unworthy servant, pardon for all my sins; bestow on me steadfast faith and the power to attack this cruel demon with assurance and fearlessness, fortified by the might of thy holy arm."

Bowdern had said that prayer on other nights, but now he could feel its strength. He made the sign of the cross again over Robbie and placed one end of the stole on Robbie's neck. With his right hand on Robbie's head, he said, *"Ecce Crucem Dómini, fúgite, partes advérsae"*—Behold the Cross of the Lord; begone, ye hostile powers!

Bishop responded, *"Vincit leo de tribu Juda, radix David"*—The Lion of Juda's tribe hath conquered, He Who is the rod of David.

His hand firm on Robbie's head, Bowdern continued, *Dómine, exáudi oratiónem meam"*—O Lord, hear my prayer.

Bishop spoke: *"Et clamor meus ad te véniat"*—And let my cry come unto thee.

"Dóminus vobiscum."

"Et cum spíritu tuo."

Robbie seemed to calm under Bowdern's hand. For a moment the shouting and the barking stopped. There was silence in the stink of the room. Then, from Robbie's mouth came the notes of "The Blue Danube"—*da da da da da, da da da da,* beautifully rendered, each note shimmering, his arms swinging in perfect rhythm with the melody. No more was his voice crude and his gestures choppy. He had the voice of an angelic choirboy, a seemingly trained voice.

Bishop, who had a better ear for music than Bowdern did, was particularly struck by Robbie's performance. After the previous outburst, Bishop, in his careful, note-taking way, had inquired about Robbie's musical abilities. His mother had told Bishop that Robbie did not sing well and, in fact, did not like to sing. Those facts explained the previous performance, but not this one.

Now Robbie swung into "The Old Rugged Cross," seemingly in a mocking riposte to Bowdern's prayer that had begun with *Ecce Crucem Dómini*. Again the music, to Bishop's ear, was of professional quality.

The singing stopped as suddenly as it had begun. Robbie awakened momentarily and Bishop casually asked him to hum along to the tune of "The Blue Danube." Robbie could not carry the melody and said that he did not know the song.

He closed his eyes and fell back into his trancelike sleep. A little while later, while Bowdern was continuing the prayers, Robbie called out to one of the priests by name. (Bishop does not record which priest.) The priest did not respond. Robbie called out again, his voice still pleasant. Once more, the priest refused to respond, following the *Ritual* instructions: Do not attempt to converse with the demoniac. In a harsh voice, Robbie called out the priest's name again and added, "You stink!" It was the first of what would be increasingly vehement attacks on the priests and Halloran.

Robbie's anger with the priest triggered a violent outburst. He began thrashing about again. Halloran struggled to hold him down. The shouting and the squirming continued until 3 a.m., when Robbie dropped into a deep slumber that Bowdern judged to be natural. He, Bishop, and Halloran waited and prayed at the bedside for another half-hour and then left. Now came another nightly ritual: the Mannheims removed soaked pajamas from the deeply sleeping Robbie, washed him, got him into fresh pajamas, and changed the sodden bedclothes.

On Sunday, Bowdern again began the session at eight o'clock and within fifteen minutes Robbie was showing signs of building to the worst evening yet. He cursed and flopped about the bed, threatening Halloran, cursing, screaming. He took delight in urinating prodigiously and broke wind loudly. He awoke for a moment at a time, complained about the urine burning him, and then fell back into the trance and continued to urinate and break wind. The room stank; the smells seemed to hang in the air like a foul fog.

For the first time, Robbie turned against the priests. "Get away from me, you assholes!" he suddenly shouted. His voice was sometimes shrill, sometimes guttural. Witnesses' recollections of Robbie's voice varied considerably. Some described his voice as unearthly—a deep, menacing voice that could not have come from a young boy. Others remembered a high-pitched, extremely irritating voice that cut into their minds like an ax. Others never could get Robbie's demoniacal laughter out of their minds.

"Go to hell, you dirty sons of bitches!" Robbie shouted.

Halloran pressed harder, fearful that the boy would leap up and harm Bowdern. But Bowdern never lost his focus on his mission. He prayed on, speaking loudly and firmly, like an officer addressing a hidden foe.

"Goddamn you, sons of bitches!" Robbie shouted. "You dirty assholes!"

Bishop duly noted these phrases. There were others, too offensive for the priest to write down. All he recorded was that Robbie also worked into his curses references to the Blessed Mother and perverted phrases from prayers to Our Lady of Fatima.

The cursing and the struggling finally ended at two o'clock.

Robbie's uncle and aunt could take no more. No one was getting any sleep. The next day, Monday, March 21, Phyllis Mannheim, worn out from grief, fear, and lack of sleep, was taken to a physician. Apparently she did not tell him the cause of her condition. Bishop does not record whether the physician prescribed a sedative.

Robbie remained seemingly oblivious to his nightly frenzies. His daily amnesia baffled everyone. "I always felt that if he had remembered what had taken place, he would have mentioned it," Halloran says. "But he never said anything to anyone who was ever involved. He never referred to anything that was ever said or done. I never had a feeling that he was putting on an act. None. If he was awake when you left, you would say 'Goodbye' and 'I'll see you again,' and he'd say, 'Okay.'"

The family gathered, Protestants and Catholics, to decide what to do next. Among the relatives were followers of Aunt Harriet's Spiritualism and believers in parapsychology. They urged alternatives other than exorcism. The Mannheims had given the Reverend Schulze their address in St. Louis and kept in touch. Apparently through him, they had met with an Episcopal priest and a local Lutheran minister. Now, hearing about the exorcism, Schulze began urging them to return home and consult his physician, who was "sympathetic to the case." But, at least for the moment, Phyllis and Karl Mannheim chose to hold off other advice and accept the recommendations of Bowdern and Bishop.

The Jesuits suggested that Robbie be put in a hospital, at least for a night, so that the rest of the family could sleep without fear of being awakened by screams. Robbie was not consulted. His parents agreed, and Bowdern immediately made arrangements for Robbie to be taken to the Alexian Brothers Hospital, an institution well known in St. Louis.

The Alexian Brothers' order, the Congregation of Cellites, was founded by monks who cared for the victims of the Black Death, which swept Europe in the fourteenth century. They were known in Europe as the Poor Brothers or Bread Brothers, the monks who succored the dying and the mad, the monks who stayed and buried the dead when others fled the plague. The name of their order commemorated their patron saint, St. Alexius, a holy man who devoted his life to helping the poor.

The Alexians opened their first hospital in Chicago in 1866, saying that they specialized in treating "idiots and lunatics of the male sex." The Brothers continued this specialty when they opened their St. Louis hospital in 1870. In segregated, race-conscious St. Louis they added a promise to treat men of any "class, nationality, religion, race or color." A new building went up in 1873. One of its two, 120-foot-long wings was reserved for mental patients. Strict rules forbade the use of chains, handcuffs, and straitjackets, but a violent patient could be put in a "security room." Bowdern arranged for one of the security rooms on the fifth floor.

Mindful of Archbishop Ritter's demand for secrecy, Bowdern knew he could trust the Alexians. The Brothers were among the first U.S. medical practitioners to recognize alcoholism as a disease. Since the 1920s they had treated alcoholics, and they had taken on a special mission, little known beyond their walls: They cared for alcoholic priests and were given the responsibility for deciding when they were cured and able to resume their religious duties.

At ten o'clock on the night of March 21, Robbie was admitted to the hospital and put into the bed in a security room. There were straps on the bed, bars on the window, and no doorknob on the inside of the door. To get out of the room, you pounded on the door until a Brother unlocked it. Brother Bruno, a longtime worker in the wing, had a keen sense of the needs of his patients and their kin. He ordered a divan moved into the room for Robbie's father, who had arrived with Robbie and the Jesuits.

Bowdern began reciting the Litany of the Saints as a prelude to the exorcism prayers and braced for another night of horror. Nothing happened.

Robbie's eyes were open in fear and he was swiveling his head around, looking first at the barred window and then at the straps that held him. He seemed more frightened by his surroundings than by what Bowdern was trying to exorcise.

For the first time, the exorcism went on without any outbursts from Robbie, who remained awake and fearfully alert. When the prayers ended, Bowdern led the people in the room—Bishop, Halloran, Karl Mannheim, and several brothers—in the rosary.

When it was finished, Bowdern rapped on the door. A Brother on duty opened it immediately and Bowdern walked out, gesturing for everyone but Karl to leave. As Bishop left the room he saw Karl Mannheim leaning over his son and praying aloud for him to sleep. At 11:30 p.m. Robbie fell into a deep and normal sleep. His father lay down on the divan and, for the first time in months, had a peaceful sleep. Robbie awoke at 6:30 a.m. and woke up his father. They returned to the home of Karl's brother and spent the day there.

One day around this time—the incident is not recounted in Bishop's diary—Karl W. Bubb, Sr., a fifty-seven-year-old professor of mathematics and physics at Washington University in St. Louis, visited the house where Robbie was staying. Bubb, a distinguished scientist, apparently had been invited to the house by a family member who, through Aunt Harriet's Spiritualism, knew of Bubb's interest in the paranormal. Bubb's mother had been a Spiritualist and had often had her son join her and others in seances.

Bubb later reported that during his visit to Robbie's bedroom he saw a table rise slowly and hover near the ceiling. A chest of drawers also reportedly moved while Bubb was in the room. As Halloran remembered the visit (which the Jesuits did not arrange), the exorcism aspect of the case greatly disturbed Bubb, who had come to see a poltergeist manifestation. As Halloran recounted the visit, Bubb jotted down some notes "and left, saying in effect, 'This isn't my territory.'"

During World War II Bubb had worked on the top-secret Manhattan Project, the mammoth scientific effort that developed the atomic bomb. At Washington University he was successively chairman of the department of applied mathematics and the department of mechanics. After his death in 1961, his papers on parapsychology—presumably including his notes on his visit to Robbie—were destroyed to protect his scientific reputation.

Bowdern, buoyed by hopes that Robbie was recovering, said that one night in the hospital was enough. The next night, Tuesday, March 22, Robbie was back in his uncle's home. About 9:30 p.m., a little while after Robbie got into the bed, it began to shake and he was again under a spell. Phyllis Mannheim called Bishop. Carrying a pyx containing the Blessed Sacrament, Bishop arrived with two other priests (not identified in the diary). The three priests knelt at the quaking bed and recited the prayers of exorcism, followed by the rosary. Shortly before midnight Robbie dropped off to a natural sleep.

Bowdern apparently interpreted Robbie's docile behavior on two successive nights as a sign that the possession was easing its grip. The priest now decided to try a new strategy: the conversion of Robbie to Catholicism. His motive seems to have been a soldierly desire to enlist the boy into the ranks of what Bowdern perceived as the strongest force that could be brought to bear on the weakening demons. Perhaps Bowdern had by now so often said the prayers of exorcism that one phrase about religious refuge was inspiring him to this action: "I adjure thee...that thou speedily depart...from this servant of God, Robert, who seeks refuge in the bosom of the Church."

Bowdern had a room set up in his rectory to accommodate Robbie and his father. Karl Mannheim, born a Catholic, authorized Bowdern to begin instructing Robbie in Catholicism. On Wednesday night Robbie and Karl moved into the rectory. Bowdern spent awhile talking to Robbie about Catholicism and teaching him prayers that Catholic children even younger than Robbie learned as a kind of primer to their religion. Contained in these four short prayers—the Acts of Faith, Hope, Love, and Contrition—were the essentials of Catholicism and, Bowdern believed, new armor for one possessed.

The Act of Faith attested to absolute belief in what Bowdern was about to teach, the tenets of the Catholic Church. The Act of Hope asked for "pardon of my sins, the assistance of Thy grace, and life everlasting; through the merits of Jesus Christ, my Lord and Redeemer." In the Act of Love Robbie prayed, telling God, "I love Thee above all things with my whole heart and soul, because Thou art infinitely lovable, and deserving of all love. I love also my neighbor as myself...I forgive all who have injured me, and ask pardon for all whom I have injured." In the Act of Contrition, Robbie said,

"I repent with my whole heart of having offended Thee; I detest my sins for the love of Thee; I firmly resolve never to offend Thee again, and by the help of The grace to avoid every occasion of sin."

Faith, hope, love—and repeated references to sin—were ringing in Robbie's mind when he went to bed at 9:30 p.m. Bowdern, Bishop, Halloran, and Karl Mannheim gathered around his bed, along with a newcomer, Father William A. Van Roo, S.J., a priest in his post-ordination tertianship.

Van Roo, whom even fellow Jesuits called brilliant, had already embarked on his life's work as a theologian by beginning studies into the influences of Arabian philosophy on Thomas Aquinas. He would become an eminent theologian on the faculty of the Gregorian University in Rome. But on this March night he was being recruited as a potential backup for Halloran. As part of his tertianship, Van Roo had just been assigned as an assistant to Bowdern, who had greeted him with, "Bill, I've got just the project for you."

Everyone around the bed joined Robbie in reciting the Acts of Faith, Hope, Love, and Contrition. Then Bowdern began the Litany of the Saints. Robbie immediately erupted, kicking, spitting, and flailing at Halloran, who pressed the boy down and desperately signaled Van Roo and Karl Mannheim for help.

While Bowdern kept saying the prayers, the three men struggled to hold Robbie. His eyes tightly closed, he twisted and screamed. But in a few minutes he snapped open his eyes and smiled up at Halloran appealingly. "Please let go of my arms," the boy said. "You're hurting me."

"I'm just going to hold my hands close to you," Halloran said.

Van Roo frowned.

Then Robbie's quiet mood abruptly ended and Halloran swiftly clamped his hands on one thin arm and motioned for Van Roo to grasp the other. Karl Mannheim held back, reluctant to grapple with his son. Van Roo frowned again. "There is no sense in having to hold his arms that hard," he told Halloran. "You're only making him uncomfortable."

Halloran, who called himself the strong-arm man of the exorcist team, thought he knew better. He had seen the pattern before: Robbie would smile, open his eyes, wait for an opening, and then lunge. This was Van Roo's first night, but he was a priest and Halloran a mere scholastic. So Halloran let go of Robbie's arm.

In a split-second, Robbie blindly lashed out, slamming a little fist into Halloran's very ordinary nose. Eyes still closed, he struck Van Roo's aquiline nose. Both Jesuits grabbed for the unerring fist, then for the other one, and pressed them down to the bed. Halloran's nose was broken, Van Roo's nose was bleeding but otherwise intact.

The two Jesuits, joined tentatively by Karl Mannheim, grimly held on. Bowdern began the prayer that had often produced a violent reaction. "*PRAECÍPIO TIBI!*" he said loudly. "I command thee, unclean spirit—"

Robbie started urinating and breaking wind. The stench was unbearable. Someone opened a window. Robbie screamed and laughed diabolically. That was the word that instantly came to listeners' minds. Diabolically.

Near the rear window was Verhaegen Hall, the old red-brick Jesuit residency full of the private rooms that Jesuits called cells. Scholastics like Halloran lived on the first floor. Priests in studies for their doctorates and priests on the university faculty lived on the second and third floors. In one of the upper rooms a young

Jesuit was reading his Office (a book of daily prayer). "I heard this wild, idiotic, diabolical laughter," he later remembered. Because of the secrecy, he knew nothing about the exorcism. "I looked toward the window from where the light was coming, but saw nothing."

Inside, Bowdern was experiencing the worst night so far. Robbie periodically awakened for moments, whimpered about the burning in his penis, then fell back into his nightmare sleep and thrashed and laughed and screamed.

"I'm in hell," he shouted, laughing. "I see you. I see you." He turned his grinning, eyes-shut face toward Bowdern. "You're in hell. It's nineteen-fifty-seven."

For the first time, Bowdern reacted to a remark from Robbie. He hesitated in his prayer. He paled and looked about, confused and anguished. He lapsed for only a moment, then summoned up new strength and resumed the prayer.

"I've got a beautiful pecker," Robbie shouted, giggling idiotically. "A willy, dilly, pilly. So round, so firm. With a red top and a hole in the middle."

He turned his face, the spittle-flecked blank face of a mad, blind man-child, to Bowdern and shouted, "Oh, you have a big fat penis!"

A towel had been draped across his loins to soak up the urine. He somehow wiggled his hands free, whipped away the towel, and started miming masturbation. The priests grabbed his hands and held them down. He shouted words that Bishop did not record, primly noting, "His expressions were lowly and smacked of the abuse of sex." When Robbie was Robbie by day, Bishop remarked in the diary, he never used obscene words.

At odd moments, Robbie awakened to report on what he was seeing and hearing in hell. The men down there, he said, used filthy words. Then he returned to his eyes-closed state, contorting suggestively, barking, singing unfamiliar songs. At 2:30 a.m. his body went limp and he drifted into natural sleep.

Halloran, grateful for being so close to home, slipped into the residence hall and into his room. His nose hurt, and he knew it was broken. He hoped that the other twenty or so scholastics on the first floor would not notice. They were all in special studies and followed a strict schedule. They had to study so much that they hardly had time for chatting with one another. None of them knew that Halloran was spending his nights holding down a demoniac.

He flopped into bed, fell asleep instantly, and got up, as usual, at five o'clock. He showered and shaved and tried to keep his faced turned away to avoid questions about his swollen nose. He joined other scholastics in the chapel and meditated before the tabernacle that held the Blessed Sacrament. Then he went to Mass, had breakfast in the refectory, and began his day with an eight o'clock class.

On a day like this one—perhaps during meditation, perhaps at other times—Halloran began to worry about his lack of reaction to what he had been seeing and experiencing. Some forty years later he would remember his feelings: "I'd be kind of disappointed, ill at ease with myself. Shouldn't I be showing more of a reaction than this? Have I got to the point where I don't really believe effectively that the devil has come here among people?" And he thought about the others. "We should be having more of a reaction to this than we are," he told himself. Looking back, he wondered, "How could I have been so flat and emotionless?" With the wisdom of maturity, he now thinks that he may have been numbed by evil.

There certainly was something numbing about it, day after day, the same prayers, the same hopes raised and smashed. But Bowdern would not despair again, and Bishop, though troubled, never had despaired, even after that first terrifying night in the rectory. Both priests believed that the departure of the demon was imminent.

The exorcism formula called for the exorcist to demand that the demon reveal the time of his departure. On the first night, when an *X* had appeared on Robbie's right leg, both priests had decided that this was the demon's signal for departing in ten days. Bishop figured departure day to be Thursday, March 24, because it was the feast of St. Gabriel, the archangel who was so high in the Litany of Saints. He also pointed out that the next day, Friday, March 25, was the Feast of the Annunciation—the day, exactly nine months before Christmas Day, when the Archangel Gabriel said, "Hail, Mary," and announced to the Blessed Virgin the incarnation of Christ. By Bowdern's count, however, March 25 was the tenth day.

Robbie remained in the rectory on Thursday, and on that night, with Bishop confident that the demon would depart, Bowdern began the litany. He had hardly got beyond Gabriel before Robbie began screaming, shouting, barking, singing, urinating, and breaking wind. Again the room filled with a foul smell.

Bowdern had invited other Jesuit priests to assist him. One of them helped three other men hold Robbie down during the worst of his violent spasms. Turning his closed eyes toward this priest, Robbie said, "You big fat ass. You ox." Robbie singled out the priest (unnamed in Bishop's diary) for special abuse. "What's the use of you being here?" Robbie asked. "You will be with me in hell in 1957." According to one of the many Jesuit tales about the exorcism, on this night, the priest, a heavy drinker, swore off alcohol for a time.

Another target was a campus handyman named Michael. Bowdern had drafted Michael for the strong-arm squad. Some wondered whether Michael's archangel name especially infuriated the demon. "Michael, pikel, likel, sikel," Robbie yelled in singsong rhyme, then shifted to direct attack on Michael's physical appearance. "Michael, you look so dirty," he said, seemingly singling out the handyman as being of a different class from the Jesuits.

This kind of social taunting was an example of phenomena that linked elements of Robbie's case to recorded cases of possession in other centuries. Because the devil, the prince of hell, was so prideful and envious, the theory went, he had a royal view of his place in the world. Accounts of medieval possessions frequently give the devil a majestic air, an attitude that Robbie often struck. Robbie's voice change, his cursing, his crude sexual allusions, his urinating and breaking wind—all can also be found in descriptions of possession cases going back to the beginning of Christianity.

Bishop noticed that Robbie's vilest talk began after midnight, desecrating the joyous feast of the Annunciation. He spoke of "kissing my pecker" and "using my stick." Turning to the priests around his bed, he said, "You have big pricks, too. And you like to rub them up and down." He again targeted one overweight priest. "You have big teats, you big ox," he said, making sucking sounds.

He swiveled his head toward Bowdern, riveting a blind gaze on the priest. "Cut out the damned Latin!" the boy demanded. "Get away from me, you goddamn bastards!"

When no one moved, he resumed his violent thrashing and cursing. Then, his voice turning coy, he said, apparently to Bowdern, "You like to stay with me. Well, I like it, too." He calmed down and fell into real sleep around 2:30 a.m.

Bowdern and Michael did the best they could to clean up the bed and air out the room without waking Robbie. Once again Halloran and Bishop trekked back to the residence hall, along with the others who had assisted Bowdern. When Bowdern finally wearily went to bed, he felt some elation with the expectation that tomorrow, on that jubilant feast, he would order the demons to depart and they would vanish from Robbie's body.

Robbie slept until 11:30 on the morning of March 25 and began another one of his normal days. Bishop, concerned about producing a record of the exorcism, wrote down only what happened during the nightly sessions. What Robbie did all day can only be imagined. Presumably his mother came with clean pajamas and, with some embarrassment, offered to help in the daily cleanup. But Jesuit residences were normally cloistered, that is, off limits to the opposite sex. There is no mention of Phyllis Mannheim's presence at the rectory during the exorcism sessions there.

Robbie, whose own skin had said *No* to school in bloody scratches, seems to have spent most of his days reading and keeping to himself. There is no more mention of his cousin, presumably because Robbie was isolated from other children. When he was staying at the rectory, Bowdern spent time with him, talking about Catholicism, giving him books to read. Robbie learned to trust and like Bowdern, but the boy did not develop a trusting relationship with any other Jesuit.

As evening neared on March 25, Bowdern prepared for what he presumed to be the end of the ordeal. Soon after Robbie went to the bedroom, Jesuit priests invited by Bowdern began to drift into the rectory. When Karl Mannheim, Bowdern, Bishop, Van Roo, and Halloran went into the room, the other Jesuits gathered outside the closed door and began to pray.

Inside the room, there was an air of calm. Robbie tossed about on the bed and fell into his trancelike state. Without cursing or making any sounds, he began what looked like a gymnastic exercise. Flat on his back, eyes tightly shut, he stiffly moved his arms in and out from his side while he scissored his legs. Like an automaton, he moved rhythmically, never tiring, never varying the movements.

As the motion quickened, he seemed to lose control, and he fell from the bed. Without awakening, he returned to the bed, resumed the movements, more gently this time, and rolled into the arms of Bowdern and Van Roo. They lifted him back into the bed and Bowdern continued reading the prayers in the *Ritual.*

Sometime after midnight, the mood changed. Robbie broke his silence by cursing his father and spitting in his face. He had been so well behaved up to then that Halloran and Van Roo had relaxed their grip on him. Suddenly he swung his body around in the bed and kicked at Bowdern and his father. They pulled back, and he kicked at a chair. At one o'clock, soon after this outburst, he fell into a natural sleep.

Outside the door, the murmur of the priests continued. The two final prayers of the exorcist are prayers of contrast—the first directed to the demon, the second directed to God. The power of those prayers of combat and faith filled Bowdern with new purpose on this night that he believed to be the night of victory.

"*Exorcizámus te!*" Bowdern began, his hand sweeping through the sign of the cross. "We cast thee out, every unclean spirit, every devilish power, every assault of the infernal adversary, every legion, every diabolical group and sect, by the name and power of our Lord Jesus Christ"—a sign of the cross—"and command thee to fly far from the Church of God and from all who are made to the image of God and redeemed by the Precious Blood of the Divine Lamb."

Again the swish of surplice as Bowdern made the sign of the cross over Robbie, sleeping on in the sleep of peace. It was as if Bowdern had never said the prayer before, so new and mighty did it feel as it surged through him. "*Non ultra áudeas, serpens callidíssime, decípere humánum genus...*

"—Presume never again, thou cunning serpent, to deceive the human race, to persecute the Church of God, nor to strike the chosen of God and sift them as wheat. For the Most High God commands thee, He to Whom thou didst hitherto in thy great pride presume thyself equal; He Who desireth that all men might be saved, and to come to the knowledge of truth. God the Father commandeth thee! God the Son commandeth thee! God the Holy Spirit commandeth thee! The majesty of Christ commands thee, the Eternal Word of God made flesh, Who for the salvation of our race, lost through thine envy, humbled Himself and was made obedient even until death; Who built His Church upon a solid rock, and proclaimed that the gates of hell should never prevail against her, and that He would remain with her all days, even to the end of the world!

"The sacred mystery of the Cross commands thee"—here, and again and again, the sign of the cross—"as well as the power of all mysteries of Christian faith! The most excellent Virgin Mary, Mother of God, commands thee, who in her lowliness crushed thy proud head from the first moment of her Immaculate Conception!" At this reference to theology—the Catholic belief that Mary was born without original sin—Bowdern paused. The image was familiar to any Catholic who wore the medal of the Immaculate Conception, which showed a radiant Mary crushing the head of a serpent. Occasionally Bowdern would pin a medal on Robbie's pajama top or place one on a chain around his neck. One such medal portrayed the Immaculate Conception on one side, the Sacred Heart on the other.

"The faith of the holy apostles Peter and Paul and the other apostles commands thee!" Bowdern resumed in Latin. "The blood of the martyrs commands thee, as well as the pious intercession of holy men and women!

"Therefore, accursed dragon and every diabolical legion, we adjure thee by the living God, by the true God, by the holy God, by the God Who so loved the world that He gave his Sole-Begotten Son, that whosoever believeth in Him shall not perish, but shall have life everlasting—cease thy deception of men and thy giving them to drink of the poison of eternal damnation; desist from harming the Church and fettering her freedom! Get thee gone, Satan, founder and master of all falsity, enemy of mankind! Give place to Christ in Whom thou didst find none of thy works; give place to the one, holy, and apostolic Church which Christ Himself bought with His blood! Be thou brought low under God's mighty hand; tremble and flee as we call upon the holy and awesome name of Jesus, before Whom hell trembles, and to Whom the Virtues, Powers, and Dominations are subject; Whom the Cherubim and Seraphim praise with unfailing voices, saying: Holy, holy, holy, the Lord God of Hosts!...*Sanctus, Sanctus, Sanctus Dóminus Deus Sábaoth!*"

Bowdern hesitated for a moment. To all those words—to *Dóminus,* and *Jesu* and *Deus* there had been no reaction, no cursing or flailing. Perhaps this was a sign that the demon already had departed. And now he turned to the prayer of hope, a prayer directed to God. The words echoed Bowdern's own hope and belief that the demon had fled minutes before the end of the feast of the Annunciation and that, finally, right had triumphed over evil.

"O God of heaven and God of earth," Bowdern cried out in an unwavering voice, "God of the angels and God of the archangels, God of the patriarchs and God of the prophets, God of the apostles and God of martyrs, God of confessors and God of virgins! O God, Who hast the power to bestow life after death and rest after toil; for there is no other God beside thee, nor could there be a true God apart from thee, the creator of all things visible and invisible, of Whose kingdom there shall be no end. Hence we humbly appeal to the sublime Majesty, that thou wouldst graciously vouchsafe to deliver us by thy might from every power of the accursed spirits, from their bondage and from their deception, and to preserve us from all harm. Through Christ our Lord."

"Amen," said the others in the room.

"From the snares of the devil, deliver us, O Lord," Bowdern prayed…we beseech thee, hear us."

He sprinkled the bed with holy water and led the way out of the room. The priests outside fell silent as Bowdern passed by, exhausted, as usual, but, tonight, strangely serene.

Chapter 11

Messages

Robbie went home to his uncle's house on Saturday. His family tried to let him have one of his usual do-nothing days. But Robbie's parents, uncle, and aunt knew what Bowdern thought. *X* meant ten days. *If Robbie gets through tonight…* So, after a dinner that they tried to keep from being a celebration, they played a game or two of something with Robbie, and Phyllis Mannheim told her son to get ready for bed. He went up the stairs as if this were just another night. To those who were watching and praying, however, this was the first night of hope.

On Saturday night, nothing happened. Robbie slept through the night. On Sunday night, nothing happened. Again Robbie and his family slept in peace. Karl Mannheim went back to Maryland, sure that Phyllis and Robbie were soon to follow.

Spring was in full bloom in St. Louis now. People lingered on their front porches, savoring the lengthening days. Flowers poked over the edges of window boxes. The dandelions began their annual invasion of the neighborhood's perfect lawns. Phyllis had to decide whether to buy Easter clothes for her and Robbie here in St. Louis or in Washington.

Easter, the day of hope. It meant more to Robbie now, for he was learning about Catholicism, and Catholics seemed to pay more attention to Easter than Lutherans did. He wondered if he would be a Catholic by Easter. He thought about the mysterious words: Examination of Conscience, Contrition, Confession, First Holy Communion.

On Monday, Bowdern dropped by to bless the house. He went from room to room, making the sign of the cross, sprinkling holy water, smiling. He was no longer issuing commands to a demon. He was reciting the Latin phrases—*In nómine Patris, et Fílii, et Spíritus Sancti*—in the usual quick, mumbling way. He talked to Robbie about his future and told him never to be afraid. In a roundabout way Bowdern asked him whether he was feeling different now, compared, say, to the last few weeks. Robbie looked puzzled. He always felt good, he said, except for being sleepy some nights.

Preparations for a return to Maryland began. Monday, Tuesday, and Wednesday passed uneventfully. Robbie's uncle, aunt, and cousins began to look forward to getting their home and their lives back to normal.

On Thursday night, Robbie and his young cousin went to bed as usual, and the adults settled in for an evening of reading and listening to the radio. They were about to go to bed themselves around eleven-thirty when Robbie came downstairs to tell his mother that he was feeling sick. *What's wrong?* she asked, wondering if he were coming down with a spring cold. *My feet are cold and then they're hot.* She told him to go back to bed and try to get to sleep. *Please come up with me. Everybody. Please.*

The adults and Robbie's cousin Elizabeth looked at each other anxiously but did not say what had just seeped into their minds. *But it's gone. It's gone,* they silently told themselves. They followed

Robbie up the stairs, and it was as if nothing had happened before this. This was the beginning all over again. *But it's gone. It's gone.*

Robbie, his eyes glazing and then closing, got into the bed. He did not lie down. He sat there, the index finger of his right hand moving along the sheet that covered his legs. The bed began shaking. He kept writing, if that was what he was doing. He kept moving that finger, back and forth. Then he said something that sounded like *blackboard*. Was that it? *Are you writing on a blackboard?* And Phyllis Mannheim remembered the Ouija board and the porcelain table top, where they spelled out the messages from Aunt Harriet. So long ago, it seemed.

Robbie lowered his head so that he could turn his closed eyes toward the sheet, as if it were the page of a book. He began speaking, slowly, forming words. He seemed to be reading what he had written on the sheet. Elizabeth picked up a pencil and looked around for paper to write on. As he spoke, she wrote. The words seemed to come from his lips in lines. He spoke in a dead, unaccented voice. It was coming from him like some kind of deranged blank verse. She could tell when Robbie came to an end of a line on the sheet. So she wrote it that way. What she wrote was:

I will stay 10 days, but will return in 4 days.
If Robbie stays (gone to lunch)
If you stay and become a Catholic it will stay away.
[name of a St. Louis relative]
God will take it away 4 days after it has gone 10 days.
God is getting powerful.
The last day when it quits it will leave a sign on my front.
Fr. Bishop—all people that mangle with me will die a terrible death.

Phyllis Mannheim left the room, went to the phone, and, trying to keep her voice from cracking, told Father Bowdern what had happened. She must have mentioned the messages' reference to Father Bishop, for he decided not to bring Bishop. He arrived at the house about 1 a.m. with Father Van Roo.

Robbie was once again in his eyes-closed, stiff-limbed posture when Bowdern and Van Roo entered the bedroom. But instead of lying on the bed, Robbie was sitting up. Bowdern scanned the messages. Following the *Ritual*'s warnings against engaging in dialogue, he went right to the prayers of exorcism.

When he reached the prayer beginning *"Praecipio tibi"*—I command thee, Robbie turned his head toward Bowdern and asked for a pencil.

Bowdern hesitated. He was never to have a dialogue with the demon. This was cleverly different. A pencil. That could start a written dialogue, but only if Bowdern were foolish enough to write responses. As long as Robbie's words were not answered, it would not be a dialogue. Still, this maneuver was interrupting the prayers of the exorcism…Bowdern made up his mind in an instant. He signaled to Van Roo to hand Robbie a pencil.

Robbie twisted around to face the headboard. A white sheet had been draped across it for some reason. Who put it there—and why—is not clear. Apparently, Robbie's uncle, during the first sheet-writing episode, decided to get a spare sheet ready.

Robbie muttered two names repeatedly: "Pete" and "Joe." While he murmured these names and some unrecorded words, he started writing rapidly on the sheet. He was severely agitated, scrawling words across the sheet, filling about three feet of white space in minutes. Elizabeth and Phyllis tried to keep a record of what he was writing, jotting his messages down as he wrote them in a big, sometimes undecipherable hand. Someone—again, it is not clear who or why—ran out, got water and soap, and began washing the sheet.

The diary on this night was not the product of Father Bishop's methodical practice of questioning witnesses and setting down what both he and they had seen. Even the absence of Bishop as a witness does not explain the diary on this night. The record is fragmentary. It raises more questions than it answers. The diary conjures up a scene of madness. The account gives the impression of frenzy, of an event spiraling out of control. It is as if, for the first time, the spell that had enthralled Robbie was spreading. On other nights, Bowdern had been the center of the scene, the calm exorcist, reciting the prayers of exorcism in his firm, commanding voice. This night, the people in the room, instead of standing or kneeling around the bed, seemed energized by Robbie's frantic writing. They became participants instead of spectators.

Robbie's uncle left the room and rushed back in with large pieces of paper. He thumb-tacked them to the headboard and stepped back. Robbie, without hesitation, went from the sheet to the paper and continued writing.

There is no mention of Bowdern or the usual saying of prayers. By allowing Robbie to have a pencil, Bowdern allowed the routine to be broken. What was it that one of the prayers called Satan? *Founder and master of all falsity.* And what did the instructions say? "Sometimes the devil will leave the possessed person…to make it appear that he has departed. In fact, the arts and frauds of the evil one for deceiving a man are innumerable. For this reason the exorcist must be on his guard, lest he fall into this trap."

Bowdern had fallen. His hopes for *X* to be Annunciation Day now were lost in the chaos of this room. He upbraided himself for allowing his own hopes and beliefs to undermine the regimen of the exorcism. And he rebuked himself for allowing this sheet and the pieces of paper to become a screen for the devil's work.

Bowdern managed to get the room under control. He composed himself, resumed the prayers, and finished them. He was once again inside the familiar experience of watching Robbie, after hours of apparent madness, slip out of the spell and into untroubled sleep. The prayers ended, and Bowdern was left with an aftermath, the dripping headboard sheet and the stack of papers. He gathered them up. For the first time, he had a record not of what others had seen of Robbie but of what Robbie had dredged from his own mind and soul.

The record was not complete. Elizabeth had not managed to get down everything that Robbie was chanting. Words, phrases, and jottings were lost during the frenetic scrubbing of the bed sheet and the changing of the pieces of paper. Bowdern, Van Roo, and Bishop analyzed what they had, and Bishop, ever the rational organizer, arranged them for the diary. He focused on statements that responded to the exorcist's demands—the answers to the command in the basic exorcism prayer: *Thou shalt tell me by some sign or other thy name and the day and the hour of thy departure.*

Bishop noted the frequency of the Roman numeral *X*, unmistakable with its crossbars at top and bottom: "This was written four times on this first occasion and was repeated several times during the exorcism, usually in answer to the question, 'diem' [day]."

Robbie also repeated, with a slight change, a line that Elizabeth had jotted down: *I will stay 10 days and then return after the 4 days are up.* Assuming that the tenth day was Friday, March 25, and that the days of absence were Saturday, Sunday, Monday, and Tuesday, the statement did not quite add up. But possession could have resumed on Wednesday without having been recognized by

Robbie's family, with no obvious outbreak until Thursday night. Bowdern, who had become convinced that he knew the day of departure, had not been at the house to assess Robbie's condition. So a mild possession on Wednesday was possible, making *the 4 days are up* factual.

During the ritual, the exorcist's commands go beyond a demand for telling the time of departure. The exorcist also commands the demon to reveal his name and speak in Latin. At one point on that chaotic night, the response came in incomprehensible marks on a piece of paper. The marks were not letters of the Roman alphabet. Another response was defiantly specific: *I speak the language of the persons.* ["language" was misspelled]. *I will put in Robert's mind when he makes up his mind that the Priests* [also misspelled] *are wrong about writing English. I will, that is the devil will try to get his mother and dad to hate the Catholic Church. I will answer to the name of Spite.*

Another statement seemed to respond to the command that the demon give its name: *I am the devil himself.* Added to this was a peculiar remark: *You will have to pray for a month in the Catholic Church.* Who was *you?* and what did *for a month* mean? Would Robbie be possessed for another month? Neither Bowdern nor Bishop could satisfactorily interpret the remark.

Much of what was written was baffling. Robbie had drawn what seemed to be a map with *2,000 ft* written on it. Bishop speculated that the cryptic map might have been connected with the attempt to find Aunt Harriet's hidden treasure. A witness said that about the time that Robbie was drawing this he spoke, saying, "Yeah, this is what I got on the Ouija board."

One drawing stunned Bishop. It was a face, unrecognizable but human. Next to it were two words: *Dead bishop.*

Bowdern got his shock from another line: *You may not believe me. Then Robert will suffer forever.*

Robbie had been learning about the Catholic Church since March 23. That was the day he had been brought to the rectory, and on that night he had broken Halloran's nose and bloodied Van Roo's nose. Bowdern had decided that the task—called giving Catholic instructions—should not be handed to casualties in his war with the demons. So he assigned Robbie to another assistant pastor, Father Joseph McMahon, a kind, gentle man who seemed to get along with Robbie. It was said in the Jesuit community that Joe McMahon would do any job well, as long as it did not involve singing or the Gregorian chant. He had such a tin ear that in chapel, as a scholastic, he had been told to move his lips but not to sing.

Robbie's parents had planned to have him confirmed in the Lutheran Church. But they told Bowdern that Robbie's choice of religion was his own business. Robbie, quite casually, decided to convert to Catholicism, perhaps to please Bowdern.

The *Ritual* instructions for performing an exorcism do not suggest that the demoniac be converted to Catholicism. But woven throughout the instructions and the prayers are assumptions that Satan mostly selects Catholics for his targets. The *Ritual*, for example, urges that the person possessed should be exhorted "to fortify himself by frequent reception of penance and Holy Communion." And one of the prayers, commanding the demon to "give place to the one, holy, and apostolic Church," is virtually a miniature catechism on Catholic dogma.

Bowdern was not a missionary aiming to garner one more soul for the Lord. Robbie's conversion had a strategic dimension in Bowdern's battle plan. Exorcism is Christ against Satan, with a

Catholic priest representing Christ. If Robbie became a Catholic, in Bowdern's view, priest and victim would be united. By bringing Robbie into the Catholic Church, Bowdern would solidify the front against the demons. In the combat metaphor of exorcism, Robbie would be better shielded by "the whole armour of God."

Now, after the relapse into possession, Bowdern moved swiftly to get Robbie into the Catholic Church. Nowadays, conversion of a Protestant to Catholicism does not usually include Baptism, since most Protestants—certainly including Lutherans—have been baptized. The Catholic Church generally recognizes baptisms by other churches as valid. But prior to the reforms of the Second Vatican Council, promulgated in the late 1960s, conditional baptism—a rite performed just in case the Protestant baptism had not been valid for some reason—was far more common than it is today. And Bowdern was not taking any chances. On his recommendation, Robbie and his parents agreed that he should be baptized a Catholic. This would be followed by instructions in the next two sacraments he would receive: Penance (Confession) and Holy Communion.

The date for his baptism was set for Friday, April 1, between 8 and 8:30 p.m. at St. Xavier, the College Church. Bowdern apparently picked the time so that the baptism would take place before the hours when Robbie's worst outbursts began. About 7:30, Robbie, his parents, his uncle, and his aunt set off for the church. Robbie was squeezed between his mother and father in the back seat. Uncle George drove and Aunt Catherine sat next to him.

At the church, Bowdern donned a surplice and stole and got ready the utensils for baptism. The marble baptismal font was at the end of the nave, near the church's main entrance, a location symbolizing entry into Christianity through Baptism. A few steps away was the olearium or ambry, a little shrine that contained the holy oils used in dispensing the sacraments of Baptism, Confirmation, and the Last Rites (Extreme Unction). By long practice, baptismal water and oil were specially blessed with prayers that exorcised the devil from them.

The usual Catholic candidates for baptism are infants. Their acceptance of the sacrament is done through proxy by their god-parents. Robbie, as a person who had reached the age of reason, could not be treated as an infant. With the permission of his parents, he would be baptized voluntarily. Such a baptism is slightly different from an infant's baptism. Elements of the rites are rooted in traditions that go back to the early centuries of Christianity, when adult converts spent weeks in preparation for baptism.

Candidates for baptism, known as catechumens, were exorcised at a special ceremony. A bishop breathed on them and hissed a command to Satan: "Depart, thou accursed one." The hissing was called exsufflation, the blowing out of the devil; in another rite, called insufflation, the Holy Spirit was breathed into the candidates. Their ears and nostrils were touched to symbolize the opening of their minds to the words of God. They turned toward the west and said, "I renounce thee, Satan, with all thy pomps and all thy works." Next, they turned to the east and said, "To Thee I dedicate myself, Jesus Christ, eternal and uncreated Light."

Thus, by Bowdern's strategy, the ancient rites of baptism, though used in the modern world to welcome babies into Christianity, would be a counter-offensive against Robbie's posses-sion. He would say over Robbie, as he would say over an infant, "I exorcise you…in the name of God the Father almighty, and in the love of our Lord Jesus Christ, and in the power of the Holy Spirit. I exorcise you through the living God…who created you for the defense of the human race...to make the sacrament [of baptism] salutary for fleeing the enemy."

On the mouth that had cursed and spat and screamed Bowdern would put a few grains of salt, evoking wisdom. Because baptism is a form of exorcism, salt, an ancient repellent of the devil, has long been a part of the ritual. On Robbie's back and chest, where the scratches had pained him, Bowdern would daub holy oil in an ancient blessing that imparted wisdom and fortitude. Then Bowdern would pour holy water from the font over Robbie's head three times in the form of a cross, while saying in Latin, "I baptize thee in the name of the Father and of the Son and of the Holy Ghost." Upon the forehead, site of knowledge, Bowdern would trace the old talisman against demons, the sign of the cross. All of this would similarly be done in the baptism of an infant, for a Catholic baptism is a form of exorcism.

While Bowdern stood by the church door awaiting Robbie's arrival, the boy and his uncle were struggling for control of the car. The fight had begun several blocks from the church when Robbie suddenly complained about pains in his feet. Then, a moment later, he said he had cold feelings and hot feelings. It was a sign, Phyllis Mannheim knew. As she frantically wondered what to do, Robbie closed his eyes and erupted. The car radio was on. Whatever was being broadcast faded away and the radio started transmitting static.

"So you are going to baptize me!" he shouted in his chilling, guttural voice. Then the awful laugh: "Ha! Ha! And you think you will drive me out with Holy Communion! Ha! Ha!"

He grabbed the steering wheel and swung the car toward the curb. "You son of a bitch!" he shouted at his uncle. George Mannheim, pushed violently away from the steering wheel, reached down and pulled on the emergency brake. The car swerved up on the curb and came to a stop against a lamppost.

Robbie spun around and seized his mother by the throat. His uncle turned off the ignition, but the radio did not stop. The static continued. The key jumped out of the ignition lock and landed on the floor in front of the rear seat. The static crackled on.

Karl yanked Robbie off his mother. George got out of the car and helped his brother haul Robbie out of the car. Catherine slipped into the driver's seat. The two men managed to pin Robbie against the car while Phyllis got into the front seat next to Catherine. Robbie kept up a stream of curses and fought as the men pinioned his arms against his sides. Karl and George pushed Robbie back in the car and pinned him down on the back seat. Catherine started the car, backed off the sidewalk, and continued to the church. She turned off the radio but static kept coming from the loudspeaker.

Robbie broke free and got his hands around Catherine's throat before Karl and George could drag him back. Catherine squirmed out of her nephew's grasp and managed to keep control of the car. By then they were near the church. She pulled up on Lindell Boulevard, in front of the church. Karl and George hauled Robbie out of the back seat. Bowdern, hearing screams and yelling, went through the baptistery to the front door and stood on the broad steps.

Under a street lamp's umbrella of light Bowdern saw Robbie, his Sunday suit torn, being wrestled to the sidewalk by his uncle and father. Bowdern could almost feel the power of the violence and evil radiating from Robbie. Phyllis and Catherine stayed in the car, too terrified to get out. The two men got Robbie to his feet and held his arms against his sides. They started dragging him toward the church steps. He was cursing, spitting, and laughing his maniacal laugh.

Bowdern, fearing some potential form of desecration, instantly decided to keep Robbie out of the church. He told the men to take the boy into the rectory, next to the church but set back from the boulevard. The baptism would go on, he said. He felt he now was in direct combat with evil.

Bowdern trotted ahead and opened the door of the rectory, then helped the two men push and pull Robbie through the door. He was shouting incoherently and spitting, great gobs of spit that splattered on the cheeks of his father, his uncle, and now Bowdern.

The men, stumbling from exhaustion, hauled Robbie into a parlor off the entrance hallway and pushed him to the floor. Bowdern got a pitcher of ice water from the refrigerator in the kitchen and poured it on Robbie's grimace. So this would be the baptism, ice water on the face of a boy turned demon.

Robbie calmed for a minute, and the men pulled him to his feet. He went limp, refusing to walk. He resumed his cursing and spitting. His father and uncle carried him to the third-floor room he had occupied before and put him on the bed. They held down his arms and legs while waiting for Bowdern.

He appeared with Michael, the handyman Robbie had taunted. Bowdern told Michael that he would be the proxy for an urgent baptism that Bowdern was improvising. Instead of a tranquil, triumphant baptism at the marble font there would be a desperate, violent ritual. Bowdern had planned an adult baptism, with a long profession of faith and abjuration of heresy. There was no time, no peace.

Bowdern stood over the bed and asked, "Do you renounce Satan and all his works?"

Robbie snarled and writhed, nearly breaking out of the grip of his father and uncle. He spat in Bowdern's face.

"Do you renounce Satan and all his works?" Bowdern repeated. The boy reacted even more violently.

Bowdern asked the question a third time, thought he saw the thrashing body weaken, and, after a long pause, asked a fourth time, "Do you renounce Satan and all his works?"

Robbie's eyes opened. For a moment his face was the face of a tired boy. "I do renounce Satan and all his works," he whispered. And in the next instant he nearly squirmed out of the hands that held him. Eyes closed, he began spitting, and, as every one of his targets later said, he never missed.

Bowdern now began to prepare to administer the sacrament of baptism. He motioned to Michael, who came closer to the bed and became a target. Bowdern told him what he had to do. Michael had to touch Robbie, acknowledging him as a candidate for baptism, and, in Robert's name, Michael had to recite the Apostles' Creed, a summary of Catholic dogma.

The first touch of holy water on Robbie's brow sent him into the worst paroxysm of rage Bowdern had yet seen that night. While Robbie writhed, spat, and cursed, Bowdern splashed him again and again. For an instant, the priest thought he saw a glimmer of the real Robbie. At that instant, Bowdern said, *"Ego te baptizo"*—I baptize thee— *"in nomine Patris"*—in the name of the Father—"

The words triggered another outburst, which Bowdern countered with another generous cascade of holy water. Using this words-then-water technique, Bowdern completed the baptism. It took nearly four hours. Convinced that Robbie was finally baptized, Bowdern began the prayers of exorcism. Bishop's last diary entry for this day shows how routine the resumed horror had become: "The usual spitting, gyrating, cursing and physical violence continued until 11:30 PM."

Robbie's Uncle George had left some time before with Phyllis Mannheim and Aunt Catherine, both of them still shaken by the wild ride to the church. Karl Mannheim chose to stay and spend another night on the divan near Robbie's bed.

Bowdern and Bishop, speculating later, wondered if the violence indicated that Robbie's demon was reacting to an attempt at a first-time baptism. This would mean, theologically and theoretically, that the demon had believed he was ensconced in the body of an unbaptized person. And that would imply that, for some reason, Robbie's Lutheran baptism had not taken effect.

Speculation about the intentions of demons is theologically and logically risky because one can never tell whether the Prince of Lies is telling the truth. But whatever the efficacy of Robbie's first baptism, the second had a devastating effect. Violence escalated. Robbie became wilder than ever before.

On Saturday, April 2, for the first time, he awakened not to one of his normal days but to nearly fifteen hours of rage. "It was evident," Bishop wrote, "that a struggle was at hand."

When the freshly baptized Robbie woke up about 9:30 a.m., he kept his eyes closed and began thrashing about on the bed. Before anyone could rush in and pin him down, he hurled a pillow at the overhead light, breaking the shade and bulb. A crockery basin was his next target, though no one was sure how he broke that.

Bowdern had decided to move quickly, following up the previous day's baptism with Holy Communion the next day.

During an interlude of calm, Bowdern and McMahon had prepared Robbie for his first Holy Communion. Preparations included an examination of conscience. "O Holy Ghost!" began the prayer for that examination. "Eternal source of light!…let nothing escape the exact research I am about to make. O Jesus!…show me now my sins…Do not permit that a criminal love for myself should now seduce and blind me…" He would have been asked to ask himself if he had been disobedient to his parents or any other lawful authority or whether he had been ungrateful to them or caused them anxiety.

Robbie the possessed boy had, of course, caused anxiety. But the theology of possession held that demons cannot enter or overcome the soul, which remains free, though besieged. Actions that Robbie the possessed boy committed were not the actions of Robbie the normal boy. His lack of knowledge about what happened during his closed-eye spells was taken as proof that awareness of possession had not entered his consciousness.

The formula for examination also had him search his conscience for any immodesty in thought, word, or deed; whether by talking, reading, dressing, or looking at unchaste objects. He looked into himself for signs of pride, vanity, covetousness, gluttony, anger, envy, sloth, deceit, rash judgments, contempt, hatred, jealousy, feelings of revenge, quarreling, or backbiting.

Although Robbie was thus taught to examine his conscience in preparation for Confession, he did not make his first confession on this day. The diary quickly moves from the thrown pillow to preparations for first Holy Communion. Bowdern gave Robbie conditional absolution, forgiving him for the minor transgressions that he would have admitted to in the confessional. Bowdern had the priestly power to decide this. Given Robbie's lapsed condition and Bowdern's full-speed schedule to bring Robbie into the Catholic Church, the waiver of Confession seems to have been part of the battle plan to have Robbie receive Holy Communion as soon as possible.

To prepare Robbie for his first Communion, Father Bowdern called in Father Bishop and Father John G. O'Flaherty, S.J., a thirty-eight-year-old Jesuit from Kansas City. Bowdern had known O'Flaherty when he taught algebra, Latin, and English at Campion High. Although O'Flaherty had not been an outstanding teacher, Bowdern spotted him as a potentially good parish priest. O'Flaherty understood people, preached pertinent sermons based on life experiences, and had a quiet reverence that was not typically Jesuitical.

Robbie lay silently on the bed when Bowdern gave conditional absolution. But, as the priest began the prayers for Communion, Robbie began to stir. Bishop and O'Flaherty moved to hold the boy down, but he merely squirmed and offered little resistance. Bowdern moved close, a particle of the Communion host in his outstretched right hand. One of the other priests held a linen cloth called a purificator at Robbie's chin.

Robbie became a whirlwind of flailing arms and legs. Bowdern pressed closer and placed the particle in Robbie's mouth. He spit it out. A deft move of the purificator and the particle landed on the cloth. Bowdern picked it up and tried again. Once more Robbie spat it out and the purificator caught it. During the next two hours Bowdern tried twice more. Both times Robbie spat out the particle, which was caught on the purificator.

O'Flaherty remarked that the day was the first Saturday of the month, a day on which services for Our Lady of Fatima were conducted in many churches, including St. Xavier. He suggested that they say a rosary in honor of Our Lady of Fatima. When the three priests finished the rosary, Bowdern tried for the fifth time and

Robbie swallowed the particle. He had made his first Holy Communion.

The mood of the room changed. The priests smiled at one another. Robbie, his eyes now open, seemed calm. Bowdern told him to get dressed for the drive home with his father. Shortly before noon O'Flaherty got behind the wheel of the rectory car. Bowdern and Karl Mannheim got in the back with Robbie between them. The priests were chatting with the boy when he suddenly lurched forward and grabbed O'Flaherty around the neck. Bowdern and Mannheim pulled the boy back to the seat and held him down for the rest of the ride.

At home, after the priests left, Robbie changed again. He was starving, he said, and he sat down to a hearty breakfast. Phyllis and Karl watched him closely. Something was happening, something new. The car incidents seemed to symbolize Phyllis' worries. Things were speeding up, out of control. All during that day Robbie swung from normal to semiconscious. One moment he was wandering around the house looking for something to do on a Saturday afternoon. The next moment he was crouched in a chair, eyes glazed or closed.

At 7:40 p.m., Bowdern and O'Flaherty returned, accompanied by Bishop and Michael. Bowdern brought with him another relic, a tiny splinter that was revered as a piece of the True Cross. It was enshrined in a small golden reliquary that Bowdern put on a bureau out of Robbie's reach.

Robbie sat on his bed in his underwear while Bowdern rapidly recited the prayers of exorcism. As Bowdern began the *Praecipio*— "I command thee, unclean spirit…"—he wondered whether the reactions of the demon within Robbie would be different now that he was Catholic. Robbie showed no response to the prayers. At one point he asked his mother for a dish of ice cream. He sat in bed eating the ice cream while Bowdern prayed on. The priest had about decided that this would be a short night when Robbie bolted out of the bed and ran downstairs.

Bowdern, fearing that Robbie would become violent, followed him to the ground floor and ordered him back to the bedroom. Robbie nodded and started climbing the stairs in the slow, sullen way of the chastised child, with Bowdern right behind him. In the hallway at the top of the stairs Robbie sprinted. He raced into the bedroom and reached for the reliquary. O'Flaherty snatched Robbie's hand away. But the boy spun and, with lightning speed, tore four pages of the exorcism prayers from an open copy of the *Ritual.*

When Bowdern reached the room, Robbie was in bed laughing a maniacal laugh, the torn pages clutched in his hand. Bowdern borrowed O'Flaherty's *Ritual* and again began the *Praecipio.*

After the words "*dicas mihi nomen tuum, diem, et horam éxitus tui, cum áliquo signo*"—Thou shalt tell me by some sign or other thy name and the day and the hour of thy departure—Bowdern paused. Startling everyone in the room, Robbie said, *"Dicas mihi nomen tuum, diem…"* Then he added, "Stick it up your ass."

At another point, when he was asked when the demon would depart, Robbie said, "Shut up! Shut up!"

That was the pattern of the next four hours: Bowdern praying in Latin…Robbie sometimes echoing the Latin or responding with a hideous laugh…Bowdern praying…Robbie mocking or twisting the Latin, laughing, cursing.

On the second round of exorcism prayers, beginning with the *Praecipio,* Bowdern glanced down and squinted. His eyes were bad. He wore thick glasses when he read, and he had been reading for hours, day after day, in ill-lit rooms. Bishop followed Bowdern's glance and gasped. Bowdern had just spoken the *dicas mihi* phrase. On one of Robbie's legs scratches began to appear: three parallel lines. Then, at the word *horam*, a brand in the shape of *X* appeared. Then the scratches erupted again, this time as *18*. Then another *18*, and another. (Bishop's diary does not specify where on Robbie's body the scratches materialized.)

At 1:15 a.m., Robbie came out of a spell and asked his father for permission to get out of bed so that he could sit on a chair. Karl helped him shakily climb out of bed and to a chair. His hands were trembling. *Please, please take me home*, he begged. He knew that his father was returning to Maryland the next day. *Please. I can't stand it. I'm going crazy.*

Never before had Robbie come out of a series of spells aware that he had been in one. On all other nights a veil had divided his normal consciousness and the consciousness of possession. Now the veil was gone. He seemed to know that he was possessed. He definitely knew that he might be going crazy.

Chapter 12

A Search for a Quiet Place

On Sunday Robbie again began his day by throwing a pillow at the ceiling light. He went back to sleep, emerged seeming dazed, fell asleep, and awoke about eleven-thirty. He did not want to get out of bed. His mother brought him his breakfast. After he had eaten, he went downstairs, looking pale and wan.

Karl Mannheim suggested a game of ball. He rounded up Robbie's two uncles and his cousin Marty. They all stood around on the broad lawn and began tossing a baseball. Robbie played listlessly, but Karl was convinced that his son was out of shape and needed only a couple of hours of ball to snap out of whatever it was that bothered him this morning. He should be happy, Karl thought.

The Mannheims had great faith in Robbie's conversion to Catholicism. Something had happened when Aunt Harriet died in the dark of winter. Now Robbie had joined this powerful religion, which was driving the poison out of him. Tomorrow, they would be going home, and the nightmare would not be coming back with them.

Karl yelled for the ball. As Robbie reared back to throw, his arm went limp and the ball dropped from his hand. He staggered around for a moment, looking as if he was about to fall down. Then he took off on a run across the lawn. Karl saw that Robbie's eyes were tightly closed. Karl and the other two men ran after the boy, who stepped up his pace and crossed the next-door neighbor's lawn. He was sprinting across the next lawn, eyes still shut, when Karl grabbed him. He spun away, but his uncles held him. He collapsed, and they carried him home.

They propped him up at the big wooden table in the kitchen. Phyllis offered him a glass of water. His eyes still closed, he shifted his body, stuck a leg under the table, and lifted it off the floor.

When he finally opened his eyes, he seemed to be poised between two states of consciousness. His parents did not have names for these states, but some specialists in possession did. They called them the crisis and the calm. In the crisis came violence and moments of seeming madness—spells or seizures, Bishop named them. In the calm state came *nothing*. Robbie had lapsed into calm, an eerie sense that suspended him outside everyday reality.

Exorcists explain this feeling as the touch of evil: Satan, while remaining hidden, projects a sinister aura that engulfs the victim. A psychiatrist who has studied cases of alleged possession does not know the origin, but he does agree that it exists: "One of the feelings that is most indicative of the spiritual nature of possession is that the possessed person has lost a human quality: the helper feels as if he or she is in the presence of something inhuman or that the possessed is empty and alienated from himself." That was the way Robbie seemed on this warm, brilliant Sunday afternoon.

Although nothing violent was happening, Robbie's parents felt jittery about his listless state. The family was heading home the next day, and they wanted to be sure that Robbie would behave on the train. So again the call went out for Father Bowdern, who was surprised. He had been feeling optimistic about Robbie. It was an optimism that got its inspiration as much from priestly hope as from the liturgical calendar.

This was Passion Sunday, the fifth Sunday in Lent and the prelude to Easter, which was two weeks away. The fourteen days of Passiontide that began that day focused on Christ's passion—his last days, the suffering and the instruments of that suffering: the scourge, the crown of thorns, the cross, the nails. The statues and crucifixes of Xavier and all other Catholic churches were draped in purple cloth as a symbol of mourning. The dark, penitential days readied the Catholic soul for the triumphant glory of Easter. Robbie's days and nights now would be caught up in that procession, and Bowdern envisioned Robbie marching from the darkness of death to the light of hope. *But what about 18 on his body? What did 18 mean? The number should have been 17. Easter was on April 17. Why wasn't the number 17?*

Bowdern arrived about 7 p.m. with Bishop, Van Roo, and O'Flaherty. The priests were gathered in the living room talking with the family. Robbie was there, looking drained and weak. Then, without warning, he lunged toward his Aunt Catherine and grabbed the collar of her dress. Uncle George moved first to seize Robbie, who, without releasing Catherine, wrested himself from his uncle's grasp. Karl Mannheim and the priests swarmed around Robbie, shielding Catherine from the boy.

Karl and George carried Robbie upstairs and angrily threw him on the bed. He lay there, looking at the ceiling and the broken lamp. George's tolerance for Robbie's spells had vanished.

Catherine had twice been attacked by her nephew. No matter how sick he might be—

Robbie started singing and shouting. For a moment George Mannheim could not understand what the boy was saying. Then he understood. Robbie was singing about Billy, his little cousin Billy, George Mannheim's youngest child. "Billy, Billy," Robbie sang. "You will die tonight. You will die tonight. You will die tonight."

Someone—Bishop does not say who—grabbed a pillow and pushed it into Robbie's face, muffling his song. Someone else pulled away the pillow to keep Robbie from suffocating. Anger was a new emotion around Robbie, and he pulled back. No reaction came to the prayers of exorcism that Bowdern had dutifully begun. About 9:30 p.m. Robbie seemed to go into natural sleep, snoring loudly. But he was restless and did not descend into deep sleep.

At midnight the priests left. Within half an hour Robbie became so violent that his father and uncle bound his arms with tape and put gloves on his hands. He whined about the pain from the tape and complained that the gloves made his hands hot. As soon as his father relented and removed the tape and gloves, Robbie flared into a rage. Karl and George grappled with him until he fell asleep at 3:30 Monday morning.

When Phyllis and Karl told Father Bowdern about Robbie's rages, he decided to accompany them back to Maryland that morning on the 9:50 train. He asked Van Roo to join him and told Father O'Flaherty to take over St. Xavier. Ordinarily, such a trip could not have been arranged so offhandedly; the superior would have to be notified, permission granted. But Bowdern, as an exorcist, had the power to make up his own mind without checking with superiors.

At the house, Robbie refused to wake up. But cold water thrown in his face stirred him enough to get him dressed and downstairs. His parents and Uncle George got him into George's car for the trip to the railroad station. His uncle took along a friend in case an extra set of hands was needed to subdue Robbie. The ride was peaceful, however, and by the time the car reached the station and the goodbyes were over, Robbie was chatting and acting happy.

The Jesuits were in one compartment on the train, the Mannheims in another nearby. During the day Robbie enjoyed himself. He spent time playing board games and watching the scenery roll by. Karl and Phyllis had their first peace in weeks. Bowdern hoped for a fast turnaround. Holy Week, the busiest time of the church year, was nearing and he had to be back to supervise the preparations.

Van Roo, looking forward to study in Rome when this was finished, hoped to use the overnight trip to catch up on the scholarly reading he had missed during the past frantic nights. The experience did not deflect him from theology to demonology. "After it was over," he said a long time later, "I never made that [exorcism] one of my interests." What he seemed to resent the most, intellectually, was being drawn into an exorcism without having a chance to study the phenomenon.

Around 11:30, when everyone was settled for the night, Bowdern heard a porter running down the aisle toward the Mannheims' compartment. Then another porter. And more running feet. Bowdern and Van Roo hurried to the compartment. Robbie and his parents were awake and in their nightclothes and robes. The boy was acting as if he were charged with electricity. Fidgeting and speaking loudly, he was jabbering at the porters. Karl explained to the priests that Robbie kept pressing the service buzzer.

Bowdern left the compartment, drew a porter aside, and told him to ignore any more service calls from that compartment. The porter, sensing something beyond mischief, asked what was wrong with the boy. Bowdern told him the boy was high-strung.

Robbie went to sleep and awakened well before the train arrived at Union Station in Washington on Tuesday, April 5. He seemed happy to be home, and once again his parents cautiously wondered whether he were whole again. When the Reverend Schulze asked about events in St. Louis, Robbie's mother and father told him that they had faith in the Jesuits' efforts. Schulze was unconvinced.

While the Mannheims were getting resettled in their house, Bowdern called on Father Hughes at St. James Church. If Bowdern had not already been aware of what Robbie did to Hughes, he would have learned about it as soon as they met. The priest still could not raise the arm that Robbie had slashed.

There is no record of the conversation between these two exorcists, strangers drawn together by an experience neither had wanted, men who had known and seen the horrors that exorcism had brought them. They could scarcely have been more unlike: Hughes, the carefree parish priest who plunged into the exorcism and earned scars from it; Bowdern, the war veteran and theologian who had had an exorcism thrust at him and now, worn and sickly, seeing no end to what he had begun. Just as people described Hughes as the easy-going Bing Crosby character in the movie "Going My Way," so parishioners of St. Xavier described their Father Bowdern as a younger Barry Fitzgerald, who played the lovable old pastor guiding the brash young curate played by Crosby. But by now Bowdern was an exhausted, desperate man.

Hughes introduced Bowdern to the chancellor of the archdiocese of Washington, the monsignor who had been the middleman between Hughes and Archbishop O'Boyle. Bowdern needed to get O'Boyle's permission to continue the exorcism, since the Jesuit was now in O'Boyle's jurisdiction. O'Boyle could not have wanted to hear anything more about this exorcism that had been botched in his archdiocese, gone to another, and now was back.

Bowdern explained that, as pastor of a large parish in St. Louis, he had to get back as soon as possible to direct the Holy Week programs. But he said he would remain in Washington until someone else could be appointed to carry on the case. O'Boyle did not respond to that idea. He simply gave permission for Bowdern to continue the exorcism in the Washington archdiocese.

Bowdern, more concerned than ever about Robbie's growing inclination toward violence, wanted the boy confined and restrained, preferably in a Catholic mental hospital. O'Boyle could have ordered the boy placed in any Catholic institution that Bowdern chose, but he left Bowdern on his own. For a bishop or an archbishop prone more to management than to miracles, an exorcism—like a statue supposedly shedding tears and causing cures—is a messy, embarrassing medieval intrusion. To an archbishop like O'Boyle, the time and energy wasted on superstition could much better be devoted to the well-being of the churches and schools in his charge.

For reasons left unexplained by Bishop and everyone else knowledgeable about the case, Bowdern did not try Georgetown University Hospital. It may have been that he did not want to get Jesuits of another province involved. Or he may have feared that the hospital, aware of Robbie's violence during his previous admission, would impair the exorcism by insisting on psychiatric intervention. Bowdern simply wanted a place where Robbie could be restrained.

He sensed that the possession had been tightening its hold on Robbie since his conversion to Catholicism. The fury of the demon, he believed, would surge beyond the limits of his or Robbie's strength. There had been demoniacs, Bowdern knew, who never recovered. To someone like Bowdern who had faith in exorcism, a failure would mean either that the exorcism had failed to dislodge the demon. Or failure could mean that the demon had fled, leaving behind the husk of a human being. He did not want a psychiatrist writing Robbie off. And he did not want Robbie injuring himself or someone he loved. Bowdern wanted to go on with the exorcism, though he suspected that the worst was yet to come.

On Wednesday, Hughes drove Bowdern to Baltimore—out of O'Boyle's jurisdiction—to inquire about a room at the Seton Psychiatric Institute, an old-line mental health facility whose patients included many Catholic priests undergoing treatment for various psychiatric problems. If the nuns who ran the institute agreed to take Robbie, Bowdern would be forced to go to still another archbishop and ask for permission to continue the exorcism. He was willing to do that if it meant that Robbie could be protected.

The nuns told Bowdern that they would take the boy in, but the institute doctors objected. If Robbie were admitted as a psychiatric patient, the doctors said, that would be fine. They were dependent upon the state of Maryland for financial aid, and Maryland would surely subsidize a juvenile psychiatric case. But an exorcism? They could not afford the professional ridicule and financial loss. The answer was no.

Hughes' superior, the Reverend William Canning, pastor of St. James, turned down Bowdern's request for the use of the rectory where Robbie first confronted Hughes. There was no room,

Canning said. That night, Bowdern called the Alexian Brothers Hospital in St. Louis. Brother Rector Cornelius assured Bowdern that Robbie had a place at the hospital whenever he needed it.

On Thursday, Robbie continued easing his way back to a normal life in his own home. School loomed again. But he would have to make up for so much lost time that his parents talked of holding him out for the rest of the school year and starting him over next fall. So, for Robbie, on this warm spring day, vacation had already started, though with chores. He spent most of the day spading up the small garden plot in the backyard and cutting the lawn.

He went to bed about 8:30 p.m. For a while the second floor was quiet. Then his parents and grandmother heard Robbie stirring upstairs. He called out to them. It was happening again.

Bowdern and Van Roo arrived shortly after nine o'clock and found Robbie writhing on the bed. The exorcist immediately began the *Praecipio*. He had spoken only a few words when Robbie squirmed, tore open his pajama top, and revealed a scratch that was rippling along his stomach even as Bowdern and the Mannheims watched. Two other scratches opened up and tore across his chest. It was as if the blade of a razor was moving inside his skin. His thin chest was heaving and he was screaming in pain. Scratched on his chest was *4*.

Bowdern prayed on. At the word *Jesu*, Robbie winced. "My legs! Look at my legs!" he cried. His mother whipped back the sheet covering him. She pulled down his pajama bottoms. Two deep, parallel slashes were slowly running down one leg from the thigh to his foot, tearing off an old scab on his ankle. Blood glistened along the scratches, which looked as if they had been made by a claw.

Robbie's eyes were open. Van Roo, the intellectual confounded by the unfathomable, stared at him, trying to understand, trying to see a pattern. Bowdern kept praying. Cries of pain punctuated many words, especially *Jesu* and *Mary.*

Robbie screamed again at *Jesu* and a great splotch of red appeared on one thigh. To the eyes of some it was the image of a devil.

There was nothing in the *Ritual* about the exorcist causing pain. Bowdern detested his role when he saw the boy wince. *Mary,* Bowdern said again and again, as he recited the rosary in English, and Robbie quailed in pain with each mention of the name. Midnight came and Bowdern marked the devotion to Mary and her sorrows. *Mary, Mary, Mary,* and pain, pain, pain.

Bowdern saw no other path. He could feel the evil radiating out from this tortured boy. The evil had to pass through him, erupt out of him, and then he would be through with it and it with him.

When Bowdern asked for the name and date of departure of the demon, the answer came etched in red, blood-flecked lines on Robbie's chest: *H E L L* and *S P I T E.* Numbers started to appear on his arms and body: *4 8 10 16.* Then came that awful voice:

"I will not go until a certain word is pronounced, and this boy will never say it."

In a waking moment Robbie told Bowdern that something was changing. In the images that Robbie had described earlier, there had been the deep pit. Now the pit had become a cave. He was in a long, dark cave. But he could see a pinpoint of light far away. Now, he said, the light was growing larger.

When Bowdern finished the third major prayer, he and Van Roo carefully examined Robbie's stomach and legs. The priests counted at least twenty scratches. Some were single stokes, others double, a few in four parallel lines. One looked like a tiny pitchfork. Robbie's hands had been in sight during the entire time. He could not have made the scratches with his hands, both priests agreed. Now, even as he lay back for the examination, he yelped, and they saw a new scratch slowly moving down his leg.

Robbie closed his eyes and began spitting and cursing. Spit splattered on Bowdern's face, then on Van Roo's. This was drenching, viscous spit in amounts that defied Van Roo's logic. By one estimate, Robbie spat half a pint in a few minutes. The priests' faces were dripping. Bowdern's glasses were so encrusted that he could hardly see. Van Roo wiped the glasses with a towel, then held it in front of Bowdern so that he could keep reading. But Robbie spat over or under the towel, never opening his eyes, never missing.

He started singing in a cackling falsetto. The priests could make out lines from ribald songs interspersed with obscenities and blasphemies (not recorded in the diary). Occasionally Robbie would hum "Ave Maria" off-key. His songs, his movements, and his curses were becoming staccato and growing in intensity. He seemed to be building to a climax. Bowdern prayed on.

Robbie's right hand began moving on his chest. Van Roo looked down. Blood. He had not noticed the length of Robbie's fingernails. With one of those fingernails Robbie was scratching two bloody words on his chest in large capital letters: *H E L L* and *C H R I S T.*

Shaken and worn, Bowdern looked at a bedside clock. It was nearly 2 a.m. Moments later Robbie warned, *I'll keep you up till six a.m.* Then, a growling voice added, *To prove it, I'll put him to sleep and then wake him up.* Robbie instantly changed states, going from a comalike seizure to a deep, natural sleep. Robbie awoke with a start fifteen minutes later. Bowdern wondered if he could hold out for four more hours. But the demon apparently had miscalculated Robbie's stamina, for Robbie almost immediately fell into natural sleep. The night was over.

Hoping that Hughes' pastor, Father Canning, would change his mind after seeing Robbie, Bowdern, invited the old priest to the exorcism session on Friday night. Bowdern said he would call the pastor when Robbie was calm enough to receive Holy Communion. Canning agreed to bring a consecrated host with him.

While Robbie played and moped through his usual calm day, Bowdern prayed for the strength to go on. He knew he had to get Robbie into a place where he could be restrained. He talked long and hard to Karl and Phyllis Mannheim and convinced them to return to St. Louis and have the exorcism continue at the Alexian Brothers Hospital. Bowdern had Van Roo arrange for the return train trip and call the Brothers to say that Robbie would be arriving at the hospital on Sunday, April 10—Palm Sunday, the beginning of Holy Week.

Robbie went into the bathroom about eight o'clock on Friday night. Minutes later his parents heard him shouting and cursing. They got him out of the bathroom and into his bed and summoned Bowdern. By the time he arrived, Robbie was relentlessly spewing spit and curses and obscenities. Bowdern had never seen Robbie so savagely diabolic. His words were so hateful and odious that Bowdern did not record them. Bishop's diary says of the session: "There was filthy talk and movements and filthy attacks on those at the bedside concerning masturbation and contraceptives, sexual relations of Priests and Nuns."

For three hours Bowdern and Van Roo prayed while Robbie splattered the priests with spit and jerked his hand up and down in a feigning of masturbation. He tore at the priests' clothes, ripped up sheets, threw pillows, sang "Ave Maria," wretchedly hummed "The Blue Danube" offkey, and acted as if he were responding to

Latin questions with jumbled Latin phrases. He spoke most of the time in a deep, gravelly voice.

Hughes and Canning pastor arrived about eleven o'clock. Canning brought a consecrated host, the Blessed Sacrament, in a pyx, which was inside a burse, a square cloth case on a cord, used for carrying a pyx around the neck. While the pastor waited in the living room, Hughes walked about the house, sprinkling holy water and saying in Latin: "Bless, O Lord, almighty God, this house, that therein be found good health, chastity, the power of spiritual victory, humility, goodness and meekness, the plenitude of the Law, and thanksgiving to"—he made the sign of the cross— "God, the Father, Son, and Holy Ghost: and may this blessing remain on the house and on its inhabitants. Through Christ our Lord. Amen."

When Hughes completed the blessing, he and Canning went upstairs and into Robbie's bedroom. Robbie was relatively calm when the priests entered. Then he exploded in a fit of cursing and swearing, his closed eyes turning toward the stunned Canning. He placed the pyx on a dresser. Robbie threw a pillow at it, but Hughes deflected it. Bowdern looked up from the *Ritual*. He sensed that Robbie had detected the presence of the Blessed Sacrament. Perception of hidden sacred objects was a traditional sign of possession. Bowdern signaled for the pastor to put the pyx back in his pocket. Another pillow whizzed past Canning as he ducked out of the room.

Bowdern now decided that Robbie could not be given Holy Communion. In a moment of calm, he gave the boy a capsule containing a mild sedative. Robbie spat it out, then picked it up from the sheet and finally swallowed it. When Bowdern tried to raise the question of taking Robbie to the St. James rectory, Canning rejected the idea even more vehemently than he had on Wednesday. The rebuff did not surprise Bowdern, but he had pressed the idea because he believed that Robbie would be more comfortable in an institution near his own home. Now there was no choice but to continue the exorcism in St. Louis.

On Saturday morning, Bowdern, Van Roo, Robbie, and his mother boarded a train for St. Louis. "R was normal all day," the diary says. "He underwent a short spell upon retiring in the evening." By now, the diary gives only the day's events that are significantly different. The urinating, the breaking wind, the obscene gestures, the screechings, the obscenities had become routine and were no longer noted. Nor does the diary disclose what that awful voice said about the priests themselves.

"On occasion," said a Jesuit familiar with intimate details of the case, "he manifested an unfathomable knowledge of the sensitivities of the exorcist and others, attempting to create a feeling of distrust and hostility between them." Another Jesuit said, "He told facts about their past life that the boy couldn't have possibly known." Hughes said, in a third-person account, that "the devil did make some disclosures that were embarrassing to the participants, but he did not profit by them." Whatever these facts or accusations were— many of them apparently intensely private—they are not recorded.

Also unrecorded day by day was Bowdern's habit of halting the Latin prayers and translating two phrases from the exorcism prayers into English. "Say what your name is," Bowdern would command, then wait for a response. Robbie usually reacted with more cursing and spitting or gibberish. Then Bowdern would demand: "Tell the day and the hour you will exit." Hearing that phrase, Robbie would become more violent.

The instructions in the *Ritual* told the exorcist to note "what particular words in the form [of the prayers] had a more intimidating effect upon the devil, so that hereafter these words may be employed with greater stress and frequency." Bowdern knew he had found a weak spot, and he hammered at it, again and again asking for the day and hour of departure. Perhaps, he thought, this question intimidated the demon because it knew that the end was near.

Bowdern hoped so. Although Bowdern was spiritually as strong as ever, he was weakening physically. Sometimes, he knew, an exorcist was stricken and had to be replaced by another. And sometimes the exorcist died during the exorcism.

Bowdern undoubtedly went over this in his mind, speculating about a replacement. Bishop was the most likely candidate. But when Bowdern and Van Roo had been setting out for Washington, Bowdern could see that the ordeal was draining Bishop. As for Van Roo, he seemed dubious about the whole idea of exorcism. He was dutiful enough, and he endured without complaint his share of spit and abuse. But his mind was on Rome and the higher reaches of theology. O'Flaherty and McMahon had seen enough to step in; both spiritually supported the exorcism.

And, Bowdern knew, ultimately any one of several Jesuits in the community could replace him. Joe Boland, a tough little ex-Navy chaplain, already had lent Bowdern a hand. So had Ed Burke, another former Jesuit chaplain who had got the Silver Star for repeatedly covering the wounded with his own body until the medics arrived on Peleliu Island. Without announcing it, the community had taken this on. It was a work of Ours, and Bowdern could take heart in knowing that, no matter what happened to him, one of Ours would bear it to the end.

Chapter 13

The Demon on the Fifth Floor

On Palm Sunday, Robbie returned to the fifth-floor security room in the old wing of the Alexian Brothers Hospital. He seemed unconcerned about being in a mental ward; perhaps he expected to stay only one night, as he had three weeks before. Brother Bruno, the gentle czar of the old wing, welcomed the boy back, chatted with him, and left him in the care of one of the Brothers who was a nurse. Bruno had talked to Brother Rector Cornelius and knew that an exorcism would be performed in the security room.

There was nothing in the medical or psychiatric textbooks about exorcism, but that did not stymie Bruno. He knew what he would do and what he would tell the others: Rely on your own good sense, follow the Alexian tradition of loving care, do what the Jesuits tell you to do—and pray. Cornelius arranged for round-the-clock prayers in the form of adoration of the Blessed Sacrament. A golden monstrance containing a consecrated host was placed between two lighted candles on the altar of the chapel. Day and night, Brothers filed in and out of the chapel to kneel and pray for the boy on the fifth floor.

The exorcism that was about to resume in the security room was officially a secret. But the Brothers at prayer knew, or thought they knew, as did many laymen on the hospital staff. Eventually, rumors about of the exorcism would spread through the hospital and into the nursing school. The news would have unnerved the members of the basketball team. Their nickname was the Blue Devils.

While Robbie settled in the hospital, Bowdern went to St. Xavier's. He celebrated Mass and, standing in the pulpit to read the Gospel account of Christ's triumphant entry into Jerusalem, he saw many faces he had not seen for some time—Palm Sunday Catholics, warming up to be Easter Catholics. At the end of Mass, they walked out carrying their palm fronds. They would stick the blessed palms behind some holy picture in a living room or bed-room, and some of them would not be back in these pews again until Christmas.

He felt weak and daunted by his double role of exorcist and pas-tor. But he was glad of his pastoral duties. There were sweet babies to baptize, shining-faced children to prepare for their first Holy Communion. There were sick calls to make. He would be carrying the pyx to places where, though there might be sadness, there would also be light and human goodness. Places where people shook his hand and smiled at him and were not driven to spit in his face and urinate on him.

In the afternoon, Michael gave him lists of things that had to be done to spruce up the grounds for Easter. *And would he be using that room on the third floor again? No, but track down Mr. Halloran and tell him he's going to be doing some driving again.* The housekeeper, following an old tradition, had devoted the three days before Palm Sunday to washing the windows and waxing and polishing every piece of furniture. Now she wanted to keep it that way until Easter. *And would Father Bowdern be careful about not having anyone in who would make a mess?*

This was being a priest, a pastor in his rectory, a man moving through joy, a man untouched by living, breathing, spitting, pissing, farting, cursing evil. How much longer could he take it?

"He looked terrible," his brother, Dr. Edward H. Bowdern, who lived in St. Louis. Four decades later, Edward remembered how he had sized up his brother with a physician's discerning eye. Father Bowdern had lost a great deal of weight. When he took off his glasses to rub his eyes, Edward saw swellings along the edges of his brother's eyelids. Sties. He had never had them before. Father Bowdern lifted an arm and grimaced. The sleeve of his cassock fell back and Edward saw pus-oozing sores and swellings. *Boils.* The physician asked and got the reluctant admission that Father Bowdern had boils on many parts of his body. Edward wanted to examine him thoroughly and treat him. It could be anemia, blood poisoning…But the priest brushed away his brother's concerns. Decades would pass before Dr. Bowdern learned why his brother looked so pale and weak. Father Bowdern never told anyone in his family about the exorcism.

By now Bowdern, who earlier had been on a light, Jesuit-style fast, seems to have been living on bread and water. His inspiration for a severe fast would have come from an instructions in the *Ritual:* "Wherefore, he will be mindful of the words of our Lord (Matt. 17:20), to the effect that there is a certain type of evil spirit who cannot be driven out except by prayer and fasting." The biblical verse refers to Jesus' response when his disciples failed in an attempt to exorcise a boy. Jesus succeeded, then admonished them, saying, "If ye have faith as a grain of mustard seed, ye shall say unto this mountain, Remove hence to yonder place; and it shall remove;

and nothing shall be impossible unto you. Howbeit this kind [of demon] goeth not out but by prayer and fasting." Given this reminder, Bowdern almost certainly went on bread and water and told no one.

Shortly after seven o'clock on Palm Sunday, Bowdern led Van Roo, O'Flaherty, and Bishop into Robbie's grim little room. Bowdern spoke briefly to Robbie, who seemed momentarily untroubled. Bowdern decided to try the exorcism prayers immediately, taking the initiative instead of waiting for a spell to begin and then reacting to it. The exorcism produced no response from a surprisingly docile Robbie. Bowdern then began the rosary. This time repetitious mention of *Mary* did not trigger an uproar of cursing and obscenities. Bowdern continued saying rosaries until about eleven o'clock, when Robbie fell asleep.

Bowdern waited a few minutes and then shook the boy awake to give him Holy Communion. Robbie could keep his eyes open for only a few seconds. He dropped off between the time Bowdern removed the host from the pyx and the time he got it to Robbie's lips. The priest was thinking of abandoning the idea when Robbie suddenly awakened and received the host. He lay back on his pillow with a smile and soon was in deep, serene sleep.

The priests signaled to be let out of the room. The Brother on duty in the wing unlocked the door and promised to keep a close watch on Robbie throughout the night. Palm Sunday had passed peacefully, and Bowdern began to hope once again that the demon, routed by the sacred force of Holy Week, was leaving Robbie.

On Monday Brother Emmet introduced Robbie to the routine in the ward. The boy picked up his room under Emmet's insistent gaze and then tagged along on Emmet's rounds. He helped

Emmet with odd jobs and began to feel he had a friend in this bleak place. The Brothers on the ward—officially, the chronic psychiatric unit—had arranged for Robbie to have full days that included some work under a Brother's supervision and study of the catechism.

Bowdern had wanted a spiritual ambiance for continuance of the exorcism, and he had found it here. Every room had a crucifix, and each morning and evening loudspeakers throughout the hospital broadcast prayers led by the hospital chaplain. But the Alexians' holy zeal did not make their hospital oppressively austere. The Brothers were invariably cheerful and tireless. There were always many non-Catholics among the hospital's 140 or so patients.

An Alexian combined intense personal faith with a commitment to give his patients both care and compassion. A Brother did not read newspapers and could not speak at meals, which he ate at an assigned chair in a dining hall. When he died, a crucifix was placed on his chair every day for a week. The food he would have eaten was given to some poor family in the neighborhood.

A Brother usually worked for about eight hours and spent eight hours a day in prayer or meditation, four hours in the morning and four in the afternoon. A Brother refrained from idle conversation, did not visit other Brothers' cells, and never walked outside alone. He fasted on Fridays. A Brother began his day at 4:40 a.m. and went to chapel for forty-five minutes of prayer, which was followed by Mass. His day ended with prayers at 8:30 p.m. He was in bed in his cell at nine o'clock.

To accommodate this religious day to the needs of the hospital, Brothers varied their prayerful schedule and employed laymen—staff workers, many of whom were recruited from a local orphanage, and nurses trained by the Alexians. All the staff members and nurses were men.

The Alexians' devotion to their religion did not cloud their medical objectivity. They were used to having youngsters as pediatric patients, including youngsters with psychiatric problems. Brother Cornelius, taking no chances, called in a non-Catholic pediatrician, swore him to secrecy, and asked him to examine and observe Robbie. Cornelius told the physician, *I want to know if there is any natural explanation for this.* The pediatrician looked over Robbie's scratches, watched his sudden shifts from violent writhing to comalike sleep. He also later said he was present when objects flew about the room. He reported back to Cornelius: *I can't give you a natural explanation for this.*

On Monday evening, Bowdern, Van Roo, Bishop, and Halloran entered Robbie's room. Bishop brought some Catholic books for children so that Robbie would have more than his catechism for reading. There was an adage, said often to young Catholic laggards: idle hands are the devil's workshop. At the hospital, the adage had extra meaning, for both Alexians and Jesuits conspired to keep Robbie active, closing his consciousness to what Bowdern hoped was the demon's waning power.

Again the prayers of exorcism went uninterrupted. Bowdern closed the *Ritual* and took his rosary beads from his pocket. Perhaps the evening would end early and quietly. But the Jesuits and Robbie had hardly reached the second decade of the rosary before Robbie shrieked in pain and clutched his chest. One of the priests leaned over, opened Robbie's hospital gown, and saw a red blotch. Soon after the reciting of the rosary resumed, Robbie screamed repeatedly. This time the capital letters *E X I T* materialized in bloody scratches on his chest, and a long scratch in the shape of an arrow ran down his chest and stomach, pointing toward his penis. *E X I T* appeared three times in different places on Robbie's body.

"His shirt was off. I saw those markings," Halloran remembered, "and there was no way in the world he could have done it with a needle or his fingernails or anything else. Not with us watching him. They would just appear. At times he would have meaningless welts all over him. The kind you would get from a thorn. That sort of thing. Very very red. I looked at them one time and they weren't there, and then the next time I looked at them, they were. Maybe ten seconds or fifteen seconds."

Robbie screamed again. He said he felt terrible pain deep in his body. He motioned to where his kidneys were, Bishop judged. Then he said his penis was burning. He began urinating in great pain. Because, in some cases of exorcism, the devil exited using urination or defecation, Bowdern once more had hope. He decided to strengthen Robbie's soul by giving him Holy Communion.

At the mention of Communion, Robbie went wild. Alexians in the room held him down and swiftly looped restraining straps around him. That night, as usual, he wore a hospital gown. As he arched his body, the gown fell away, revealing scratches and blotches branding his body. *H E L L* erupted on his chest, then on a thigh. The instructions in the *Ritual* said that the exorcist should repeatedly say any word that made "the evil spirits tremble," and this Bowdern did. With each mention of *Holy Communion* or *Blessed Sacrament*, Robbie's body curled upward and more scratches slit his skin.

"I'm giving Communion!" Bowdern shouted, bending close to the grimacing, eyes-closed face. Somehow, Robbie snaked a hand out of the restraints and punched Bowdern squarely in his testicles.

"How do you like that for a nutcracker?" Robbie said in a voice that cackled triumphantly.

Bowdern staggered back. The Alexians tightened the restraints, and Robbie's body arched against them. From these contortions apparently came reports that he could curve his body backward until the back of his head touched the back of his feet. This had been reported in other possessions, but it is not mentioned in Bishop's diary. Halloran says he never saw it happen.

Bowdern did not relent. He talked about the Last Supper, where, on the eve of his crucifixion, Jesus instituted the sacrament of Holy Communion. As Bowdern spoke, "scratches appeared from R's hips to his ankles in heavy lines," Bishop wrote, "seeming as a protest to Holy Communion."

To protect the consecrated host from desecration, Bowdern had kept the pyx far away from Robbie. Now he went to the table where he had placed the pyx, opened it, took out the host, broke off a particle, and returned to the bedside. He reached out his right hand, the particle held between his thumb and index finger. Robbie, his eyes still closed, turned toward Bowdern. A voice Bishop identified as the devil's spoke and seemed to say something like *I will not allow him to receive.*

Bowdern tried again and again, each time inspiring a full repertoire of writhing, barking, cursing, spitting, and snorting. Bowdern replaced the particle in the pyx and said that he would bestow spiritual Communion. He explained that Robbie had only to *want* to receive Jesus in Communion and miraculously Jesus would come, and it would be as if the sacred host had entered him.

"I want," Robbie began, "I…want to receive you in Holy—"
Before he could say "Communion," a torrent of anger and pain
burst upon him. He cursed and screamed, sending chills down
the spines of the Alexians, newcomers to exorcism. Throughout
the ward, patients, nurses, and staff people heard the screams.
They were all used to screams, but never had they heard anything
like this.

Finally it was over. Robbie fell into a sleep of exhaustion,
Bowdern knocked weakly for the door to be opened, and the men
stumbled out. The meticulous Bishop for once did not record the
hour that the night's exorcism ended.

On Tuesday night the priests and Halloran and the Alexians
returned to the room. Bowdern, who had put in a full day as a pastor, looked strong, somber, and as determined as ever. Thinking
back, Halloran said of him, "He would have carried on the exorcism on the ledge of a sixteen-story building."

Bowdern knelt at the side of the bed, rapidly went through the
litany of the saints and the Our Father, then, as usual, recited the
fifty-third psalm. But there was a new, firm timbre, and the music
of the psalm emerged: "*Deus, in nómine tuo salvum me fac: et in
virtúte tua*"—Save me, O God, by thy name, and further my cause
by thy power. O God, hear my prayer; give ear to the words of my
mouth. For proud men have risen against me, and men of violence
have sought my life; they have not set God before their eyes. But
see—God is my helper; the Lord supporteth my life.

"Let the evil recoil upon my foes, and cut them off in thy faith-
fulness. Gladly will I sacrifice unto thee. I will praise thy name, O
Lord, for it is good. In every need He hath delivered me, and mine
eye hath seen the confusion of my foe. Glory be to the Father and
to the Son…"

Everyone looked toward the bed, where Robbie lay, eyes closed, body twitching. "Preserve thy servant," they said in response to Bowdern, and he said, "Who places his trust in thee, my God." As usual, all words were said in Latin.

Then, as he had done on so many nights, the exorcist launched the prayer-and-reply clockwork of responsive prayer. Tonight to the usual responding voices of the other Jesuits were added the voices of the Alexians.

"Esto ei, Dómine, turris fortitúdinis," Bowdern began—Be unto him, O Lord, a fortress of strength.

"A fácie inimíci," the chorus responded—In the face of the enemy. And the Latin phrases continued. They meant:

"Let the enemy have no power over him."

"And the son of evil do nothing to harm him."

"Send him, Lord, aid from on high."

"And from Sion [Zion] watch over him."

"And let my cry come unto thee."

"Dóminus vobíscum," Bowdern concluded—The Lord be with you.

"Et cum spíritu tuo," the others said—And with thy spirit.

Bowdern swung into the invocation prayer that was a prelude to the first prayer that summoned the evil spirit. Robbie was arching his body and screaming in anticipation.

"Praecípio tibi," Bowdern proclaimed in his most authoritative voice. When he got to the first command, as usual now, he switched to English: "Thou shalt tell me by some sign or other thy name and the day and the hour of thy departure. I command—"

"Stick it up your ass!." came the shout from the bed. The words were followed by chilling, high-pitched laughter.

The voice changed. *I am the devil. I will make him awaken and he will be pleasant. You will like him.* Robbie instantly snapped his eyes open, smiled, looked around, and spoke with an eerie sweetness. In a moment Robbie's eyes closed and his body tensed. *I am the devil and I will wake him up and he will be awful.* Robbie reawakened cranky, whining, and cursing the men who were holding him.

When the prayers of exorcism ended, Bowdern started a round of rosaries, watching Robbie expectantly. No marks appeared on his body this night. Bowdern again repeatedly tried to give Robbie Holy Communion. *I will not let Robbie receive Holy Communion!* said the voice that had identified itself as the devil's. Robbie nodded off in what seemed to be natural sleep, and Bowdern ended the session.

Because Robbie had shown such a consistent pattern of daytime stability, Bowdern did not believe that the boy was in danger during the morning or afternoon. He seemed to live the life of boyhood by day and the life of a tortured soul only by night. Bowdern felt that Robbie was most open to grace in the morning, so on Wednesday morning he asked the hospital chaplain, Father Seraphim Widman, to give Robbie Holy Communion. Widman readily agreed.

Since the Alexian Brothers were not priests, they had to acquire chaplains outside of their own ranks. The St. Louis Archdiocese had no priests to spare from the parishes in and around the city. So the Alexians got their chaplain from a small religious order, the Missionaries of the Most Precious Blood.

Widman, technically a missionary assigned to the hospital, was just far enough outside the control of the archdiocese to be an objective evaluator of priests, including Jesuits, who were in the hospital suffering from alcoholism and mental breakdowns. He certified whether a priest in treatment was spiritually capable of celebrating Mass in the hospital chapel. This step took the priest to the threshold of release from the hospital.

There were priests in the hospital who could, presumably, aid Bowdern. But, under the delicate arrangement between the chaplain and priestly patients, even those certified to celebrate Mass could not perform any religious duties in the hospital. Widman could have represented a jurisdictional problem for Bowdern. The exorcism was taking place in Widman's domain, but he had little say in how this potent rite was being conducted. Bowdern diplomatically drew Widman into the exorcism by asking him to give Robbie Communion and instruct him about Catholicism. There was no friction between Widman and Bowdern.

After receiving Communion, Robbie faced another day of doing chores for Brother Emmet. So, when Halloran dropped by and suggested a spring day in the country, Robbie eagerly accepted. Though Halloran had been drafted onto Bowdern's strong-arm squad, he wanted to be more in Robbie's life than a wrestler in a Roman collar. Robbie seemed to have no memory of what happened during his seizures, but Halloran felt that the boy disliked him. The outing was Halloran's way of befriending Robbie and draining away the hostility.

Robbie checked out of the hospital in the custody of Halloran and another young Jesuit scholastic, Barney Hasbrook. Halloran proposed a short drive to White House, a Jesuit estate that stretched for seventy-five acres along the bluffs overlooking the Mississippi River. The estate, which the Jesuits used for a retreat center, was entwined with Jesuit history. Records of the Society indicate that Father Jacques Marquette, the Jesuit missionary and explorer, sailed past the site in 1673. White House got its name from a post-Civil War lobbying effort to move the nation's capital to St. Louis. Promoters pointed to the land on the bluffs as the future site of the White House. The Jesuits bought the land in 1922 and established the St. Louis House of Retreats.

Hasbrook drove and Halloran and Robbie sat in the back seat of the parish car as it headed south along the river for the twenty-minute drive. Halloran had no idea what to do with Robbie when they reached White House. His vague plan was to let Robbie walk around the grounds, which sweep from the large limestone main retreat house to the edge of the bluff, about a hundred feet above the river.

The two Jesuits took Robbie into the chapel and showed him relics of the North American Martyrs enshrined in the walls. Then they all strolled along the terraced lawn toward the bluff. Across the river lay the rich river-bottom farmlands of Illinois. The view occupied Robbie only for a few minutes. Halloran wished for a baseball and a bat and gloves, but there was no ballplaying on the hushed, landscaped grounds. A path led along the bluff to the Stations of the Cross, large white statues that commemorated Jesus' last hours as he carried his cross through Jerusalem and up the hill of Calvary.

Halloran pointed to the stations, partially visible through the evergreens south of the house. "The Stations of the Cross," he said, "the things Our Lord went through during his Passion. Would you like to see that?"

"Yes, I'd like that," Robbie said.

Halloran led the way to the first station. The two Jesuits genuflected in front of a stone plinth about four feet high. Above it was a white statue showing Jesus held by Roman soldiers before a man on a throne. A plaque said, Jesus Is Condemned to Death. Robbie genuflected awkwardly. This was the way it started, Halloran told Robbie. He explained that Catholics walked from station to station, genuflected, and stood for a few minutes thinking about what happened along the way of the cross.

Robbie seemed intensely interested. He looked up at the statue, which seemed to be larger than life. And what was the next one?

They walked down the path, which curved outward to the brink of the bluff. Here the drop was steep. Halloran, who knew the terrain, placed himself between Robbie and the brink. They stopped at the station labeled Our Lord Accepts the Cross.

There were fourteen stations, Halloran said as they walked to the third along the path. The Mississippi glinted through the leaves of the oaks to their left. To their right, up a swale of lawn, the stations marched on. At the third, Jesus Falls for the First Time, Robbie stood and gaped. Jesus, felled by weariness and pain, was on his hands and knees under the weight of the cross. A soldier was scourging him. The Jesuits interpreted the event for Robbie. Jesus, they said, was carrying more than the cross; he was carrying the sins of the world. "We adore you, O Christ," went the prayer that was to be recited at each station, "and we bless you because by your holy cross you have redeemed the world."

They walked on. The Mother Meets the Son. Jesus' Blessed Mother, the Virgin Mary—at *Mary*, Robbie started—knelt at the side of the road. Jesus, weighed under the cross, sees her suffering a mother's pain. At Simon of Cyrene Takes Up the Cross, Halloran told the story of how the soldiers forced a man named Simon to carry Jesus' cross because he was now too weak to bear it. At the next station, Veronica wiped the blood-stained face of Jesus, and Halloran told how some people believed that Jesus rewarded Veronica by leaving the print of his face on her towel.

Halloran turned away from the station and looked down. The path ran close to the edge here and the ground fell off to a sheer, bush-fringed cliff. Halloran started to feel anxious. He walked faster: Jesus Falls the Second Time, Jesus Meets the Women of Jerusalem. A white knot of kneeling, weeping women watched Jesus stagger by. Halloran looked down at Robbie. Something was happening to him. "Let's get out of here," Halloran said, turning to Hasbrook.

Jesus Falls the Third Time...Jesus Is Stripped of His Garments...

Just before the eleventh station, Jesus Is Nailed to the Cross, Robbie started to scream and run. He ran up the lawn, then turned and dashed toward the edge of the cliff. Halloran sprinted along the brink and threw himself at the boy, tackling him before he went over.

Robbie fought and pummeled Halloran. Hasbrook ran up and helped pin Robbie to the ground. The boy had never gone wild in daylight. Halloran hoped that it would be a short rage. But he sensed that he and Hasbrook were beginning a long struggle.

They half-dragged, half-carried the boy to the car. "He was wild," Halloran remembered. He held Robbie down in the back seat while Hasbrook started the car and roared out of the grounds and onto the main road. "I was afraid we would be arrested for kid-napping, the way it must have looked to anybody seeing us in the car." Halloran needed all his strength to keep Robbie down. He still managed to wiggle free for an instant and lunge over the seat to grab the steering wheel. Hasbrook kept his eyes on the road and got them back to the hospital.

The Brothers took Robbie in and calmed him down. He was bright and cheerful when Bowdern led Halloran and the rest of the exorcism group into the room shortly before nine o'clock. Father

McMahon had given him some puzzle gadgets to play with, and, sitting on the side of the bed, he told the priest how much he enjoyed them. Bowdern, though disturbed by Halloran's report on the incident at White House, took Robbie's tranquillity as a sign of progress. The priest signaled that he was about to start the prayers. Robbie lay back on the bed. Halloran, McMahon, and Bishop knelt around it. A Brother on duty knelt nearby.

Bowdern knelt, opened the *Ritual* and began the litany of the saints.

Robbie flew into a rage. Halloran grabbed him, and the Brother swiftly moved to help. Two other Brothers, stationed outside, unlocked the door and rushed to the bed.

Robbie calmed slightly under restraint. He opened his mouth to speak. To some in the room the voice did not seem to be Robbie's. *God has told me to leave at eleven tonight*, the voice said. *But not without a struggle.* Then came, by Bishop's testimony, the most violent eruption he had witnessed. For twenty straight minutes the boy tossed and twisted, cursed and grimaced. Bowdern went on with the prayers. At the *Praecipio,* he did his usual English translation of the when-will-you-depart question but demanded a response in Latin. The response came in what kids of the day called pig Latin: *Ick-stay it-ay up-ay your-ay ass-ay.* Then the voice did its own translation: "Stick it up your ass!" He mocked the real Latin with clear and distinct, imitations of the Latin words. He began singing in a falsetto: "Stick it up. Stick it up."

He damned and threatened everyone in the room. He yelled "Fire! Fire!" at the top of his lungs. A Brother rose and signaled for the door to be opened. He knew he had to patrol the ward. When a patient went into a frenzy in one room, the contagion of fury spread through the wing. Already there were muffled screams and poundings at door after door. Brothers in white habits strode along the dim corridor. Burly nurses slipped into the rooms of violent patients and restrained them.

In Robbie's room, Bowdern never wavered. He finished the prayers and began a rosary. The Brothers added their voices, and the words of the Hail Mary filled the little room. The space filled with the hum of voices, and it was as if nothing could penetrate this immense, endless bulwark of words.

At fifteen minutes before the promised eleven o'clock departure, a church bell tolled. Robbie began simulating the peal, stretching out the sound in a remarkable imitation. "Bong! B-o-o-n-g-g-g. B-o-o-n-g-g-g..." At eleven, the bell tolled again, and the room fell silent as everyone waited for the end. How would it be? Would there be a visible exit? Would there be a great, booming sound, as in other recorded exorcisms?

Robbie laughed and again began imitating the bell. "Bong! B-o-o-n-g-g-g. B-o-o-n-g-g-g..." The instructions in the *Ritual* had warned of disappointments like this. Never trust the word of the devil.

The rosary murmur never ended. The Alexians would recite more than fifty decades of the rosary this night. At midnight Bowdern decided to try to give Robbie Holy Communion. *I will not permit it,* said the voice coming from Robbie's mouth. Bowdern tried and tried again. Finally, as he had done before, he resorted to spiritual Communion. *Just say it. Just say, "I want to receive you in Holy Communion."*

The voice laughed—the loud, rising and falling laugh that chilled the spine. Robbie seemed to waken. *I want...want...* He could not say *Communion.*

The next morning, the morning of Holy Thursday, Father Widman experienced no problems in giving Robbie Holy Communion. During the afternoon, Halloran dropped in. They began talking about what this day of Holy Week commemorated. Halloran remembered the scratches and pain that mention of Communion apparently had inspired on Monday. He specifically asked, "Would you like to know about it?"

"Yes, that would be good," Robbie replied.

Since Robbie was so calm and had received Communion only hours before, Halloran saw no danger in continuing to talk about Communion. He started to describe the Last Supper on the first Holy Thursday. There, Halloran said, Jesus broke a piece of bread and gave it to his apostles, saying, "This is my body." He went on, telling how the Last Supper was the origin of the Mass and how Communion was a central element of the Catholic faith.

Robbie started to squirm.

"What's the matter?" Halloran asked

"My legs are hurting," Robbie replied.

Halloran lifted the sheet and pulled up the legs of Robbie's pajamas. He was covered with welts—his legs, his chest, his abdomen, his arms.

"Oh, I wish you'd stop," Robbie said. "I can't stand this any more."

Halloran suggested that they pray together. The pain eased, and the welts started fading away.

Brother Cornelius bought a statue of Our Lady of Fatima and placed it in the main ground-floor corridor. He dedicated it with a petition to Our Lady that she intercede for Robbie. The Brothers promised that their community would give special devotions to Our Lady of Fatima if Robbie were spared further affliction.

After Mass at Xavier's on Thursday morning, Bowdern, robed in purple vestments and holding aloft a golden monstrance, led a procession from the main altar down the main aisle to a side aisle. He placed the monstrance, which contained the Blessed Sacrament, on the side altar amid banks of flowers and glowing candles. He then stripped the main altar and the other side altar, removing all altar linen and candles. The ceremony reminded the faithful that Jesus had been stripped of his garments for scourging. His Passion had begun.

As Bowdern entered Robbie's room on Holy Thursday night, Catholics were streaming into churches to pray before the Blessed Sacrament. By custom they would go to seven churches that night, a night of such universal and solemn devotion that Bowdern must have felt the surge of spiritual power enveloping him and the others in the room.

The prayers and the rosaries flooded the room. Robbie accepted the prayers in peace.

On the morning of Good Friday, a day of mourning and loss, Bowdern stood before the main altar at Xavier's and held up a crucifix veiled in purple. "Behold the wood of the Cross," he said, "on which hung the Salvation of the World." Then, in three stages, he unveiled the cross and kissed the feet of the crucified Jesus. One by one his parishioners came forward to kiss the feet.

Catholics revere the three hours from noon to three o'clock as the hours when Jesus suffered and died on the Cross. At noon in St. Louis Cathedral the *Tre Ore*, the devotion of the three hours, began. A St. Louis radio station broadcast the service. In his room, under the watch of praying Brothers, Robbie listened attentively to the three hours of prayers, hymns, and sermons on the seven last words of Jesus.

Brother Rector Cornelius had bought a second statue, this one of St. Michael the Archangel. One of the prayers Cornelius believed to be especially effective was a prayer to St. Michael, "most illustrious prince of the heavenly hosts," the defender against "the rulers of this world's darkness." The prayer ends with a vision that invokes a pit like the one that Robbie had seen: "Lay hold of the dragon, the ancient serpent, no other than the demon, Satan, and cast him bound into the abyss, so that he may no longer seduce mankind."

On Holy Saturday, Cornelius brought the statue to Robbie's room. He talked with Robbie for a few minutes, said a few prayers, and had the statue placed on a table in the corner of Robbie's room. The statue, about three feet high, portrayed a winged Michael, his head bared, his body sheathed in mail armor under a red and yellow robe. He held in two hands a spear that he was about to drive down the throat of a writhing demon pinned to the ground by Michael's feet.

Holy Thursday, Good Friday, and now Holy Saturday—three days of peace in the room on the fifth floor. On this day, called the Day of Rest of the Lord's Body in the Tomb, the catechumens of early Christianity had renounced Satan and become Christians in preparation for the glory of Easter. Bowdern expected that Robbie's torment would follow that ancient timetable and he would find peace during the triumph of Easter. After midnight on Saturday, as the first minutes of Easter ticked by, Bowdern talked to the Brothers to make arrangements for Robbie to be awakened at 6:30 on Easter morning, given Holy Communion, and be taken to Mass in the Alexians' chapel.

Shortly before 6:30 on Easter Sunday, Father Widman left the elevator and, head bowed, started down the fifth-floor corridor.

Before him walked a Brother in a white habit, ringing a small bell to signal that the priest was carrying the Blessed Sacrament. The two men entered Robbie's room. Brother Theopane, who was on nurse's duty, knelt.

While on duty, Theopane wore over his ankle-length black cassock a white scapular, a cloaklike garment that slipped over the head and hung down to the waist in back and front. On this warm morning he had ducked out of the scapular and folded it over a chair. He looked toward it, as if planning to put it on for Widman's benefit.

The priest motioned for him to stand and told him to wake Robbie. The Brother gently shook Robbie. He did not open his eyes. Theopane shook him again, a bit more strenuously. Robbie remained in apparent sleep. Theopane turned questioningly to Widman. The priest put the pyx on a table, went to the bed, and grabbed Robbie by the shoulders. He shook him vigorously, then slapped his face. Robbie woke up, groggy and sullen.

Widman took the host out of the pyx and, holding the host between the index finger and thumb of his right hand, made the sign of the cross over Robbie's closed eyes. He told Robbie to sit up. The priest said a short Communion prayer and brought the host toward Robbie's lips. They remained closed. *Open your lips!* Robbie turned away. *Open your lips!* Widman tried a second time, and a third. *Open your lips!* Finally, on the fourth attempt, he succeeded in getting the host into Robbie's mouth.

Widman said a post-Communion prayer and left to start a busy Easter. His was the voice that boomed from the hospital's loudspeakers at morning and evening prayers, and he had two Masses to celebrate. Theopane, who had knelt when the Blessed Sacrament was being proffered to Robbie, went back to the chair next to the bed and resumed silently reading from a book of prayers to the Blessed Virgin. He did not notice that Robbie was out of bed until the prayer book was torn out of his hands.

Theopane tried to grab the boy, but he darted away and yanked the scapular off the other chair. Theopane tried to pull it away from Robbie, who spat a viscous glob into the Brother's face. Stunned and confused, he wiped his face while Robbie jumped up and down on the scapular. As he trampled the garment, a deep voice coming from him said, *I will not let him go to Mass. Everyone thinks it will be good for him.* Theopane summoned help. Reinforcements subdued the boy and got him back in bed.

At St. Xavier Church, Bowdern, resplendent in white and gold vestments, was celebrating the first of his Easter Masses. Later in the morning a duty nurse managed to get word to him: He was needed urgently at the hospital. Something had happened.

Robbie was thrashing and cursing in his bed when Bowdern arrived. A few minutes after he entered the room, the boy quieted down. Bowdern left, his hope of a triumphant Easter shattered.

In late afternoon, some Brothers took Robbie outside to toss a ball around and enjoy a few hours of fun. He seemed relaxed and even happy. As dusk was falling, Emmet, the Brother who had taken a liking to Robbie from the start, told Robbie it was time to go inside. They entered the hospital by a basement door and headed for the elevator. Suddenly, Robbie stopped, turned, and smashed his fist into Emmet's face. Emmet reeled back. But, well experienced in handling disturbed patients, he reacted quickly. He reached out to twist Robbie around and pin his elbows behind him. Robbie was too fast for him. He pummeled Emmet, driving him against the wall in the deserted basement. Emmet shouted for help.

By the time other Brothers reached Emmet, he was exhausted and battered. Astounded that the slight little boy could do this, a Brother stepped forward—and was stopped by a solid punch. Several Brothers grappled with Robbie. He kept screaming, *I'll kill you! I'll kill you!* They got him down and, holding his arms and legs, managed to carry him into an elevator, and down the corridor to his room, where they strapped him, screaming and spitting, to his bed.

Bowdern was again summoned. Robbie, eyes closed, was arching his body against the restraints, spitting and screaming. During the prayers of exorcism a voice thundered from Robbie. It sounded like the one that had said, *I will not let him go to Mass.* The devil, as witnesses called the voice, said he would again show his power: *I will have Robert awaken and ask for a knife.* Emmet, Theopane, and the other Brothers looked at each other anxiously. He had threatened to kill his oppressors.

In an instant, Robbie awakened and asked for a knife. He said he wanted to cut an Easter egg. He went back into his closed-eyes daze and the prayers resumed. In a few minutes, the voice said, *I will have Robert awake and ask for a drink of water.* His eyes opened and he asked for water. A trembling hand held a glass out to him. He drank the water and promptly closed his eyes and fell back on the bed.

The Easter Sunday exorcism session, the one that Bowdern had not expected to perform, ended with taunts and curses from whomever or whatever was on the bed. Robbie seemed to be under the absolute control of an unknown force. The boy seemed weary of it all. But who was Robbie now? And this voice. Was it the voice of something that had taken the boy away forever?

Easter Sunday seemed like a turning point. The voice, the devil's voice, as Bishop called it, now spoke more frequently and authoritatively, that was sure. And there was something in the air, something that touched each man in a different way. Witnesses did not agree on what they saw and heard and felt and smelled. When they entered that room, they seemed to conjure up horrors that simultaneously existed in their minds and in the room itself.

Witnesses told of feeling a chill go through them when they were in the room. Bowdern, they said, wore an overcoat over his surplice and cassock. The stench was almost unbearable for Bowdern, says an account based on eyewitness interviews. This same account says Robbie's "stomach distended and his features were so distorted that he seemed altogether a different person."

Other stories told of Robbie's ability to understand Latin and that he sometimes read the minds of people in the room. One report says that the "diabolical personality" within him sensed the goodness and sins of those who entered the room and "bellowed and roared" whenever "a person in the state of grace walked into the room." When a physician entered the room during one of Robbie's spells, there was no reaction. Bowdern supposedly turned to the doctor and said this was a sign that he was not in a state of grace. According to the account, the flustered doctor went out and came back about half an hour later. He was greeted by roaring. In the interval he had gone to Confession and cleansed himself of sin.

Physical and psychological experiences in the room continued to intensify on April 18, the Monday after Easter. Robbie awoke at eight o'clock, kicked the Brother at his bedside, and leaped out of bed. Another Brother rushed in. Robbie seized a bottle of holy water, threatened to throw it at them, then hurled it over their heads. The bottle smashed against the ceiling, showering the

Brothers with water and shards of glass. This was a particularly terrifying incident because holy water was supposed to repel demons, not provide ammunition for them.

The Brothers were still cleaning up the glass when Father Widman arrived, preceded by a bell-ringing Brother. The chaplain had brought Holy Communion. Robbie spat in his face. Widman pulled back, clutching the pyx. The host within it, like holy water, was supposed to repel evil.

Widman urged Robbie—if Robbie were still there—to make a spiritual Communion. Robbie spat again, and, as usual, did not miss. Widman, wiping his face, thought he heard *I can't*. But a moment later, Robbie sputtered the formula: *I want to receive You in Holy Communion*. He fell back on the bed, exhausted.

He has made spiritual Communion, Widman thought, and he heard a voice say something. As Bishop recorded it, the message was something like: *One devil is out. Robert must make nine Communions and then I will leave.*

Whatever was said, Widman stayed for more than an hour, trying to get Robbie to make nine more spiritual Communions. Robbie seemed unable to speak. Widman shortened the formula to *I wish to receive you*, knowing, theologically, that those few words were still sufficient for a valid spiritual Communion.

The voice of the devil, as Widman thought it to be, laughed and said, *That isn't enough. He has to say one more word, one little word. I mean one BIG word. He'll never say it. He has to make nine Communions. He'll never say that word. I am always in him. I may not have much power always, but I am in him. He will never say that word.*

Widman left, defeated and wondering what was the word? Robbie started singing incomprehensible songs. He was urinating profusely, threatening the Brothers, cursing. Suddenly, he calmed and smiled. He was a boy who was hungry. He sensed the stinking mess he was in and asked for a bath. The Brothers decided to wait for thirty minutes to see whether he would change moods again.

At noon they brought him a tray bearing a glass of milk and a piece of cake and ice cream. He smiled and hurled the glass, which shattered against a wall. No Brother would approach him now. He looked vicious and exuded a loathing that the Brothers seemed almost able to touch.

Father Van Roo arrived and spent most of the day in the room trying to understand this phenomenon so alien to his intellect. To him, theology was the foundation of faith and meaning. What did theology have to do with this filth, this evil senselessness? "I was sort of a monitor," he remembered. "I would sit at his bedside. I watched his eyes…It was all unpredictable; I can't recall a pattern."

Late in the afternoon, after Van Roo left, the Brothers brought in a tray and arranged a place setting on a small table. They wanted Robbie to get out of the bed so they could bathe him, get him into fresh pajamas, and change the urine-soaked sheets. Robbie got out of bed, walked to the table, smiled, and picked up a plate of chipped beef. He stepped quickly to the window, turned and, holding the plate like a discus, threatened to brain anyone who moved.

One Brother dived under the bed. Robbie laughed. But the Brother had not tried to escape. He crept toward Robbie's feet and, when he lunged to seize them, the other Brother sidestepped to clutch the boy's arm. Robbie turned and threw the plate, which smashed against the wall, strewing chipped beef around the room.

Bowdern had spent much of the day re-reading instructions in the *Ritual*, instructions that by now he had practically memorized. And, between tales of terror coming from the hospital, he had read accounts of other cases of possession. He felt that he had missed something. The *Ritual* had warned him to be on guard "against the arts and subterfuges," and, he believed he had done that; he had been on guard.

No, the demons had not fooled him. He had fooled himself. He had put too much stock into his theory that the demons would follow a liturgical calendar and depart on Easter. What did Easter have to do with it? His theory was based on human reason. He remembered how he and Ray Bishop had misinterpreted the *X* as a sign of the demons' exit in ten days. That all seemed so long ago…Numbers. There had been so many. *4, 8, 10, 16, 18.* That was the most recent one. *18.* Today was April 18. Well, who knew? And what had the boy said about a word, a certain word? "I will not go until a certain word is pronounced. And this boy will never say it."

He called Bishop and O'Flaherty and told them they would be going to the hospital at seven o'clock. O'Flaherty would drive. And he had a new plan. *I'll be asking for responses in English.* Back on March 31, the demon had said that he did not respond to Latin because he used the language of the person possessed. *We'll accommodate him. And we're pinning medals on Robbie no matter what he says. And as soon as he goes into one of his spells we put a crucifix in his hand.*

And if Robbie claimed he was free of the demons, Bowdern vowed he would pay no heed. He would follow a sentence in the instructions to the letter: "Yet the exorcist may not desist until he sees the signs of deliverance." Bowdern wanted a sign, an unmistakable sign.

When the priests walked in, they found Robbie being held down by the Brothers. They had just carried him in, they said.

Moments before, he had turned into a nice little boy and begged for a chance to telephone his mother. They escorted him to a telephone and he had gone wild. They had shoved him down and hauled him back, but it had been close. They were still full of dread over what he could have done if he had escaped. He was murderous today, murderous.

Instead of reading the prayers in his usual commanding voice, Bowdern shifted to a quiet tone. At the *Praecípio,* he asked the demons, in Latin, for a sign that would tell the day and hour of their departure. Then, switching to English, he said that the response could be given in English.

Nothing happened. Bowdern resumed the prayers in Latin. During a prayer to God as "Creator and Defender of the human race," he traced the sign of the cross on Robbie's brow. He said a few more words and then traced three crosses on the boy's chest, saying *"Tu péctoris hujus intérna custódias. Tu víscera regas. Tu cor confírmes."* When Bowdern came to *Tu víscera regas,* Robbie asked the meaning. "Keep watch over his reason, rule thou over his emotions, bring cheer into his heart," Bowdern said. Robbie nodded and then repeated the Latin words.

Bowdern forced a crucifix into Robbie's right hand. He thrashed around. Two Brothers held him. He slipped his hand away and threw the crucifix to the floor.

Minutes later he came out of his trance for a moment and asked about Latin. O'Flaherty suggested that he try to learn the Hail Mary in Latin. *"Ave Maria,"* the priest began...In fifteen minutes Robbie could recite much of the prayer without assistance. O'Flaherty continued to hold Robbie's attention by telling him the story of the children who saw Our Lady of Fatima. Robbie appeared to pay strict attention. He asked for an eighth-grade

Catholic school book and thumbed through it, stopping now and then to read a few paragraphs of a short story or a snatch of poetry. He abruptly closed the book and balanced it on his knees, then on his head.

O'Flaherty and Bowdern exchanged glances. Something seemed to be working. Then the book went sailing across the room and thumped against the wall.Robbie's eyes were closed, his body stiff. Bowdern kept saying the prayers. It was about 9:30 p.m.

Another shift. Robbie said he wanted to recite the rosary while Bowdern and the Brothers responded. Bowdern nodded and smiled, handing Robbie a rosary. Robbie clutched the crucifix that dangled from the circle of beads and, falteringly, started to say the prayer that began the rosary, the Apostles' Creed. "I believe in God, the Father Almighty, Creator of heaven and earth; and in Jesus Christ…" Next came the Our Father, three Hail Marys…at the start of the first decade he stopped and said something vague about mysteries. Somebody prompted him, "Glorious, the Glorious Mysteries." The person directing the saying of the rosary is supposed to cite mysteries (as Catholic liturgy refers to certain events from the life of Jesus and his mother) for the reciters to contemplate as they tell their beads. *The Resurrection.* It was the first of the Glorious Mysteries.

There was about Robbie tonight a wavering reverence. He said that he felt he had to pray whenever he was able. *Can I make spiritual Communion on my own?* But he was beset by doubt, wondering what it was that sent him in and out of possession. *If I pray will that make me…?* His voice trailed off. He tried to make a spiritual Communion. *I want…I want.* And in an instant he was gone, stiff and blind to the world of prayers, in another trance-like sleep.

Eyes tightly closed. he squirmed and whined about the religious medals that had been slipped around his neck. *They're hot. They hurt.* This night they would not be removed. Bowdern slipped the crucifix into Robbie's hand again. He did not drop it.

Widman stepped up, holding his most precious belonging, the crucifix he had held when he was ordained a priest. He blessed Robbie and asked him to kiss the image of Jesus. Robbie violently turned his head away and soared into a rage.

He "spit into the exorcist's face with uncanny accuracy, invariably hitting the priest in the eyes," according to a report for which O'Flaherty is said to have been the source. One of the Jesuits held a pillow between Robbie and Bowdern as a shield. Then, "the boy's tongue began to flick out and his head to move to and fro in the gliding fashion of a snake. Suddenly he would make a quick movement above, beneath, or alongside the pillow and spit mucus into the exorcist's eyes."

Bowdern kept reciting in his new quiet voice. Robbie was screaming and arching his body against the torment. Bowdern said his last "Amen." There came then absolute quiet, a quiet that seemed to fill the room. Bishop surreptitiously checked the time. It was 10:45 p.m.

From Robbie came a new voice, a clear, masterful voice, rich and deep: "Satan! Satan! I am Saint Michael, and I command you, Satan, and the other evil spirits to leave the body in the name of *Dominus.* Immediately!. Now! NOW! NOW!"

Dominus. That, Bowdern realized, was the *word,* the word that the demon had said that Robbie would never speak.

Now began, says Bishop's diary, "the most violent contortions of the entire period of exorcism." In what Bishop believed "was the fight to the finish," for seven or eight minutes Robbie screamed and twisted on the bed. Then he calmly said, "He's gone!"

Robbie looked around at the priests and Brothers and said he was feeling fine.

It was over. They all knew it. The demon was gone. The Brothers got up from their knees and embraced each other, tears in their eyes. Bishop and O'Flaherty patted Bowdern on the arm and waited for his smile, his tears, his prayer of thanks. But Bowdern was neither smiling nor crying. He looked grim and fierce. He was waiting for the sign.

Robbie was radiant as he told the priests what he had just seen in his mind's eye. It was a dream, yet more than a dream. There was something real about it. He said that he saw a beautiful figure, with flowing, wavy hair, standing in a brilliant white light. He wore a white garment that clung closely to his body and seemed to be made of mail. Robbie sensed that the figure was an angel in bodily form. In his right hand the angel held a fiery sword, and with his left hand he pointed down to a pit or cave, where the devil stood amid flames, surrounded by other demons. Robbie could feel the heat of the fire.

The devil, laughing madly, charged toward the angel and tried to fight him. The angel turned toward Robbie and smiled, then faced the devil and uttered the word *Dominus*. The devil and his demons ran back to what was now clearly a cave. After they disappeared into it, Robbie saw bars on the entrance and letters spelling out *S P I T E*.

As the demons vanished, Robbie said, he felt a tugging in his stomach. Then something seemed to snap, and he was suddenly relaxed and happy, the happiest he had been since the night of January 15.

The next morning Robbie awoke from a deep sleep, repeated his beautiful dream to the Brother seated next to the bed, and got ready to attend Mass and receive Holy Communion in the hospital chapel. Father Van Roo, the consummate intellectual drawn into an experience beyond reason, said the Mass. When time came for Van Roo to distribute Holy Communion, Robbie joined the other patients and Brothers walking to the altar rail. He knelt there, raised his head and opened his mouth. Van Roo placed a consecrated wafer on Robbie's tongue. The boy seemed serenely happy. But Bowdern still did not have his sign.

Robbie returned to his room. In the afternoon, he took a nap. When he awoke, he seemed not to remember anything about his ordeal. He rubbed his eyes and stood up. "Where am I? What happened" he asked the Brother sitting by his bed.

At that moment, an explosion that sounded like a gunshot resounded through the hospital. Everyone, from Brother Rector Cornelius to the cooks and the patients, heard it. Cornelius, other Brothers, nurses, all rushed to the elevator or stairway to get to the fifth floor. The Brother in the room had thrown open the door. Robbie was standing by his bed, smiling.

The great sound still reverberated through the corridors. Bowdern had his sign. There is a prayer for the deliverance, and somewhere, sometime, Bowdern said it: "We beseech thee, O almighty God, that the spirit of iniquity may no longer have any power over Thy servant, Robert, but rather that he may depart afar and nevermore return…"

Chapter 14

The Secret Unlocked

When Robbie left the hospital, Brother Rector Cornelius, a short, dark-eyed, taciturn man, went to the fifth-floor corridor of the old wing, had the statue of St. Michael removed from the room where Robbie had stayed, turned a key in the door, and declared the room permanently locked. He and his Brothers would keep the secret of the exorcism. The Jesuit community, out of respect for the promise that Bowdern had made to Archbishop Ritter, joined in the secrecy.

The Reverend Luther Miles Schulze had not made such a promise. Soon after the Mannheims returned home in April, Schulze noticed that they were not coming to his church on Sundays. He dropped by to ask them whether they had left the church. They told him that Robbie had converted to Catholicism and they were also planning to convert.

Schulze apparently felt that the conversion released him from whatever confidential relationship he had had with the Mannheims. On August 9 he told a meeting of the Washington, D.C., branch of the Society for Parapsychology that he had seen a poltergeist in the home of a "Mr. and Mrs. John Doe" who lived in a Washington suburb. Using "Robbie's" actual first name, he told his fellow parapsychologists that the poltergeist manifestations centered on the boy. He then told about the strange events that occurred when the boy spent a night in the minister's house. He concluded his address by saying that the boy was later taken to a city in the Midwest.

During March and April, Schulze had been in correspondence with Dr. J. B. Rhine, the pioneer of parapsychology, telling him in detail about a family in his congregation that was "being disturbed by a Poltergeist phenomena." Schulze had told how he had taken the boy into his home. "Chairs moved with him and one threw him out," Schulze wrote. "His bed shook whenever he was in it. When he was in bed with me, mine vibrated. There was no apparent motion of his body. I then made a bed on the floor for him and this glided over the floor…The family mentioned other such phenomena as chairs moving, tables over turning, objects flying through the air, and scratching and drummings. Their floors are scratched from the sliding of heavy furniture." Rhine suggested that Schulze arrange for the boy to be seen by Dr. Winfred Overholzer at St. Elizabeth's in Washington, known as the United States Government Hospital for the Insane. Schulze, instead, gave the family the names of two "very devout Christian women, one of whom holds prayer circles regularly in her home in which some illnesses have been cured. The other is the daughter-in-law of a Dr. Vincent, retired Presbyterian missionary to China who had experiences with similar cases."

Schulze's letters to Rhine contain details that apparently were in his lecture. The news accounts of Schulze's address did not identify him, though he did make himself available for an interview. No exorcism is mentioned in that interview, which kept all identities secret. But, in what may have been a garbled report of Schulze's remarks at the meeting, one newspaper reported that when the boy was in the unnamed Midwestern city *three* exorcisms were performed, one each by a Lutheran minister, an Episcopal priest, and a Roman Catholic priest. (There is no record of an Episcopal exorcism and there is no Lutheran exorcism rite.)

Exorcism was such an exotic idea that reporters abandoned their interest in the poltergeist and concentrated on the alleged exorcisms. Reporters began calling contacts in the chancery of the Archdiocese of Washington. The queries set off a chain reaction. Spokesmen for Archbishop O'Boyle would not give any information to the Washington press. But details of the exorcism were leaked to *The Catholic Review*, a nationally circulated, semiofficial weekly newspaper. In the edition dated August 19, the Catholic paper published a three-paragraph story under a Washington dateline:

> A 14-year-old Washington boy, whose history of diabolical possession was widely reported in the press last week, was successfully exorcised by a priest after being received into the Catholic Church, it was learned here.
>
> The priest involved refused to discuss the case in any way. However, it is known that several attempts had been made to free the boy of the manifestations.
>
> A Catholic priest was called upon for help. When the boy expressed a desire to enter the Church, with the consent of his parents he received religious instruction. Later the priest baptized him and then successfully performed the ritual of exorcism. The parents of the afflicted boy are non-Catholics.

The "diabolical possession" had not been "widely reported"; there had only been mystifying reference to three exorcisms. The phrases in *The Catholic Review* look suspiciously like a rationale for the archdiocese to get some controlled publicity on the exorcism through the Catholic press. But the story only succeeded in whetting the appetites of the Washington press corps.

Jeremiah O'Leary, a young assistant city editor on *The Washington Star-News,* spotted the story, tore out the item, and pasted it to a pink assignment sheet, intending to send out a reporter to learn more about the exorcism. "As a lifelong Catholic," O'Leary later wrote, "I had a vague awareness there was a phenomenon known as diabolical possession and that the church had some kind of track record for the casting out of devils by means of the ritual of exorcism."

He checked with his superior, Daniel Emmett O'Connell, the acting city editor, who said, "I think that's one we'd better leave alone." O'Leary persisted and O'Connell let him take the story idea to Charles M. Egan, the news editor. Egan reluctantly approved but told O'Leary to get on the story himself rather than assign a reporter.

O'Leary "sprayed phone calls to every priest of the many I knew" and wrote a short story that was printed on the afternoon of August 19 on an inside page of his newspaper. The following day, *The Washington Post* published on its front page a long and detailed story of the exorcism, which the newspaper said had been performed in Washington and in St. Louis. The exorcist was described as "a Jesuit in his 50's."

Among the readers of the story was William Peter Blatty, an undergraduate at Georgetown University. Blatty, then in his junior year, was thinking about becoming a Jesuit. Instead, he became a writer and, in 1970, wrote a book inspired by the *Post* clipping. The book had the same title as the movie that was later based on it, "The Exorcist."

While doing research for the book, Blatty tracked down Father Bowdern, who by then had left St. Louis University and was in charge of retreats at White House. Bowdern told Blatty about the diary but said that he could not help him because of his promise to Ritter and fear that the boy's life would be disturbed by publicity.

"My own thoughts," Bowdern wrote Blatty, "were that much good might have come, if the case had been reported, and people had come to realize that the presence and the activity of the devil is some thing very real. And possibly never more real than at the present time...I can assure you of one thing: the case in which I was involved was the real thing. I had no doubt about it then and I have no doubt about it now."

At Bowdern's request, Blatty, in fictionalizing the exorcism, made the demoniac a young girl to further hide the identity of the boy who is called "Robbie" in this book. Linda Blair played Regan, the possessed girl, and the setting of the exorcism was transferred to Washington, with cooperation from the Jesuits at Georgetown University and Fordham University. Although Blatty based the book and movie on the 1949 exorcism, he drew from other cases and from his imagination. But, by having Regan become possessed in the midst of hatred—produced by her fighting parents—Blatty established a psychological climate that experts in possession recognized.

"We often see that," said a priest who has been involved in several possession cases. "The victim is innocent, but there is intense hate or some other powerful evil all around the victim." This priest, a Jesuit, said that he had understood that the hate surrounding

Robbie was racially motivated. In that segregated era, the Ku Klux Klan was active in suburban Maryland, and, in St. Louis, bigotry still seethed in the wake of the desegregation of the archdiocese and the university.

The main set of the movie, a reproduction of the interior of a Georgetown townhouse, was built in a warehouse in New York. Father Thomas Bermingham, S.J., of the Jesuit community at Fordham University, became a technical adviser on the film, along with Father John J. Nicola, who, while not a Jesuit, had been taught by Jesuit theologians at St. Mary of the Lake Seminary in Mundelein, Illinois. While studying in Rome, Nicola had written a doctoral thesis on possession. Nicola, then assistant director of the National Shrine of the Immaculate Conception in Washington, was available to give assistance there. Bermingham and Father William O'Malley, S.J., were available in New York.

The director, William Friedkin, recalls getting a call from the production manager one morning at four o'clock. "He said, 'Don't bother to come to work...The whole set burned down...And nobody had any inkling of how or why it happened'." So many accidents befell the set in New York that Friedkin asked Bermingham to exorcise the warehouse. Bermingham told Friedkin that there was not enough evidence of Satanic activity to warrant an exorcism. But Bermingham gave a solemn blessing in a ceremony that was attended by everyone then on the set, from Friedkin and Max von Sydow (who played Father Merrin, the exorcist) to teamsters and grips. "Nothing else happened on the set after the blessing," Bermingham says. "But around that time there was a fire in the Jesuit residence in Georgetown."

Friedkin says he talked to Father Bowdern "at some length before we got started" and learned details of Robbie's exorcism.

Friedkin also says he received a tape from Rome of an actual exorcism and mixed the "incredible wails" of the demoniac into the soundtrack of "The Exorcist," mixing it with the moans and cries of Linda Blair, the actress who played the demoniac Regan in the film. "I believe that this case was as advertised," Friedkin says. "I believe it was demonic possession, whatever that means."

When the movie was released in 1973, it inspired widespread interest in exorcism. In Daly City, California, near San Francisco, for example, Father Karl Patzelt, a Catholic priest performed a highly publicized exorcism at the home of a young airline employee. Panzelt later performed about half a dozen more exorcisms. A new archbishop, concerned about the publicity, ordered Patzelt to end his career as an exorcist.

In St. Louis, Bishop's diary remained a secret. The security room on the fifth floor of the Alexian Brothers Hospital stayed locked. Everyone who worked in the hospital, from the thirty or more Brothers on the hall to the laymen in maintenance shops, knew why the room was locked.

As the years went by, tales about the locked room were passed on to the new Brothers who came to the hospital. They knew that the room was in the wing for extremely ill mental patients. Brother Bruno and the others who had worked in this wing were certainly used to dealing with madness there. So why the locked room? In a wing of madmen, what kind of madness could keep that one room locked?

Several years after the locking of the room, one of the Brothers was working as a first-aid man at Camp Don Bosco, a boys' summer camp operated by the Archdiocese of St. Louis near Hillsboro, Missouri. He was a gentle, friendly man who stood six feet, four inches tall and weighed more than two hundred pounds. He was sitting at a table in the mess hall with several other young men of various religious orders. They were talking and enjoying their meal, hardly noticing the radio playing in the background. Then came a song based on the theme of the Woody Woodpecker cartoons—a song with Woody's jangling, maniacal laugh: "Ha-Ha-Ha-*Ha*-Ha"

The burly Alexian lunged across the table and yanked the radio cord from the socket. "I can't stand that song," he said. He sat down, trembling, and broke into a sweat. When he calmed down, he told his table mates that night after night in the spring of 1949 he and other brothers had been kept awake by wild, spine-chilling laughter coming from one of the rooms in an old wing of the Alexian Brothers Hospital.

Another Brother told of loud banging on the door of his cell, as the Brothers called their quarters. Night after night he would answer the knocking, only to find no one there.

To those few brothers who knew the secret of the room, what had happened there transcended earthly madness. Down the years, even after the Brothers who knew the secret had died, and even after the memories of the room had faded, the Brothers still kept the room locked.

In May 1976, work began on a new hospital. In the first phase of construction, old outbuildings were torn down and a new six-story tower with two-story wings was built. Finally, in the last phase, in October 1978, after the patients were moved out of the 110-year-old original hospital building, the contractor ordered that structure torn down.

Workers first combed the old building for furniture that was to be taken out and sold. One of them found a locked room in the old psychiatric wing and broke in. The room was fully furnished—dust-covered bed, bedstand, chairs, a table with a drawer. Before removing the table, the worker, out of curiosity, went through the drawer. In it he found some papers. Neither he nor anyone else would ever know how or why that report was in that table in that room, which presumably had been locked since 1949.

The furniture, including all that had been found in the locked room, was sold to a company that owned a nursing home five blocks away. By then, the exorcism in the hospital was fairly well known in St. Louis. Furniture salvaged from the hospital was locked in a room on the fourth floor of the nursing home and never used. When the nursing home itself was later torn down, many of the demolition workers, like the staff people and the city inspectors before them, refused to go to the fourth floor.

The papers that the workman found seemed to be some kind of a log or diary. The typewritten pages were accompanied by a letter addressed to Brother Cornelius and dated April 29, 1949. "The inclosed report," the letter began, "is a summary of the case which you have known for the past several weeks. The Brothers' part of this case has been so very important that I thought you should have the case history for your permanent file."

The worker handed the papers to his boss, who passed it on to the administrator of the hospital, a layman. The administrator read the letter, which was signed by Father Raymond J. Bishop, a Jesuit from St. Louis University. Then the administrator turned to the pages of the diary. Words on the pages—*Satan...diabolical...a huge red devil...exorcism*—stunned him. Horrified, he realized that the report revealed the secret of the locked room.

His daughter, who was attending a secretarial school in St. Louis, managed to get a look at the document before her father whisked it out of sight. She recognized *Halloran*, the name of one of the Jesuits mentioned in the diary. She told her father that Halloran was a Jesuit and the uncle of one of her classmates. The administrator gave the pages to the Jesuit's brother, a lawyer. The secret was quickly locked up again, this time in a safety deposit box.

When I began working on this book, I found a Jesuit who had been part of the exorcism. He was Father Walter Halloran, S.J. he told me that he thought there was a diary. Through his brother, he acquired the diary, which he had not seen before, and verified it as a carbon copy of the diary that Father Bishop had kept through those long nights in 1949. Father Halloran had the pages copied and returned them to the safety deposit box. He then sent the copy of the diary to me, agreeing to let me use it as the preliminary source for this book.

After the first edition of this book was published, I was given the name of the Alexian Brother who was in charge of keeping track of contents of the hospital when it was being torn down. He told me that he had never heard the story of the finding of the diary. But, like all the other brothers at the hospital, he knew what had happened in one of the fifth-floor rooms. Beginning sometime around 1958, he said, the old section of the hospital stopped being a psychiatric unit and rooms in it were mostly used for storage. During the demolition, he entered the room he knew to be the exorcism room. He remembered that it was full of furniture.

By then, a huge battering ball had smashed down much of the old building, and he realized that within a day the room would be gone. "They had knocked down much of the front of the building," he recalled, "and, for some reason, the room was still there.

All around it was destroyed. The only way to get to it was up a back stairwell."

He does not know why, but he decided to check the room one last time. He made his way up the stairwell and entered the room. "Somebody had been in there," he told me. "There were markings all over the wall. Bad words, written with spray paint or crayon. There were a number of burned-down candles on the floor. It made me creepy. Who would know it was that particular room?"

He stood there—innocent about satanic cults—and felt that "something had taken place in that room," something he could feel. He sensed that more than one person had been there. He went down the stairwell and never saw the room again, for it became part of the last rubble of the old hospital.

Afterward, when he talked about his experience, a knowledge-able priest suggested that the room had been used for satanic rites. When I pressed him for more details about what he saw, the Brother could not provide any. He could only remember the feeling of a group having been there, and the thought, *They somehow knew about that room.*

Father Bishop kept the secret of his diary to his grave, as did Father Bowdern. There is some tantalizing evidence that he was involved in at least one other exorcism. In June 1950, the bishop of Steubenville, Ohio, aware of the 1949 exorcism in St. Louis, wrote to Archbishop Ritter and asked for help. The Ohio bishop said that a young man in the Steubenville diocese was attacking priests and nuns, and diabolical possession was suspected. Ritter, through his chancellor, asked Bowdern to look into the matter. There the meager record ends. Halloran says Bowdern never mentioned another exorcism.

The Alexian Brothers kept the secret. People connected with the case believed that revelations about it would disclose the identity of the person who was the subject of the case, the boy I have called Robbie. His name, which I know, has never been revealed, and I will never reveal it.

Robbie was a normal, typical American boy of the times. What happened to him, I believe, happened without any action or provocation on his part. He seems to have been an innocent victim of horror. It was as if, on a clear day, with no cars coming from either direction, he stepped off the curb and was hit by a car neither he nor anyone else had seen. He was, I believe, a victim of a strange, incomprehensible event, an unearthly event whose cultural and psychological roots are deeper than Christianity's.

The only person who could possibly know exactly what happened is Robbie himself. But he does not want to talk about that terrible winter and spring of 1949. People who have gently probed Robbie's memory say that he does not even remember what happened. He went on to a Catholic high school and remains a devout Catholic. His parents converted to Catholicism and received their first Communion on Christmas day, 1950. I have been told that the boy of 1949 grew into a man who lives a happy and rewarding life. I have also been told that he named his first child Michael after the archangel.

Like Robbie, the Jesuits involved in the exorcism walked out of that nightmare of evil unscathed. None of the lethal predictions of death in 1957 came true. Bowdern, who remained pastor of St. Xavier's Church until 1956, went on to other assignments, ending his Jesuit career as Confessor of Ours at Xavier's. He died in 1983 at the age of eighty-six. Father Bishop, after twenty-two years at St. Louis University, was sent to Creighton University in Omaha,

Nebraska, where he taught for twenty more years. He died in 1978 at the age of seventy-two. Father O'Flaherty, who served as pastor and assistant pastor at Xavier's and other churches until 1976, went into retirement at Regis College in Denver, Colorado, and died of pneumonia in St. Louis University Hospital in 1987 at the age of eighty. Father Halloran and Father Van Roo are still alive.

The only priest scarred by the exorcism was Father E. Albert Hughes, and his breakdown lasted only a few months. In 1973 he returned as pastor of St. James. "He was far holier," a parishioner remembers. "He became more aware, more spirit-filled, more understanding." He would never talk about what happened in 1949. His reluctance appeared to be deep-seated, but he was also under official restraint from making any written observations on his own. In May 1950, however, at the invitation of theologians at Georgetown University, Hughes lectured for more than an hour to a gathering of faculty members and students. He spoke from what appeared to be his official report to Archbishop O'Boyle. That report, like the one made by Father Bowdern to Archbishop Ritter, remains in secret files accessible only to the archbishop. But the archivist of Georgetown attended the lecture and took eight pages of notes based on Hughes' report. That set of notes is one of the sources for this book.

Many parishioners at St. James were aware that their pastor had played some mysterious role in the possession case made famous by the movie. And the nuns at St. James School told their pupils just enough about the exorcism to "put the fear of the devil in us," as one remembers.

In 1980, Father Frank Bober arrived at St. James as Father Hughes' new assistant. Bober, who had heard rumors about the exorcism, finally summoned the nerve to ask Hughes about it. "It was on October 8," Bober remembers. "We talked for about two hours, and I think I convinced him that other young priests like me would be educated by knowing about the exorcism. He talked about having a seminar. He wanted them to know about Satan and his power." Hughes always believed, Bober says, that Robbie wounded him with "a surge of Satanic power." But he said that the experience deepened his faith. "He told me," Bober recalls, "that it made him more aware of the tremendous power of the priesthood. The power of Christ through the priesthood brought the entire situation to a positive conclusion."

After finally unburdening himself about the exorcism, Hughes seemed exhausted. He told Bober that they would have to postpone continuance of the talk, and plans for the seminar, to another day. Four days later, on October 12, Father Hughes had a heart attack and died. He was sixty-two years old. Some parishioners believe that Robbie, then a forty-five-year-old man, attended Father Hughes' funeral.

Although the clergymen who were involved in exorcism kept the boy's identity secret, his neighbors in Mount Rainier knew him and treated a house at 3210 Bunker Hill Road as a menace to the neighborhood. Since the first edition of this book, doubt has been cast on that address as Robbie's. (See Chapter 2 notes in Sources.) I believe that the family at sometime occupied that house and resettled in nearby Cottage City. At least once after 1949, neighbors walked around the outside of the abandoned house on Bunker Hill Road, sprinkling holy water.

For years the house stood empty. Once in a while a couple of neighborhood teenagers would enter on a dare. They called the place "The Devil's House." Kids throwing stones broke most of the windows. Doors hung open. Tramps, as they were called then, sometimes slept there, got high on cheap wine, passed out, and scurried away in the morning. Occasionally, usually in winter, a tramp would start a fire to keep warm, and the fire would get out of control. A neighbor would see the flames and call the Mount Rainier Volunteer Fire Department.

A fire truck would speed out of the squat brick fire headquarters a few blocks away. The volunteers would briskly do their job, roll up their hoses, and return to headquarters. They had quickly put out a fire, but there was something troubling about it, something beyond reach of explanation. Putting out a fire at that house was not the same as saving a real, living house.

In April 1964, after a winter of several calls to the empty house, the volunteers started talking among themselves. None of them liked to go into that house. There were the usual risks—a fall through a rotting floor, a misstep on a staircase, smoke poisoning. And there was the fear of somehow being trapped by, well, who knew what? It was a house that lured firemen to flames, endangering them, making them save it. Some of the volunteers wished that the house would just burn down.

The mayor and the Mount Rainier volunteer firemen believed they knew what had happened at the house in 1949. So, when they began talking about what to do, they easily reached an agreement. The captain of the volunteers got what he decided was the proper permission for what he called a training exercise at the Devil's House. On a warm spring day in April 1964 the trucks rolled to the corner where the house stood. A pumper hooked up to a hydrant and men ran hose to the outside of the house. Around two sides of the property they ran perforated hose and turned on the water, sending up a shield of spray to protect the houses next to and in back of the house.

Small, silent groups of neighbors gathered on the sidewalks across the street. A couple of volunteers in boots, helmets, and glistening coats disappeared into the house. Through a broken window people could see flames crawling up the walls of a room. A few younger men, the students of this training exercise, entered behind a powerful jet of water.

They called it a controlled fire: set a room afire, send in a crew to put out the flames. Each room was burned and all of the men got practice in entering a room and extinguishing a fire. Then, when all the training was over, the volunteers lined up around the edge of the property. Men went in carrying cans. From outside they could be seen, again going from charred room to charred room. Moments after they emerged, flames began crackling throughout the house.

The volunteers stood there watching until the house burned to the ground.

Later, men came and carried off the charred wood and the blackened concrete foundation. A bulldozer filled in the cellar and smoothed the ground. When I first saw the site, seven crumbling concrete steps rose from the sidewalk where the house stood. Spindly trees struggled up from cracks in the steps, which ended at the edge of a lot covered with weeds and brush. A rusty pipe, half hidden in the brush, emerged from the ground in the middle of the lot.

The owner of the property had made elaborate arrangements to remain unidentified. Land records show that the property has had the same titular owners, two local businessmen, since 1952. I talked to one of the two men listed. He turned out to be a real estate dealer. He said his name had been used by a relative, who was also a real estate dealer. That man, who at first declined to talk, finally admitted that he was not the real owner. "The actual owner does not want to be identified," he told me. When I asked if the owner's wish for anonymity was based on the house's notoriety, the real estate man professed not to know anything about the history of the Devil's House.

In June 1992 the owners of record sold the lot, for $22,500, to the Maryland-National Capital Park and Planning Commission. After Robert M. Arciprete of the commission bought the lot, a staff member came into his office and told Arciprete something he did not know: "You sold the Exorcist lot!" Mount Rainier Mayor Linda M. Nalls said in 1993 that she did not know the dark history of the lot. But she hoped to bury the past by using the lot to enlarge an adjacent school playground. When I went back to the site recently, children were playing on what had been the site of the Devil's House.

The final secret is what did happen, first in Maryland and then in St. Louis. Did demons possess Robbie? Or did religious belief mask a psychiatric phenomenon?

The Roman Catholic Church has never said whether demons possessed Robbie, despite what seems to be enough ecclesiastical evidence to render a verdict. Father Bishop's diary is the most detailed chronicle of a possession written in modern times. And to this diary can be added the reports in the secret archives of the two archdioceses and in the archives of the Society of Jesus. A priest who has seen some of those archives told me that the major ecclesiastical report on the exorcism was signed by forty-eight witnesses. Bishop's diary lists nine Jesuits who saw Robbie under possession.

The Roman Catholic Church should have enough information to make a declaration about this exorcism. But the leaked story in

The Catholic Review is the only semi-official Catholic report ever issued on the case.

Archbishop Ritter, following Church procedure, appointed an examiner—a Jesuit professor of philosophy at St. Louis University—to investigate the case. The examiner had the authority to interview participants under oath. According to a Jesuit who is familiar with the results of that investigation, the examiner concluded that Robbie was not the victim of a diabolical possession. Buttressing that report were statements by psychiatrists at Washington University. They said they saw no evidence of the supernatural or preternatural.

"The examiner said it could be explained by a psychosomatic disorder and some kinesis action that we do not understand but which is not necessarily preternatural," I was told. (The examiner apparently did not further explain his reference "kinesis action," but many specialists in parapsychology believe in the existence of psychokinesis, the movement of objects by mental power.)

"When Archbishop Ritter got the report," according to my Jesuit source, "he asked everyone to stop talking about it. It's not that they were hiding anything. It just was that they felt that the overall effect of the thing was counter-productive."

Neither the examiner's report nor any other was ever released. "There was never any authoritative statement made as to whether this was a true case of possession," Halloran says. "I remember talking to Father Bowdern about it, and he said they will never make a statement about it."

As Halloran quotes him, Bowdern said, "Really, what difference does it make? Make a statement about it and you'd have a whole group of people who would want to destroy it, and you'd have another group of people who want to make it a true exorcism. I don't think they [Church authorities] are ever going to say a word about it. I think they will never say whether it was or it wasn't." And then, Halloran remembers, Bowdern paused and added, "You and I know it. We were there."

Yes, Halloran was there, but, looking back at what he saw and touched and smelled, he says, "I should never feel comfortable or capable of making an absolute statement. You know, you have some things that are considered characteristics of exorcism. For instance, if this little kid exhibited prodigious strength. Well, he didn't. And the other thing is an ability to use foreign languages without having any experience in them. Say if a person were possessed he might be able to speak Swahili. Another thing is feats of dexterity, walking up a wall, and things like that. These never happened. I don't have the faintest idea why the devil would need a possession. Satan would certainly have more effective means to spread evil than possessing someone."

Halloran, himself a target of Robbie's fist, does not believe that the boy's strength was more than an agitated adolescent could summon. As for Robbie's use of Latin, Halloran attributed this to Robbie's hearing repetitious phrases from the exorcist.

Halloran was a U.S. Army chaplain in Vietnam. "I saw more evil in Vietnam," he says, "than I saw in that hospital bed." He believes in evil, in an evil of place. He remembers talking to a Jesuit back from a long assignment in Africa. "He told me that in the place where he was working at first he felt he was in constant confrontation with the presence of evil. It never stopped, he said, until he established the presence of the Blessed Sacrament. Then, he said, it seemed that that power was broken. To Halloran, this was "a practical example of evil." But he spoke as a Roman

Catholic about what to him was the awesome power manifest in the Blessed Sacrament.

Finding evil outside a religious framework taxes the rational mind, especially in the age of psychiatry. In the Judeo-Christian tradition, the existence of evil is dogma. But, like the demons who tormented the man in the country of the Gadarenes, the theories of evil are Legion.

King Saul is the only person in the Old Testament who is possessed by "an evil spirit from God." The idea that evil could somehow be connected with God was an Old Testament concept. The New Testament, with its many references to possession and exorcisms, reflects new thinking about the spread and control of evil: The powerful fallen angels, led by Satan, inhabit and torment human beings. But the demons can be expelled by Jesus. He orders them out, and they leave, bitter and angry—yet obedient to God's will through Jesus' command.

At the time of Christ, popular belief in Galilee held that demons caused mental illness. The power to cast out those demons was a great power, just as it is today. As a modern Catholic theologian has noted, "the difference between the ancient conception of demonic possession and the modern conception of mental disease is, for the most part, only a difference of terminology. Although demon possession is called neurosis or psychosis today, the cure is the same, i.e, suggestion."

Demoniacal possession faded from Judaism, but another form of possession appeared among Jews in medieval Europe: the belief that a dead soul could enter a living body. Narratives of Jewish exorcisms resemble records of Christian exorcisms. But the possessor, the *Dybbuk,* is the spirit of a dead person. In Christian accounts, the possessor is one of the devil's legion of demons or the devil himself. Modern Judaism does not accept possession in any form.

Christianity, from the beginning, debated the existence of evil and Satan. What emerged from the debate was the idea that God created all things. Satan and his demons were created good in their nature but became evil by their own will. They are the fallen angels, divinely created beings who, through pride, envy, and finally despair, turned against God.

The first epistle of John personifies the devil, saying Christ came to overthrow him: "For this purpose the Son of God was manifested, that he might destroy the works of the devil."

The struggle between good and evil will not be easy, the New Testament warns. The demon is so strong and resolute that he dares to tempt Christ. Elsewhere in the Gospels Christ cites exorcism as further proof of his spiritual power and kingship: "But if I cast out devils by the Spirit of God, then the kingdom of God is come unto you." Christ's role as an exorcist gave Christianity the basis for the solemn belief that Satan could possess a human being and that God, through the ritual of exorcism, could drive Satan out of the victim.

Father Juan Cortes, S.J., a psychologist with a long interest in demonic possessions, questioned even Christ's exorcism. He examined the records of all known exorcism cases, including Robbie's, and concluded that there was no evidence of any possessions anywhere. He believed that "misinterpretations of the written words and expressions of the evangelists" were "primarily responsible for the deep belief in the minds of so many (in earlier times and at present) concerning both possessions by demons and the convenience and even necessity of expelling such demons through the performance of exorcisms."

Some of the misunderstanding, he wrote, may have occurred because the words "devil" and "demons" were erroneously thought to be interchangeable. By his interpretation, the biblical expression translated as "possessed by demons" should be read as "afflicted by harmful forces," by "strange, unknown powers," or by "evil spirits," the last in the sense of the modern phrase, "I'm in bad spirits today." The Gospels, he wrote, "contain no cases of possession by the *Devil*...no real, clear-cut cases of *possessions* by demons can be found in them..."

The exorcisms of Jesus, by Cortes' interpretation, were cures of diseases, not true exorcisms. As Cortes explained it, "When the possessed were healed, the invisible cause, mistranslated as 'devil,' had to be expelled and, consequently, the unwarranted but long tradition of exorcisms (or casting out devils) by Jesus became a reality. However, the method Jesus used in his healings of those afflicted by one or other type of illness (internal or external) was exactly the same: his presence, his touch, his word, his will or command. There is no reason to consider some healings as exorcisms while excluding the others."

In the modern world, people of many cultures believe that they can be taken over by aggressive spirits of evil. And every culture has a ritual for exorcising the demons, whether they be from the afterlife or from some hellish realm of evil. The exorcist, representing communal authority and benign supernatural power, treats the mad person by extracting the demon. If the exorcism does not work, the possessed person is consigned to whatever fate the community deems just. He or she may be a witch or a warlock and condemned to death. Or the community may decide to pity the mad person as an ill-fated prey of demons.

In cultures where psychiatry is a healing force, the psychiatrist often is the exorcist. Psychiatrists I talked to offered several possible explanations for the phenomenon. A specialist in multiple-personality disorders said that an exorcist does essentially what he is trying to do: Get rid of the entity that is inside the tortured patient. "I've dealt with several multiple-personality patients who thought they were possessed by Satan," he said. "They are highly susceptible to self-suggestion and amazingly open to hypnotic suggestion." In a typical case, he told of holding up his hand in front of a patient and telling her that his hand was slowly disappearing. "She believed that she saw it disappear. Inside her mind, there was no doubt that my hand had disappeared, any more than there was a doubt about being possessed. That belief is so deep that it is extremely difficult to dislodge. In the multiple-personality patient, every nerve ending can be a person." Usually, those nerve-ending persons are human personalities. Occasionally, however, the dweller within is a demon or Satan.

He said he did not know how his patients became possessed, although he almost invariably finds a history of sexual abuse in early childhood. He wondered whether there was any such history in Robbie's case. He was particularly interested in how Aunt Harriet haunted the early stage of the possession and how Robbie reacted when confronted by the Stations of the Cross, particularly the one showing Jesus being stripped of his garments. "Was there some kind of sexual encounter?" he wondered. "Was there guilt and a suppression of memory?"

Other psychiatrists have suggested Tourette's syndrome as the medical cause of possession. Victims of this disorder uncontrollably curse and scream, grunt and twitch and may involuntarily shout four-letter words. Some specialists on Tourette's syndrome say that Regan, the young girl under possession in "The Exorcist" film showed so many Tourette symptoms that she resembled, in an exaggerated way, some of their patients. Robbie, however, seemed cured of whatever had ailed him, and, at this stage in research, Tourette's syndrome is incurable.

Dr. Judith L. Rapoport, a world-renowned specialist in obsessive-compulsive disorder (OCD), believes that demoniacs may be victims of scrupulosity, a form of OCD long recognized by the Catholic Church and defined as "habitual and unreasonable hesitation or doubt, coupled with anxiety of the mind, in connection with the making of moral judgments." She calls victims of scrupulosity "innocent sinners" who make "a thousand commitments to God."

The founder of the Society of Jesus, St. Ignatius Loyola, "provided the Catholic Church with its first definition of scrupulosity through a description of Loyola's own obsessive behavior, and his insight into its irrational yet distressful force," she writes. As an example, she offers this from his *Spiritual Exercises*:

> After I have trodden upon a cross formed by two straws, or after I have thought, said or done some other thing, there comes to me from "without" a thought that I have sinned, and on the other hand it seems to me that I have not sinned; nevertheless I feel some uneasiness on the subject, inasmuch as I doubt yet do not doubt.

Robbie is an unlikely example of scrupulosity: he was not a Catholic and he showed no signs of religious fanaticism.

Rapoport also suggests a very rare mental illness, childhood schizophrenia. Generally, schizophrenia is a disorder of late adolescence or young adulthood. But, she says, "there are atypical cases of children—mostly boys—who develop normally until, say, the age of eight, when they start having typical schizophrenia symptoms, such as hearing voices." She told of examining a boy who heard voices, including the devil, "who is telling him to hurt people and do dangerous things."

Father Nicola, the priest who was one of the advisers for "The Exorcist," later advised psychiatrists who believed that their patients were in need of exorcism. He inevitably counseled against exorcism unless there were what he called preternatural signs, such as the ability to read minds or speak a language previously unknown to the demoniac. When I talked to him, he said he did not believe that Robbie had been diabolically possessed.

Nicola said the Catholic Church was trying to stay in the middle road about possession while still maintaining theologically that there is a devil operating in our world. "The Church walks a tightrope," he told me. "If the Devil is operative in the world, then let's do the exorcism. On the scientific side, science says that possession is not possession. It's a matter of seeing what faith and nature each might show." Like some other specialists on exorcisms, he cautiously wondered if parapsychology might hold some answers to the inexplicable phenomena associated with possession.

Father Herbert Thurston, S.J., an authority on the occult, writing about demoniacs, also wondered about forces we do not yet understand: "That there may be something diabolical, or at any rate evil, in them I do not deny, but, on the other hand, it is also possible that there may be natural forces involved which are so far as little known to us as the latent forces of electricity were known to the Greeks. It is possibly the complication of these two elements which forms the heart of the mystery."

There is, finally, I think, something of the fable to exorcism, if a fable is a veil thrown across the face of truth. One day I was talking to a Jesuit theologian about possession and about the intricacies of good and evil. He rattled off the books I should read on the subject and he showed the proper Jesuit contempt for anything less than hard-edged reason. As the interview ended, he asked me casually if I had heard what had happened in Xavier's after the end of the exorcism. No, I hadn't. And then he told me—told me as if this, too, was important to a discussion of good and evil.

Soon after the successful end of the exorcism at the hospital, he said, something strange happened in St. Francis Xavier Church. It was night, and the church was in partial darkness. Several Jesuits had gathered in the church for a service. Suddenly, the shadowed loftiness of the great soaring apse blazed in light. The Jesuits looked up and saw, filling the immense space above the altar, what Robbie said had seen—St. Michael, flaming sword in hand, defending the good and warding off evil.

The Exorcist Diary

Author's Note: I obtained this diary from Father Walter Halloran, who participated in the exorcism and, many years later, acquired a copy of the diary under the strange circumstances that I describe on page xiii. Accompanying the 24 pages of the diary was a letter, dated April 29, 1949, from Father Bishop to Brother Cornelius, the rector of the hospital. The letter said:

The inclosed report is a summary of the case which you have known for the past several weeks. The Brothers' part in this case has been so very important that I thought you should have the case history for your permanent file.

We have been informed by the Chancery Office on two different occasions, March 16 and April 27, that the case is not to be publicized. I fear that the news has already broken in various parts of the city through individuals asking for prayers and perhaps through some who took part in the case. The difficulty of keeping some of the facts secret is practically beyond our control right now, but insofar as we are able we should not make this case public until we have a definite statement from the Chancery Office. [*Note: No such statement was ever issued.*]

One of the finest benefits that has come to me as a result of this case is a high appreciation of the work and religious devotion of the Alexian Brothers. The prayerful assistance of your Community was certainly a strong factor in winning a battle against Satan. Your own co-operation to the extent of establishing public devotion to Our Lady of Fatima will always be associated with the inspirational aspects of the case.

The [**NAME DELETED**] family has been won over completely by the wholehearted charity of your Brothers. There is little doubt that the intention of becoming a Catholic has been deeply influenced by the Christlike attitude of the Brothers who worked with [**NAME DELETED**].

It will always be a distinct privilege for me to remember you and your Community at the Holy Sacrifice [*of the Mass*].

*The diary begins with a section called "CASE STUDY," in which the boy's name, address, and other information is recorded. I have deleted identifying information in this section. Elsewhere in the diary, where family names are given, I have omitted them with [***NAME DELETED***]. I have changed two names that appear frequently, indicating the changes by making the first reference, i.e.,* **Robbie** *and* **Harriet***, in bold type. There are occasional misspellings; where necessary for clarification, I have indicated this with the conventional* [sic]. *The diary that was given to me had been photo-copied from the original typescript; the photo-copy contains a few unintelligible words. I have indicated them with* [unreadable]. *The writer of the diary uses "R" to identify the boy; I have retained that identification.*

Case Study

[NAME AND ADDRESS DELETED.] Son of [NAMES DELETED.]

Birth: [MONTH,DAY DELETED]1935. Religion: Evangelical Lutheran; baptized six months after birth by a Lutheran Minister.

Maternal Grandmother—practicing Catholic until the age of fourteen years.

Paternal Grandfather—Baptized Catholic but no practice.

Father—Baptized Catholic but no instruction or practice.

Mother—Baptized Lutheran.

[NAME DELETED]and his mother visited in St. Louis at [NAME AND ADDRESS DELETED.]

Background of the Case.

On January 15, 1949, at the home of **Robbie** in Cottage City, Maryland a dripping noise was heard by Robbie and his Grandmother in the Grandmother's bedroom. This noise continued for a short time and then the picture of Christ on the wall shook as if the wall back of it had been bumped. By the time the parents of R returned home there was a very definite scratching sound under the floor boards near the Grandmother's bed. From this night on, the scratching was heard every night about seven o'clock and would continue until midnight. The family thought that the scratching was caused by a rodent of some kind. An exterminator was called in who placed chemicals under the floor boards, but the scratching sound continued and became more distinct when people stamped on the floor.

This scratching continued for ten days and then stopped. The family finally believed that the rodent had died. The boy, R, seemed to think he still heard the noise but the family did not hear anything for a period of three days. When the sound became audible again, it was no longer in the upstairs bedroom but had moved downstairs to the boy's bedroom. It was heard as the sound of squeaking shoes along the bed and was heard only at night when the boy went to bed. The squeaking sound continued for six nights, and on the sixth night scratching again was audible. The mother, grandmother and boy while lying on the bed on this night heard something coming toward them similar to the rhythm of marching feet and the beat of drums. The sound would travel the length of the mattress and then back again and repeat this action until the mother asked "Is this you, Aunt **Harriet**?" Harriet [**LAST NAME DELETED**]had died in St. Louis two weeks after the first sounds were heard in the ome [*sic*] of R.) The mother continued asking questions but had no verbal reply. She asked this question, "If you are Harriet, knock three times." There were waves of air striking the grandmother, mother and the boy, and three distinct knocks were heard on the floor. The mother asked again, "If you are Harriet, tell me positively by knocking four times." Four distinct knocks were heard. Then there followed claw scratchings on the mattress.

When the mother or the Grandmother paid no attention to the mattress scratching, the entire mattress would begin to shake. The action at times was very violent. On one occasion the coverlet of the bed was pulled out from under the matress and the edges stood up above the surface of the bed in a curled form as though held up with starch. When the bystanders touched the bed spread, the sides fell back to normal position. The scratching on the mattress has been continuous since the first night it was heard.

On February 26, 1949, there appeared scratches on the boy's body for about four successive nights. After the fourth night words were written in printed form. These letters were clear but seemed to have been scratched on the body by claws.

Since Mrs. [**NAME DELETED**] is a native St. Louisan she thought of leaving her home and taking the boy to St. Louis in order to avoid some of these strange manifestations. It seems that whatever force was writing the words was in favor of making the trip to St. Louis. On one evening the word "Louis" was written on the boy's ribs in deep red. Next when there was some question of the time of departure, the word "Saturday" was written plainly on the boy's hip. As to the length of time the mother and boy should stay in St. Louis, another message was printed on the boy's chest, "3½ weeks." The printing always appeared without any motion on the part of the boy's hands. The mother was keeping him under close supervision. There seemed to be a sharp pain when the marks occurred so that the boy doubled up and uttered a rather terrifying sound. The markings could not have been done by the boy for the added reason that on one occasion there was writing on his back. Even in St. Louis the writing continued. There was some question of sending R. to school during his visit here, but the message, "No," appeared on his wrists; also a large "N" on both legs. The mother feared disobeying this order.

Other Manifestations.

An orange and a pear flew across the entire room where R. was standing. The kitchen table was upset without any movement on the part of R. Milk and food were thrown off the table and stove. The bread-board was thrown on to the floor. Outside the kitchen a coat on its hanger flew across the room; a comb flew violently through the air and extinquished blessed candles; a Bible was thrown directly at the feet of R., but did not injure him in any way. While the family was visiting a friend in Boonesboro, Maryland, the rocker in which R. was seated spun completely around through no effort on the part of the boy. R's desk at school moved about on the floor similar to the plate on a Ouija board. R. did not continue his attendance out of embarrassment.

Witnesses.

Since the beginning of the above-enumerated incidents there have been fourteen different witnesses to testify and verify different phenomena. Two Lutheran Ministers were called in on the case. One of the Ministers invited the boy to his home and slept in the same bed with him. During the night the clawing sounds on the floor were heard as they were in R's own home. The Minister prayed but the action became stronger. R. was tied to a chair, and the chair tipped over. A Psychiatrist was consulted but declared that he did not believe the phenomena. His report was that the boy was quite normal. R. was irritated with the questions and procedure. A Physician gave R. a complete physical check-up and found him to be a normal boy, but somewhat high-strung. A Spiritualist was called in to use his formulae for ridding people of spirits, but he had no success. (It should be remarked here that Aunt Harriet believed very much in Spiritualism and often consulted Spiritualists.).

Father Hughes, Catholic Priest of St. James Parish at Mt. Rainier, Maryland, was asked for his advice and he suggested blessed candles, holy water and definite prayers. He did not meet the boy in person. The mother took the bottle of holy water home, sprinkled all the rooms, and when she placed the bottle on a shelf, the bottle flew across the room, but did not break. When she held the lighted candle along side of R. at night, the whole bed, mother and son moved back and forth with the swaying of the mattress. Prayers ordinarily aggravate the phenomena. Father Hughes was seeking permission from the Bishop for an exorcism about the time when the [**NAME DELETED**] were going to St. Louis. Consequently, he was unable to proceed with his plan.

St. Louis.

Different displays were witnessed by two aunts of the boy, four uncles and four cousins in St. Louis. The printing, "No School," was seen by four different people. The swaying of the mattress, the upsetting of bedroom furniture and the scratching on the mattress were observed by the entire group.

March 9, 1949, the violent moving of the mattress and the scratching on the boy's body was observed by the mother, an aunt, an uncle, a cousin of college age, a friend of the family, and by Father Bishop.

One of R's cousins who is in Father Bishop's class asked Father Bishop whether he could give any assistance to the case. Father Bishop consulted Father Kenny and with Father Reinert, the President of the University, and decided that it might be well to have the boy say some prayers and that we could give him the Priestly blessing.

Furthermore, Father Bishop agreed to go to the home of the [NAME AND ADDRESS DELETED] so that he might bless the house and room where R. slept. A second class relic of St. Margaret Mary was pinned on the bed of R.

Even after the blessing of the house and in spite of the relic, the swaying was evident and the scratching appeared. The relatives of the boy said, however, that Wednesday night was the most peaceful they had had since R. arrived in St. Louis.

Day by day events in St. Louis.

Monday, March 7, 1949.

Home of R's non-Catholic aunt and uncle. Five or six relatives present. Spirit questioned through an alphabetical medium, on porcelain kitchen table. Letters of alphabet written on paper were underlined whenever the table moved. A code of messages became evident. Phenomena indicated that the spirit was not the devil but the soul of the deceased Harriet. Spirit confirmed again to all present that she was Harriet by moving a heavy bed two or three feet with no one of the bystanders near the bed. All the group saw this action. Furthermore, writing appeared on R's body while he was reading a comic book. There was sharp pain. The writing was done through his clothes.

When R. retired, there was violent shaking of the bed and scratching on the mattress. Hardly any relief through the night.

Tuesday, March 8, 1949.

At the home of R's Catholic aunt, two cousins and non-Catholic uncle. Shaking of mattress, scratching, stool upset several feet away from the bed. Phenomena observed by cousin who spent the night with R. Mattress continued to move in the direction of the uprights of the bed, even when cousin lay along-side of R. All other members of the family observed the violent shaking of the mattress and heard the scratching sound.

Wednesday, March 9.

At home as of Tuesday. Father Bishop blessed the entire house and used a special blessing in R's room and on his bed. A second class relic of St. Margaret Mary was safety-pinned to the extreme corner of R's pillow. Shortly after R. retired the mattress on his bed began to move back and forth in the direction of the bed uprights. The boy lay perfectly still, and did not exert any physical effort. The movement in one direction did not exceed more than three inches, the action was intermittent and completely subsided after a period of approximately fifteen minutes. When Father Bishop sprinkled St. Ignatius Holy Water on the bed in the form of a Cross, the movement ceased quite abruptly, but began again when Father stepped out of the room. During the course of the fifteen minutes of activity a sharp pain seemed to have struck R. on his stomach and he cried out. The mother quickly pulled back the bed covers and lifted the boy's pajama top enough to show zig-zag scratches in bold red lines on the boy's abdomen. It should be remarked that during the fifteen minutes the boy was not out of view of six observers. When the mattress shaking subsided, there was peace for the remainder of the night, i.e. after 11:15 PM.

Thursday, March 10.

Same place as Tuesday and Wednesday. Same people present in the home as of Wednesday with the exception of Father Bishop. Shaking of mattress, and scratching which beat out a rhythm as of marching soldiers. Second class relic of St. Margaret Mary was thrown on the floor. The safety pin was opened but no human hand had touched the relic. R. started up in fright when the relic was thrown down.

Friday, March 11.

Same place as above. Same observers as of Thursday with addition of Fathers Bowdern and Bishop. Father Bowdern had concluded the Novena service in the College Church at 9:00 PM. It was arranged that the relatives of the boy would take the two above-mentioned Priests to the home of R. Since the Novena service was in honor of St. Francis Xavier, Father Bowdern, the Pastor, thought it proper to take the first class relic of Xavier along for a Novena Blessing. He likewise carried a crucifix containing first class relics of several of the North American Martyrs and of St. Peter Canisius.

Shortly after R. had retired at 11:00 PM, he called downstairs that he had been frightened by a strong force that had thrown some object against the mirror in his bedroom. With safety pin opened, the relic of St. Margaret Mary had been thrown against the mirror and the sound was like a pellet striking the glass. Another occurrence was a cross mark scratched on R's left, outer forearm. The pain was similar to that produced by a scratch of a thorn. The cross remained evident for approximately forty-five minutes.

Father Bowdern read the Novena prayer of St. Francis Xavier and then blessed R with the relic (a piece of bone from the forearm of St. Francis Xavier). Then the crucifix reliquary was safety-pinned under R's pillow. There was no shaking of the mattress or scratching at this time.

After the above blessing the group of observers went downstairs to review some of the history of the case, when a loud crash was heard in R's bedroom. The boy was dosing when the bottle of St. Ignatius Holy Water was thrown from a table two feet from R's bed into a nearby corner, a distance of approximately six feet. The bottle did not break. Then Father Bowdern put his Rosary around R's neck, and both Priests recited the Rosary, one Priest on either side of R's bed. Father Bowdern taught R several ejaculations to Our Lady of Fatima. With a blessing to R, and to the family the Priests left the home about 12:30 AM Saturday.

Five minutes after Fathers Bowdern and Bishop left R's home, there was a heavy scraping noise in R's room. A bookcase was moved from along side the bed and turned completely around facing the entrance to the room. The stool at the dressing table moved from the table to the bed, about two feet. The stool was moved back to its position and in a few moments, it was turned over. Mother and R. were in bed when crucifix with relics was moved from under the pillow to the foot of the bed. The relic of St. Margaret Mary was lost in the room.

Then followed violent scratching and shaking in rhythm. The five people in the home then decided to ask questions of the spirit. There is some question about an amount of money which was concealed by Aunt Harriet before she died. Through many different questions it seemed that the map which would locate the money hidden in the metal strong box would be found in the attic of

Harriet's home, but only [**NAME DELETED**], the father of R who lives in [**ADDRESS DELETED**] could find it. When [**NAME DELETED**]'s name was suggested the bed shook violently. Further questioning revealed that the money was for [**NAME DELETED**], the daughter of [**NAME DELETED**]. Whenever the questioners wanted the bed shaking to stop they called, "Harriet, stop" and the bed stopped as though Harriet were listening for a question.

On the night that Harriet died she told everyone in the house to go to bed at 10:00 PM and she died between 2:00 and 2:30 the following morning. The striking parallel indicated is that the bed shaking and noise always ceases by 2:30 AM.

Saturday, March 12, 1949.

Fathers Bowdern and Bishop arrived at the home of R at 11:45 PM. Before the arrival of the Priests that evening the bookcase in R's room was moved away from the wall quickly and with precision. (The bookcase with books would weigh more than fifty pounds). Then again just before the Fathers went upstairs to R's room, a quick, scraping noise was heard. The bookcase had swung around from the wall to the side of R's bed in an arc of five or six feet. Father Bishop replaced the bookcase, and then Father Bowdern blessed R. with the relic of St. Francis Xavier and Holy Water. The Fathers prayed the Rosary aloud and then prayed silently from 12:00 to 3:00 AM. R. had a very normal sleep and there were no manifestations of an evil spirit.

Sunday, March 13.

The family was alone. There was shaking of the mattress and scratching on the under surface. The phenomena did not persist more than one and one-half hours.

Monday, March 14.

The Priests were not present. A stool was thrown over R's bed and landed with a loud crash, but nothing was injured. The mattress shook, as on many previous occasions. The shaking continued for about two hours.

Tuesday, March 15.

There was the usual mattress shaking. The relic of St. Margaret Mary was thrown from the pillow. The mattress movement continued for two hours.

Wednesday, March 16.

Permission was granted by the Most Reverend Archbishop Joseph E. Ritter that Father William S. Bowdern, S.J., Pastor of the College Church in St. Louis might read the prayers of exorcism according to the Roman Ritual. Fathers Bowdern, Bishop, and Mr. W. Halloran, S.J., arrived at the [**NAME DELETED**] home between 10:15 and 10:30 PM. Shortly after 10:30 R. was sent to bed and Father Bowdern helped him to examine his conscience and make an act of contrition. Then Father Bishop, Mr. Halloran, R's mother and the uncle and aunt of R were called into the bedroom in order to prepare for the exorcism. All those present knelt down beside R's bed and acts of Faith, Hope, Love and Contrition were recited together (R said the prayers too).

Next Father Bowdern in surplice and stole began the prayers of exorcism. R was awake and the overhead light in the bedroom was kept burning. R kept his hands outside the bed covers. On the first "Praecipio" there was immediate action. Three large parallel bars were scratched on the boy's stomach. From then on at the names of Our Lord and His Blessed Mother, and St. Michael scratches appeared on the boy's legs, thighs, stomach, back, chest, face and throat. These scratches were sharply painful and caused red marks on the body, and the marks raised up above the surface of the skin, similar to engraving. Only one scratch pierced the outer layer of the skin, similar to a very slight laceration and caused a small amount of blood to flow. This scratch appeared on R's left leg. R recoiled under evident pain as each mark was made. R stated that some of the marks felt like thorn scratches, others like brands. The brand marks were the more painful.

The most distinct markings on the body were the picture of the devil on R's right leg and the word "HELL" imprinted on R's chest in such a way that R could look down upon his chest and read the letters plainly. The imprint of the devil and "HELL" appeared at the repetition of the "Praecipio" demanding the evil spirit to identify himself. The devil was portrayed in red. This [*sic*] arms were held above his head and seemed to be webbed, giving the hideous appearance of a bat. All the room observers agreed that the above two signs could not be mistaken for other designs. In further answer to the prayer "Praecipio" two letters "GO" and a third pointed away from the crotch, an indication which might have meant that the devil would leavy [*sic*] by way of urination or excrement. To the question how many demons? a single line was scratched on R's right leg. There were at least four heavy brand marks in the form of an "X". This impression may have indicated that the exorcism would take ten days, or that the devil would depart at 10:00 o'clock. At least during the first days of the exorcism the "X" had no significance. The markings on the legs seemed to be long scratches with no special meaning. Marks were made on the boy's body more than twenty-five *sic*] different times during the course of the evening, each mark causing the boy to double up with pain.

The next phase of the reaction took the appearance of quiet sleep. R seemed to relax and there were no painful scratches. The prayers were continued by Fathers Bowdern and Bishop alternating. When the prayers to St. Michael was begun, R began to stir in his apparent sleep. He smiled and then laughed. Next he began sparring. He struck the board back of his bed strong blows with his fist, and then began punching the pillow with more than ordinary force. As he swung his arms in violence he spoke of the conflict which appeared to him In all the manifestations since the beginning in January there were no words spoken by R when he seemed to be under the influence of the devil. The family had not seen such violent reaction as was shown on this night and the following. Evidently the exorcism prayers had stirred up the devil. Holy Water was sprinkled on R and he came out of his apparent sleep. R was asked what he was doing and what he saw. He said he was fighting a hugh [*sic*] red devil who felt slimy and was very powerful. The devil was trying to prevent him from getting through the iron gates at the top of a pit that was about two hundred feet deep and was very hot. R wanted to fight that devil and felt that he was strong enough to overpower his enemy. R mentioned that there were other smaller devils.

When the exorcism prayers were continued, R fell back into the tantrum stage, and after some deep breathing, he would go into strong combat with the devil who was trying to keep him down in the pit. There was hand to hand wrestling.

From 12:00 midnight on, it was necessary to hold R during his fights with the spirit. Two men were necessary to pin him down to the bed. R shouted threats of violence at them, but vulgar language was not used. R. spit at his opponents many tines. He used a strong arm whenever he could free himself, and his blows were beyond the ordinary strength of the boy.

R could be brought back to a waking condition for brief periods by dousing him with Holy Water. As the night wore on, it became almost impossible to keep R from falling into the fitful and apparent slumber during which he went through violent byrations. [*sic*] It was about 5:00 AM of the 17th before the tantrums began to moderate themselves. When R was awakened from this more moderate state, he was so limp and weak that he could not sit up or hold his eyes open. He could not stay awak long enough to drink a glass of water. (The need for water throughout the night was always the first request of R upon awakening). He complained of the intense heat from which he had suffered in his combats.

The last phase of the night's demonstrations consisted in an apparent sleep in which R began to sing. He sang with a high-pitched voice and with tremendous volume such songs as "Swanee" and "Old Man River." The tunes were not completed and were garbled versions, together with full arm gestures and a wild attempt at interpretation. In the song stage, R was more amenable and did not have to be subdued physically except in a few instances. His muscles became relaxed and his whole bodily attitude was one of composure. During the singing phase R awakened several times on his own, i.e. without slappings and Holy Water.

About 7:30 AM, R began a natural sleep and continued quite peacefully until 1:00 PM of the 17th. Then he ate an ordinary meal and participated in a game of monopoly.

Thursday, March 17.

Fathers Bowdern, Bishop and Mr. Halloran arrived at R's home between 9:00 and 9:30 PM. R's father had flown in from Maryland because of the extraordinary events of the preceding evening. R declared that he was very sleepy about 9:00 PM. His parents helped him to get ready for bed, but had difficulty in keeping him awake long enough to remove his clothes. R fell into the deep tantrum sleep as on the previous night. It was necessary for the father and uncle to hold him with considerable force because of his tyrating.[*sic*] By means of Holy Water and several sharp slaps on the boy's face Father Bishop was able to bring R. back to consciousness. But in a few moments R was back in his wild nightmare. This state is not like natural sleep because of the threshing action and the shouting did not bring R back to consciousness. He could not be awakened by ordinary means. At times it was impossible to bring him to.

The prayers of the exorcism were continued while the family prayed the Rosary. The commands of the formula caused violent reactions in R. The new phase of the case emphasized diabolical spitting. R spit at the three men who were holding him. He spit at Father Bowdern who was reading the prayers of the exorcism and tore his stole. He spit at Father Bishop who was blessing him frequently with Holy Water. R spit directly in the faces of his father and mother and his uncle. His eyes were shut tight, but he was able to aim well in spite of the cloth held near his face. When R was conscious, he did not know that he was spitting during the tantrums, nor did he know that he was fighting with those who held him. He fell exhausted after each ordeal, but yet his pulse did not vary much from normal.

There were no scratches clawed upon the boy's body in the course of the evening, but the thrashing action was every bit as severe as it was on the preceding night. The threats to those who were holding R were not vulgar, yet were loud and eerie. Occasionally R hummed a little tune or sang phrases from "Swanee River." His melody was false and the pitch was extremely high.

Natural sleep came to R at 1:30 AM. Then the Fathers departed.

Friday, March 18.

R had a spell about 1:00 PM. His father held him tight in his arms while the mother and aunt prayed the Rosary. The struggling ceased in about one hour's time. Fathers Bowdern, Bishop and Mr. Halloran, SJ, arrived at R's home at 7:00 PM, chatted and played a game with R. He retired at 8:15 PM. R prayed the Rosary with the clergy at his bedside. The novena prayers to Our Lady of Fatima were recited in common. Next the Fathers began the Litany of the Saints, as indicated in the exorcism ritual. In the course of the Litany, the mattress began to shake. R was awake. The shaking ceased when Father Bowdern blessed the bed with Holy Water. The prayers of the exorcism were continued and R was seized violently so that he began to struggle with his pillow and the bed clothing. The arms, legs, and head of R had to be held by three men. The contortions revealed physical strength beyond the natural power of R. R spit at the faces of those who held him and at those who prayed over him. He spit at the relics and at the Priests' hands. He writhed under the sprinkling of Holy Water. He fought and screamed in a diabolical, high-pitched voice. During one of his quieter reactions he was moving his feet in rhythmical fashion. Father Bowdern held the Blessed Sacrament three or four inches from the sole of the moving foot. The movement stopped on the foot which was nearer the Blessed Sacrament. This manifestation of the power of the Blessed Sacrament showed up time after time without fail.

For short intervals R became conscious, but knew very little of what had happened. He felt the pain in his arms from the strong arm tactics that he used, and which were used on him.

When the exorcism was taken up again, R went back into his tantrum even when he was trying to repeat some short prayers with Father Bowdern. R stood up in bed and fought all those around him. He shouted, jumped, and swung his fists. His face was devilish, and he snapped his teeth in fury. He snapped at the Priest's hand in the blessings. He bit those who held him.

By 12:00 midnight there were signs of change. R stood up in bed; then he dropped to his knees and quietly went through salaams. The salaams were repeated four or five times. On several occasions *in* the process of bowing R said "Our Lady of Fatima, pray for us," and also repreated the words of the "Hail Mary." The next stage was beating out a rhythm on the pillow, something similar to the rhythm of trotting horses. Then R rose again and began his strong fight for the eviction of the devil. His gyrations were in all directions. He pulled off the upper part of his underwear, and held his arms high above himself in supplication. Then he made as though he were trying to vomit from his stomach. His gestures moved upwards, close to his body. He seemed to try to lift the devil from his stomach to his throat. He asked that the window be opened and then in a happy, victorious mood he said sweetly, "He's going, he's going..." and finally, "There he goes." His body fall limp upon the bed in a perfectly relaxed condition. Everything seemed to indicate conquest. In a moment he was normal and seemed relieved. The whole family knelt around the bed and said prayers of thanksgiving. The mother was beside herself with joy. R was asked what his experiences were during the latter part of the night. He said that he saw a huge, dark cloud of black vapor in front of him passing out from his vision. A figure in black robes, cowl, and white [*unreadable*] walked away in the cloud.

R got out of bed, put on his bathrobe and saw the Fathers off. He was very happy. R. seemed to have made a complete recovery at 1:00 AM, and it was about 1:30 when the clergymen departed. About 2:00 or a little after R felt strange sensations in his stomach and in a few moments he began to call out fearfully, "He's coming back! He's coming back!" Father Bowdern was called at 3:15 AM and the three exorcists went back for more of the formula. No evident progress was made, and about 7:30 AM, the boy dropped off into a natural sleep.

Saturday, March 19.

The exorcists arrived at R's home at 7:00 PM. R retired at 8:00 PM, and the routine of the exorcism was begun again. Violent shoutings with fiendish laughter were a part of the phenomena. The shouting resembled the barking of a dog, and the snapping of R's teeth was truly diabolical. It should be stated again that the violent reactions always followed upon the prayers of the exorcism. There had been no violence from the boy before the exorcism was begun on the night of March 16.

When the exorcist asked for a sign through the prayer "Praecipio" on three or four different occasions R urinated, seemingly without control. He complained upon awaking that the urine burned him. Previous to the urination R doubled up with pain in his stomach and he woke up crying. He complained too that his throat hurt him.

Songs were sung very beautifully in a clear voice and with real finesse. The best rendition was the "la la" of the "Blue Danube" with excellent and flowing gestures of interpretation. Another song was the hymn the "Old Rugged Cross." The striking thing about the singing on this night was the professional ability shown. R cannot sing well in normal life, nor does he like to sing. Father Bishop hummed the tune of the "Blue Danube" after R was awake, but R was unable to carry the melody. He said he did not know the song. He made this same affirmation several days later.

Another performance of the evening was a playful call for one of the Fathers present. R repeated the call over and over again in a very pleasant voice but when no response was given, R's voice turned hard and the expression became, "Father_____you stink."

Then followed violence and demoniacal fighting until R was wholly exhausted at 3:00 AM, and he fell into a deep slumber. The exorcists waited a half hour and then departed.

It is worthy of mention that God seemed to have pity on the boy when he became exhausted. The devil was not permitted to disturb R after he had fallen into his natural sleep. However, R was tried to the point of exhaustion every night of the exorcism.

Sunday, March 20.

R [*unreadable*] his tantrum at 8:45 PM with more violence than on any previous occasion. All the violence followed on the prayers of the exorcism. The high point of the evening were urinations which really burned R, breaking wind through the rectum three different times, and the cursing of the exorcists.

Some of the vulgarity follows:
Get away from me-
You ass holes-
Go to hell, you dirty sons of bitches-
God damn you, sons of bitches-
You dirty ass holes-
And occasionally R would use prayers to Mary and Our Lady of
Fatima. Action ceased at 2:00 AM.

Monday, March 21.

The family of R was losing sleep, and the mother had to be
taken to a physician, so it was thought best to take R to a hospital
so that the other members of the family might relax. Since R was so
boisterous in his tantrums, it was decided that the Alexian Brothers
would have a room away from the regular patients where R could
scream without harm to the rest of the hospital. Then too the
Alexian Brothers have equipment for holding patients in bed when
there is violence. R was put to bed at 10:00 PM, but he feared the
surroundings of the hospital: the barred window, the bare room,
the straps on the bed, and the knobless door. His whole reaction
was one of intense fear. Father Bowdern began the Litany of the
exorcism and continued on through the entire formula. Several of
the Brothers were present beside Father Bishop, Mr. Halloran, SJ
and R's father. When the exorcism was completed, all knelt for the
Rosary. R did not fall asleep nor was there any discernible reaction
on the part of the devil. The exorcist group left the room while R's
father read prayers for his boy during the space of a half hour. One
of the most edifying scenes since the beginning of the case was to
see the father using prayers to get his son to sleep. At 11:30 PM R
fell into a sound, normal sleep, and continued peacefully through

the night. His father slept on a divan in the same room. R awakened at 6:30 AM and was taken home for the day.

Tuesday, March 22.

R went to bed at his uncle's home about 9:30 PM. Shortly after he retired the bed began to shake and it seemed that operations were in progress again. R's mother called Father Bishop, and he with two other Priests drove out to the home and arrived there with the Blessed Sacrament at 11:00 PM. The three Priests knelt at the bedside of R and began the prayers of the exorcism. The bed shook during short intervals on three different occasions. When the exorcism was completed, the Rosary was recited and R went off into a natural sleep. The Fathers departed at midnight, and no further action took place.

Wednesday, March 23.

Father Bowdern arranged that R might have a room at the College Church rectory. Two beds were provided so that R's father might sleep in the same room with his son. R took a brief instruction on the Catholic religion and then went to bed at 9:30 PM. Short acts of Faith, Hope, Love and Contrition were recited by all the group, including R. Immediately upon the first invocations of the Litany R went into his tantrum. He fought and kicked, and spit so that three men could scarcely hold him. In the course of the evening R broke Mr. Halloran's nose and caused Father Van Roo's nose to bleed. The first blows were accurate, quick, and deadly, although R's eyes were shut. At the "Praecipio" R urinated rather copiously and on coming to himself complained of the burning sensation. There were four or five such urinations during the evening. Several times there was passing of wind through the rectum.

The language of R became abusive and dirty. He met one of the Fathers in hell and stated the year as 1957. He indicated surprise at finding the Father in hell. The vile and filthy talk which followed makes anyone shudder. R spoke of his penis as a "beautiful pecker, a willy, dilly, pilly…so round, so firm with a red top and a hole in the middle." He pulled the towel from his loins and shook his body in a suggestive and shimmy fashion. His expressions were lowly and smacked of the abuse of sex. When R came to normal from time to time he would say that the men down there were using filthy language. R was never accustomed to filthy expressions in his regular life.

With more contortions, barking and singing R finally went off into natural sleep at 2:30 AM. His body was limp and completely fagged out.

Thursday, March 24.

At the Rectory. Reactions began at 9:45 PM, and continued until 2:30 AM. Father Bishop thought that this would be the last night since it was the Feast of St. Gabriel, and the next day was the Feast of the Annunciation. Father Bowdern believed that the "X" mark on R from the first night of the exorcism should be interpreted as the 10th day, so he did not expect the devil to leave until the following night.

R had great physical strength. Four men were holding him. R ran the gamut of shouting, screaming, barking, singing, kindly expressions, urination and passing foul air. One of the assisting Fathers was met in hell in 1956. He was called a big fat ass and an ox. Michael, the workman who helped R was constantly in R's bitter imprecations, or in silly rhymes, "Michael, pikel, likel, sikle… Michael, you look so dirty."

The filthiest talk was given out after midnight on the Feast of the Annunciation. R spoke of kissing his pecker, and using the stick for pleasure. Then he would say, "Isn't it pretty?" He turned upon the Priests at his bedside, "You have big pricks too, and you like to rub them up and down…You have big teats, you big ox." Then followed a sucking sound. He called to the exorcist to…cut out the damned Latin…Get away from me, you God damned bastards."

About 2:00 AM R noted from his tantrum that the bystanders were going to stay on to the end. In a coy tone he remarked, "You like to stay with me. Well, I like it too."

The Blessed Sacrament had no noticeable effect in the course of the night.

R slept from 2:30 to 11:30 AM.

Friday, March 25.

At the Rectory. R was very restless and could not sleep. The group of Priests prayed outside his door. For brief periods R fell into fitful tossing which was not real sleep. On one occasion R fell out of bed, but was not hurt. Next he walked awkwardly into the arms of Fathers Bowdern and Van Roo. Shortly before midnight, he lay prone on his back with his arms stiff at his side. He began a leg and arm movement as a gymnastic exercise. His arms moved out straight from his body and then moved back in straight lines to the side of his body. There was no noise.

After midnight there was some pitching about, but not for long intervals. R cursed his father and spit at him, and then he kicked at the Priests at his bedside. He pushed the nearby chair with his foot several times and finally fell into a deep sleep at 1:00 AM. This was Friday night, the 10th night since the exorcism was begun. Perhaps the "X" given on the first night was to mean 10 days. On Monday night the [**NAME DELETED**] home was blessed by Father Bowdern. No disturbances occurred Monday, Tuesday, or Wednesday nights, and R was getting back to normal life.

Thursday, March 31.

At 11:30 PM R went downstairs and complained that he was feeling ill, and that his feet felt cold, then hot. When the family went up to the bedroom with him the disturbances began. First the shaking of the bed. He began to write on the sheet with his finger, explaining between spells that he seemed to be reading from a blackboard. They were unable to make out what he was writing on the sheet. Then he began to talk, telling what he saw on the blackboard. Notes taken by his cousin are as follows:

I will stay 10 days, but will return in 4 days

If Robbie stays (gone to lunch)

If you stay and become a Catholic it will stay away.

[**NAME DELETED**]

God will take it away 4 days after it has gone 10 days.

God is getting powerful.

The last day when it quits it will leave a sign on my front.
Fr. Bishop—all people that mangle(sic)[*this sic appears in diary*] with me will die a terrible death.

Family called Rectory about midnight. Fathers Bowdern and VanRoo arrived at the house at about 1:00 AM and Father Bowdern began the rite of exorcism.

At the "Praecipio" R (in a spell) called for a pencil. At this point and frequently at the beginning of subsequent spells he addressed one or both of two persons: "Pete" (most frequently) and "Joe." Taking the pencil, he began to write with it on the head of the bed, which was covered with a white cloth. R's type of spell and writing was repeated perhaps eight or ten times. What he wrote was recorded for the most part. The family washed away the writing a few times, making room for more, and [**NAME DELETED**] fastened large sheets of wrapping paper to the bed. The following is a record of most of the writings, though it is not complete. Some of the things written were repeated:

1). In answer to the first set of questions he wrote the Roman numeral X. (It was clearly the numeral, with crossbars at top and bottom). This was written four times on this first occasion and was repeated several times during the exorcism, usually in answer to the question, "diem."

2). I will stay 10 days and then return after the 4 days are up.

3). I am the devil himself. You will have to pray for a month in the Catholic Church.

4). (In answer to the command to give "nomen lingua Latina.")I speak the language of the persons. (word language was misspelled).

   I will put in Robbie's mind when he makes up his mind that the Prests (sic) [*this sic appears in diary*] are wrong about writing English.

   I will, that is the devil will try to get his mother and dad to hate the Catholic Church. I will answer to the name of Spite.

5) In 10 days I will give a sign on his chest he will have to have it covered to show my power.

6) He drew a strange thing that looked somewhat like a map, with "2,000 ft" written on it (apparently connected with early dreams about hidden treasure and a map to find it). I believe that it was in this connection that he spoke also, saying "Yeah, this is what I got on the Ouija board."

   He drew a face also, and wrote the words: "Dead bishop."

7). You may not believe me. Then Robbie will suffer forever.

8). When commanded to give a sign in Latin, he wrote meaning less marks on the paper, not even letters of the Roman alpha bet.

Friday, April 1.

R had been taking instructions on Catholic doctrine since Wednesday, March 23 under the direction of Father McMahon. R's father and mother leaving R's choice of religion to himself. They had agreed that R would not be confirmed in the Lutheran church, as had been planned previously.

With the relapse into possession after five days of respite the mother, father and R agreed that the proper thing to do was to have R baptized a Catholic. Sponsors were picked and the baptismal party was to arrive at the College Church between 8:00 and 8:30 PM. As the party of five relatives drove from R's home, R felt a strange sensation in his feet. There were alternations of hot and cold feelings, and then R went into one of his spells. He began by saying, "So you are going to Baptize me! Ha ! Ha!—And you think you will drive me out with Holy Communion! Ha! Ha!" R grabbed the steering wheel of the automobile and his uncle was forced to pull up to the curb in order to subdue the violence. R stiffened and fought. It was a major task to remove him from the front seat and force him into the back of the car. R's father and uncle held R in the back seat while the aunt drove. Even with careful supervision R leaped up to seize his aunt as she drove. An interesting sidelight is that the radio in the car would not operate while R was in a spell, although it worked before and after.

At the College Church Rectory another hard struggle made it almost impossible for [*unreadable*] men to carry R from the car to the Rectory. Inside the door of the Rectory R shouted and spit. He was thrown on the floor of one of the parlors and continued his physical violence. Even ice cold water had little effect upon him. The father and uncle were completely exhausted from the battle.

R was carried to the third floor or the Rectory and placed on the bed. There was little hope that the Baptism could be administered at the baptismal font in the presence of the chosen sponsors. Michael, the workman, was chosen as proxy. R was in and out of his seizures for short periods but there was not enough time for the long profession of Faith and abjuration of heresy. Father Bowdern had R repeat the words of a briefer form. Then the regular procedure for the Baptism of infants was followed. However, when R was asked, "Dost thou renounce Satan?" he went off into a spell. The action was repeated three or four times, but R went off before he could answer the question with the words, "I do renounce him."

Finally R was normal long enough to give the answers. When Father Bowdern came to the Baptism proper the physical resistance exceeded any violence of the evening. R remained conscious for the words, "Ego te baptizo in nomine Patris" and then there was a violent upheaval. None-the-less, the Baptism was completed with a generous amount of baptismal water. It seemed from the reaction that the Lutheran Baptism had not been administered properly, or that it had not taken effect.

After the Baptism the prayers of the exorcism were continued. The usual spitting, gyrating, cursing and physical violence continued until 11:30 PM.

Saturday, April 2.

R awakened at 9:30 AM, but was not calm. He threw a pillow at the light and broke the shade and bulb. The crockery basin in his room was likewise shattered. This was the morning when R was to receive his first Holy Communion. Fathers Bishop and O'Flaherty were called in to assist Father Bowdern in the preparation for Holy Communion. It was evident that a struggle was at hand. There was no difficulty in going through the conditional confession. Perhaps this quietness indicated again that the Baptism of the preceding night had taken effect.

When Father Bowdern began the prayers for Holy Communion, R went into his spell, kept his eyes shut and his mouth closed, but he was not hard to hold at this time. R rallied for brief moments yet whenever Father Bowdern brought the Eucharistic particle near R, the boy went into his spell. On five different occasions when the particle was placed in R's mouth, he spit it out onto the corporal or purificator which was helways [sic] held in front of his mouth for caution.

After nearly two hours of vain attempts Father O'Flaherty suggested that we pray the Rosary in honor of Our Lady of Fatima, especially since this was the first Saturday of the month. When the Fathers had completed the Rosary, another attempt was made with Holy Communion. This time R was able to swallow and he had made his first Holy Communion under extraordinary opposition.

R finished dressing himself and prepared to leave for home. Father Bowdern asked Father O'Flaherty to drive the car while he himself, R's father and R sat in the back seat. It was about 11:45 AM. Only a few minutes after the car was in motion R jumped up off the seat and grabbed Father O'Flaherty and had to be pulled off with force. R was not normal on the road for more than a few minutes at a time.

At home he came to long enough to eat a fairly good-zized) [sic] breakfast. During the remainder of the day there were only brief intervals of consciousness. The Sacraments had stirred up Satan more than any other Priestly administration. The family was nervously worn from the long day of fighting. Fathers Bowdern, Bishop, O'Flaherty, and Michael arrived at R's home at 7:40 PM. Spells continued. There was no response to the "Praecipio" before 8:40 PM. One short spell of less than a minute occurred between 8:40 and 11:15 PM. During this period R. ate a dish of ice cream.

At 11:15 R ran downstairs and sat on the arm of a parlor chair. He was becoming so nervous that he could scarcely stay in the bedroom. Father Bowdern feared that R would become violent downstairs so he asked R to go back to the bedroom. R trotted up the stairs in boyish fashion, turned into his bedroom and ran straight for the reliquary of the Holy Cross. Father O'Flaherty caught his hand in time, but R reached for the open ritual and tore four pages out of the exorcism formula. He grasped with lightning speed.

Then followed a spell in which Father Bowdern commanded that R should respond in Latin to the "Praecipio,"—"Dicas mihi nomen tuum, et horam exitus tui finalis." The only responses were a repetition of the Latin words followed by a remark, "Stick it up your ass," or by "No!", or by a laugh of ridicule.

At 12:15 spells continued with the same type of responses to the "Praecipio." There was jumbled mockery of the Latin questions. However, at this stage writing appeared on the boy. The letters "GO" were printed in red as they were on the first night of the exorcism. At the command, "dicas mihi tiem," three parallel scratches appeared on R's thigh. At "horam" and X was branded. Three [*unreadable*] were branded on different parts of R's body.

At 1:15 AM, R was so nervous that he begged to get out of bed and sit on a chair. His hands trembled in a nervous frenzy. He begged his father to take him back to Washington on Sunday; he could not stand the ordeal any longer; he feared going crazy. Relief came at 1:40 in a natural sleep.

SUNDAY, April 3.

At 7:00 AM, R threw a pillow against the ceiling light, but then went back to sleep. There was another short seizure at 8:30, but R went back to sleep until 11:30, then took breakfast.

About 12:00 noon, R walked downstairs but went into spells several times, but there was nothing of a serious note until 4:00 PM. R engaged in a ball game with his father, two uncles, and a cousin. At one point he tried to throw the ball to his father, but began to stagger as a drunken man. His father rushed to his assistance when the boy began to run in a straight line across the lawns of two of the neighbors. He ran with his eyes shut and with high speed. Three men closed in on him and carried him back home. In the kitchen R lifted the heavy kitchen table with one of his legs.

R ate very little supper and seemed abnormal. On one occasion he wrapped his legs around a leg of the table and was pulled away by means of strong [*unreadable*] force.

Fathers Bowdern, Van Room [*sic*] Bishop and O'Flaherty arrived at the ome [*sic*] at 7:00 PM. Within a few minutes R had a spell in which he grabbed at his aunt and would have torn her dress if several men had not come to her assistance.

R was carried upstairs fighting but came to himself shortly after he was thrown upon the bed. This was Passion Sunday, so the Fathers thought that God would put an end to R's suffering on this night. The exorcism was begun in full but there was no response at the "Praecipio."

One new feature of this evening was a kind of devilish prophecy concerning R's little cousin [**NAME DELETED**].Shouting and singing in rhythm, R repeated over and over for about ten minutes, "You will die tonight. You will die tonight." It was hard to quiet R by any means but a pillow on his face.

From 9:30 to 12:00 there was no disturbance except snoring and restless sleep. The Fathers departed at midnight, but more trouble began at 12:30. It became necessary to bind the arms of R with tape and to place gloves on his hands. Then he complained of the pain from the adhesive tape and the heat of the gloves. However, when the tape and gloves were removed, R went about his violence again. It was 3:30 before quiet came.

Monday, April 4.

Arrangements were made that the [**NAME DELETED**] family was to go back to Washington, D.C. by train at 9:50 AM. R's father had lost a lot of time from his work, and the strain upon the St. Louis [**NAME DELETED**] was beginning to tell. Fathers Bowdern and Van Roo were to accompany R and his parents on the trip.

It was difficult to arouse R from his cleep [*sic*], but cold water dashed in his face brought him out sufficiently so that he could be dressed. He was taken to the railroad station accompanied by his father, mother, uncle and friend of the family. There was no difficulty boarding the train. R walked and chatted normally. What happed [*sic*] on the trip and thereafter will form another report.

Jesuits who saw Robbie under possession:

Rev. George Bischofberger, SJ
Raymond J. Bishop, SJ
Joseph Boland, SJ
William S. Bowdern, SJ

Edmund Burke, SJ
John O'Flaherty. SJ
William Van Roo, SJ
Mr. Walter Halloran, SJ
Bro. Albert Schell, SJ

CONTINUATION OF CASE STUDY INCLUDING THE TRIP TO WASHINGTON, D.D., AND THE RETURN STAY IN ST. LOUIS.

Monday, April 4.

En route to Washington there was no trouble on the train all day. One short spell of violence occurred when R retired at 11:30 PM.

Tuesday, April 5.

R awoke normally on the train and was taken to his home in [**ADDRESS DELETED**] and without a mishap. In the course of the morning Fr. Bowdern met Fr. Hughes, the assistant pastor at St. James Church at Mt. Rainier, and found that he had made arrangements with the Chancellor of the Archdiocese of Washington that Father Bowdern would have full permission to continue with the exorcism. Neither the Pastor nor the assistant at St. James, in whose parish R. lives was able to assume the full responsibility of the case because of lack of room for the boy. It was thought advisable by all concerned that R should not be kept at home. Fathers Bowdern and Hughes tried several hospitals in Washington, but because of the nature of the case no one was willing to accept the burden.

Wednesday, April 6.

Fathers Bowdern and Hughes drove to Baltimore to inquire about a room at the Seton Institute. The Daughters of Charity were willing to take the boy but the Doctors objected since the case was not considered psychiatric, and furthermore, since the hospital was dependant upon the State of Maryland for aid, each patient had to be accounted for on the records. It would have been strikingly bad to include the treatment of exorcism.

With disappointment in Washington and Baltimore Father Bowdern decided to call again on his devoted friends, the Alexian Brothers in St. Louis. He called long distance and was assured a place for R through the kindness of Brother Rector (Cornelius).

R was normal during the entire day. He took some exercise in the afternoon. Upon retiring he had one very slight spell which lasted only seconds and may have been a nightmare.

Thursday, April 7.

At [**ADDRESS DELETED**] R was normal all day. He worked in the afternoon, spaded a little and cut the lawn. But the evening spell lasted for five hours, from 9:15 PM to 2:15 AM.

 (1) Branding: R was awake. During the exorcism at the "Praecipio" at least twenty brands appeared on R's body. Many occurred at the name of Jesus as he recited the Hail Mary. The first mark was clearly a number "4". Some other marks ray have been the number "4" also, but were obscure. Mother [*sic; should be 'Other'*] marks: a single stroke, double strokes, seemingly a pitch fork, several times four strokes or claw marks of various

lengths on belly or legs. One set of such claw marks from thigh to ankle tearing off a scab near the ankle.

When these marks occurred, the boy's hands were kept away from his body. One branding occurred on his leg just as he started to lie down after the preceding mark had been observed. Most of the branding occurred under his clothing or at least under the sheet covering him.

2) Spitting, violence.

3) Singing: humming the "Ave Maria."

4) Filthy talk.

5) Writing on his own body with fingernail the words "HELL" and "CHRIST" in large capital letters.

6) Through R the devil said he would keep the Priests until 6:00 AM. He made this statement at 2:00 AM when everyone was fagged out. He said he would prove his threat by having R awaken immediately. R awoke with a start, but the Fathers were relieved when sound sleep came fifteen minutes after 2:00. It seemed throughout the possession that whenever R was completely exhausted God permitted him to go off to sleep and commanded the devil to be quiet.

Friday, April 8.

R was normal all day. There was a five-hour session in the night from 8:15 PM to 1:20 AM.

1) Began when R was alone in the bathroom, a few minutes after the Priests arrived. Two and one-quarter hours of great physical violence. Half hour of crying. continued with shorter spells until 1:20 AM: violence, spitting, nonsense jumbling of Latin questions, singing

Blue Danube, Ave Maria, and so forth. There was filthy talk and movements and filthy attacks on those at the bedside concerning masturbation and contraceptives, sexual relations of Priests and Nuns.

2) Irritated and impatient after the long struggle. Fathers Hughes and Canning arrived with the Blessed Sacrament about 11:00 PM. The house was blessed by Father Hughes. R twice threw pillow in direction of the Blessed Sacrament. He took one sedative, spat it out, then finally swallowed it.

Saturday April 9.

On the return trip to St. Louis R was normal all day. He underwent a short spell upon retiring in the evening.

Sunday, April 10.

When R returned to St. Louis he was sent immediately to the Alexian Brothers Hospital. There the Brothers took him into one of their private living rooms for the day. Fathers Bowdern, O'Flaherty, Van Roo and Bishop arrived at the Hospital shortly after 7:00 PM. R was taken to the fifth floor where he occupied the same room which was assigned him on his earlier visit. The exorcism was completed and several Rosaries recited but no disturbances occurred. R went into a good sleep about 11:00 PM, but the Fathers decided to awaken him after midnight in order to give him Holy Communion. R was so fatigued that it seemed almost hopeless to keep him awake for more than seconds at a time. When the Fathers were planning to abandon the experiment, R became quite normal and was able to receive Communion without special effort. The Blessed Sacrament brought peace to R. He settled back on his pillow with a smile and was soon in deep sleep. Nothing disturbing happened throughout the night.

Monday, April 11.

Brother Emmet kept R occupied with manual work on his Hospital floor, and what was most valuable, won the friendship and confidence of R so that the psychiatric surroundings were more understandable and agreeable.

Fathers Bowdern, Van Roo, Bishop and Mr. Halloran arrived at the Hospital at 8:00 PM. Father Bishop brought some Catholic readers and stories for R so that he would have more than his catechism for study and reading. R went to bed at 9:00 PM, and the exorcism was completed. The evening gave every reason for expecting quiet. While the Fathers were reciting the Rosary R felt a sting on his chest, but upon examination only a blotch of red was observable. The Rosary was continued until R. was struck more sharply by a branding on his chest. The letters were in caps and read in the direction of R's crotch. "EXIT" seemed quite clear. On another branding, a large arrow followed up the word "EXIT" and pointed to R's penis. The word "EXIT" appeared at three different times in different parts of R's body. R felt terrible pains in his kidneys and in his penis. He cried from the burning sensations. When he urinated, he complained of even more severe pain.

At midnight, the Fathers planned to give R Holy Communion, but Satan would have no part of it. Even while the institution of the Blessed Sacrament was explained to R his body was badly scratched and branded. The word "HELL" was printed on his chest and thigh. Upon the explanation of the Apostles becoming Priests and receiving Our Lord at the Last Supper, scratches appeared from R's hips to his ankles in heavy lines, seemingly as a protest to Holy Communion.

When Father Bowdern attempted to give R a small particle of the Sacred Host, the boy was taken off by a quick seizure and the devil said that he would not allow R to receive. After four or five attempts it was thought that a spiritual Communion would have to suffice. But even the expression of the words "I want to receive You in Holy Communion" was cut off by a seizure at the word "Communion."

From all further indications during the evening, it seemed that the attempts to administer the Sacrament of the Eucharist roused the devil more than ordinarily. He went through his usual routine of fighting, barking, cursing, swearing, spitting and [*unreadable*], but kept on longer than usual. There was no quiet sleep until 9 PM. One of the edifying events of the night was the devotedness of the Alexian Brothers to constant prayers and their professional attitude at the bedside.

Tuesday, April 12.

Action began after the exorcism prayers were completed. During the general recitation of the Rosary by the Fathers and Brothers the regular performance began, but with the omission of writing on R's body. The noise and singing were very disturbing to everyone. R gave no response to the "Praecipio" except to imitate the Latin words, then laugh, or say, "Stick it up your ass."

One new phase was the display of the devil's power over the senses and external personality of R. In one instance the devil said he would have R awaken and the boy would be pleasant and attractive. The devil's promise was true. A few minutes later the devil said he would have R awaken, but this time he would be offensive. True to the promise R came out of the spell very irritable and he complained quite bitterly to those who held him.

Several attempts were made to give R Holy Communion after midnight, but each trial was unsuccessful. The devil showed definitely that he was not R speaking, for he said, "I will not let Robbie receive Holy Communion." It was about 1:30 AM before quiet sleep followed.

Wednesday, April 13.

R received Holy Communion on arising in the morning without encountering difficulty. During the afternoon R was taken out to the White House (Retreat House) and shown the chapel there as well as the outdoor Stations of the Cross. At the fourteenth Station, when R was farthest away from the automobile he went into a spell and had to be carried back to the car by force. The seizure lasted about twenty minutes.

In the evening R was ready for bed at 8:45. He was bright and cheerful and enjoyed especially some trick gadgets that Father McMahon ahd [*sic*]given him. As he sat on the bed, and before any prayers were begun, R went off into a quick but violent seizure. It seemed to the exorcists that this would be an important evening. R spoke almost immediately and said that God had commanded him to leave at 11:00 o'clock tonight, but that he would not leave without a struggle. He proved the latter part of his promise by showing relatively more physical power than at any previous time. He stayed in his first spell for twenty minutes while Father Bowdern worked on the exorcism and the Brothers prayed the Rosary in honor of Our Lady of Fatima.

In the "Praecipio" Father Bowdern ahd [*sic*]always been insisting in getting response in Latin, and he kept up his demands. The devil ignored the command, answered in pig Latin, playfully imitated the commands, or used the common expression "Stick it up your ass." He began singing the words, "stick it up, stick it up." In no instance up to this point in the case has the devil answered in Latin, although his imitation of Latin was clear and distinct.

Filthy talk and damning threats to those at the bedside continued as on other evenings. A new note of the evening was the loud nuisance shouting of "Fire!" At 10:45 R began to imitate the sound of a large church bell sounding out the 11:00 o'clock hour. He sustained the "ng" sound at the end of the word "bong." After 11:00 PM the same cathedral bell sounds were repeated, but it was very evident that the devil had deceived everyone by his first remark of the evening.

After midnight unsuccessful attempts were made to give R Holy Communion. Satan said again that he would not permit Holy Communion. He laughed at each of the attempts. R could not repeat the word "Communion," before he went into his spell.

The Brothers had prayed valiantly for several hours around midnight. They completed more than fifty decades of the Rosary and their prayerful assistance is worthy of the highest comment. Round-the-clock adoration of the Blessed Sacrament was begun by the Brothers on Monday or Tuesday evening.

Holy Thursday—Good Friday—Holy Saturday, April 14, 15, 16.

R received Holy Communion from the Hospital Chaplain, Father Widman, on Thursday morning. The Fathers arrived for the prayers of exorcism in the evening. Rosary was continued by the Brothers. There were no reactions before or after midnight on Thursday. The Fathers were informed this night that Brother

Rector purchased a new statue of our Lady of Fatima and had it placed in a conspicuous spot on the first floor corridor of the Hospital. It was dedicated to the Blessed Virgin with the petition that Our Lady of Fatima would intercede for R in his ordeal. The Brothers promised Community devotions to Our Lady of Fatima should R be spared from further affliction.

No disturbances of any sort occurred on Holy Thursday, Good Friday, or Holy Saturday. R listened attentively to the Tre Ore service broadcast over WEW on Good Friday.

Or Holy Saturday, Brother Rector bought a small colorful statue of St. Michael the Archangel. The statue was placed in R's room. It should be remarked here that one of the most effective prayers of the exorcism was that dedicated to St. Michael.

After midnight of Saturday, arrangements were made that R should be awakened for 6:30 Communion, and that he should attend the second Mass in the Brothers' chapel, Easter morning.

Easter Sunday, April 17.

Father Widman, Hospital Chaplain, made three unsuccessful attempts to give R Holy Communion in his room. After some waiting and slapping of R, the fourth attempt succeeded.

Brother Theophane, who was on nurse duty in R's room, was reading the Office of the Blessed Virgin. It was about 6:45 AM, when he came to the "Regina Caeli" R jumped out of bed, then grabbed the Office Book from the Brother and reached for the scapular from the Brother's habit, which was placed on a nearby chair. R fought and spit at the Brother and trampled the scapular underfoot in an Indian war dance. The devil said, "I will not let him go to Mass. Everyone thinks it will be good for him." It was impossible to get R to the chapel because of his frequent seizures. Father

Bowdern was called to the Hospital and shortly after his arrival the spell was broken. There was no further reaction until evening.

In the evening R was spending little time with the Brothers at recreation outside the Hospital. Brother Emmet was escorting R back to the basement floor of the hospital when R went into a fighting spell. The Brother was alone and shouted for help, but it was some time before the other Brothers heard him. Brother Emmet was quite exhausted from the struggle. R was carried into the elevator and placed in his fifth floor room. The Fathers immediately began the prayers of exorcism, and the usual indications of violence continued. The devil showed his power again by saying that he would have R awaken and ask for a knife. He had threatened to kill those who molested him while in his seizure. When R came out of the spell, he asked for a knife so that he might cut an Easter egg. A little later the devil said that he would have R awaken and ask for a drink of water, and R carried out the plan.

There was no response to the "Praecipio" except taunting remarks to the exorcists. Everyone, including R, was becoming weary of the long performance. R did not begin to sleep until midnight. The Fathers left the Hospital at 12:45 AM.

Monday, April 18.

8:00 AM—R awoke in a spell, kicking at the Brother at the bedside. He jumped out of bed, seized the Holy Water bottle, threatened to throw it at the Brothers, then sprinkled Water toward them. Finally, he threw the bottle over their heads, smashing it against the ceiling.

8:15 AM—Father Widman attempted to give R Communion. It was impossible. Spitting: Unable to make even spiritual

Communion: Made one Spiritual Communion. The devil then seized him and said that one devil was out, and that R had to make nine Communions (sacramental or spiritual apparently) and then he would leave his body. R continued for an hour unable to make spiritual communion or to receive the Sacrament.

10:00 AM—There were more spells when attempting Spiritual Communion. R was able to say: "I wish to receive you." (That is all the Priest attempted to have him say, since it was sufficient). The devil laughed and said: "That isn't enough. He has to say one more word, one little word, I mean one BIG word. He'll never say it. He has to make nine Communions. He'll never say that word. *I am always in him.* I may not have much power always, but I am in him. He will never say that word." Several spells: violence, singing, urination.

11:30 AM—R said he was very hungry, and wanted a bath and food. We put him off until noon. Then gave him a tray: cake, ice cream, milk. He threw the glass against the wall, scattering broken glass all over. Violence intermittent until about 1:30 PM. R was very discouraged and disgusted and mean.

In the afternoon, the Brothers brought a serving of chipped beef and arranged R's tray on a little table in his room. R picked up the plate, ran over to the window, held the plate in an almost perpendicular manner in the palm of his hand and dared the Brothers to step closer. One of the Brothers crawled under the bed to catch R at his feet, the other circled the bed to restrain R's arms, but the plate was fired mightily against the opposite wall. No one was hurt but the plate was broken to bits.

On the trip to the Hospital on this evening the Fathers had decided that in the "Praecipio" Father Bowdern would ask for the responses in English. Moreover, the medals were to be left on R in spite of his protests to the contrary. A crucifix was to be placed in R's hand when he was under his spell. These resolutions were discussed and carried out because of the information gathered from the reading concerning several other cases of possession.

Fathers Bowdern, O'Flaherty and Bishop arrived at the Hospital at 7:00 PM. Father Van Roo had been with R during the greater part of the day, but was relieved by the Brothers shortly before the evening meal.

R asked to telephone his mother, but on his way to the telephone he went into a spell and had to be carried back to his room, in a fighting mood.

Father Bowdern read the rite of exorcism quietly. When he came to the words "Tu pax confirmes, Tu fiscera regas," he blessed R with signs of the Cross. Immediately, R repeated the expressions perfectly and asked their meaning. Several times later he repeated the Latin. The signs of the Cross and the Crucifix were very effective. R fought hard when the Crucifix was forced into his hand. In one instance R threw the Crucifix out of his hand.

Next Father O'Flaherty began teaching R the first half of the Ave Maria in Latin because R had expressed a real interest in Latin. In the space of fifteen minutes R could recite a good portion of the prayer unassisted. After the memory lesson Father O'Flaherty told R the complete story of Our Lady of Fatima to which R paid strict attention. A little later he asked for a Catholic reader containing eighth grade prose and poetry, and then thumbed through several stories as he sat in bed. Finally, in a boyish way, he took to balancing the book on his knees and on his head.

R went into a spell while he held the book on his knees and immediately the book was thrown into the corner of the room. From 9:30 until 11:00 PM, R was in and out of seizures. During his quiet moments the most impressive prayer of the evening was R's leading of the Rosary, while the Fathers and Brothers answered. R's reverence seemed truly remarkable.

R was more co-operative this night than he had ever been before. He felt that he had to pray whenever he was out of his seizure. He asked whether he could make Spiritual Communions on his own, and he wondered whether through his prayers he himself could bring on a seizure. His efforts at Spiritual Communion brought on spells at different times. Whenever he became normal, he reverted to prayer. He stated several times that he saw more light each time he went into a spell. The light seemed to be at the end of a dark tunnel.

R complained several times that the medals on his neck were hot and he asked that they be removed, but the medals were not taken off. Father Bowdern forced a small reliquary crucifix into R's hand when he was in a spell. The reaction to the medals and the cross was exceptional. When Father Widman blessed R with his ordination crucifix and asked R to kiss the image, R went into a spell.

During all of the above seizures Father Bowdern continued the "Praecipio" and asked that the responses be given in English. This procedure was a change from the regular routine. In the commands up to this time, Latin had been insisted upon. The devil in one instance, March 31, had written that the Priests were wrong in asking for Latin answers, and he stated that he used the language of the person possessed. While Father Bowdern used the "Praecipio," Father Bishop repeated over and over again the exorcism prayer to St. Michael.

Author's Note: The 24-page, single-spaced, photo-copied typescript that Father Halloran gave me ended at this point. Apparently, other pages were lost or overlooked when this copy was found at the Alexian Brothers Hospital (see page 224). I obtained pages 25 and 26, the final pages, from another source, a priest who had a complete file on the St. Louis exorcism. He uses the file as a guide for other exorcisms, as was Father Bowdern's intention. Page 25 continues the events of Monday, April 18:

At 10:45 PM, the most striking event of the evening occurred. R was in a seizure, but lay calm. In clear, commanding tones, and with dignity, a voice broke into the prayers. The following is an accurate quotation:

"Satan! Satan! I am Saint Michael, and I command you,
Satan, and the other evil spirits to leave the body in the name
of Dominus, immediately—Now! NOW! N O W!"

Then there were the most violent contortions of the entire period of exorcism, that is since March 16. Perhaps this was the fight to the finish. Father O'Flaherty and the Brothers were weary and sore physically from the exertion. After seven or eight minutes of violence R, in a tone of complete relief said, "He's gone!" Immediately R came back to normal and said he felt fine.

R now explained what he saw. He said there was a brilliant white light and in that light stood a very beautiful man, with flowing wavy hair that blew in the breeze. He wore a white robe that fitted close to his body. The material gave the impression of scales. Only the upper half of the body of this man was visible to R. In his right hand he held up a wavy and fiery sword in front of him. With his left hand he pointed down to a pit or cave.

R said he saw the devil standing in the cave. R felt the heat from the cave and saw the flames. First the devil fought, resisting the angel and laughing diabolically. Then the angel smiled at R and spoke, but R heard only the one word "Dominus". As the angel spoke, the devil and about ten of his helpers ran back into the fire of the cave or pit. After the devil disappeared the letters "Spite" appeared on the bars of the cave. As the devils disappeared into the pit R felt a pulling or tugging in the region of his stomach. As the devils disappeared, he felt a snapping, and then felt relaxed completely. He said that this was the most relaxed feeling he had since the whole experience began in January.

R related his visual experience at 11:00 PM. This time was approximate to the time that the manifestations of the devil began in [**ADDRESS DELETED**] the evening of January 15, 1949.

After 12:00 midnight, R led another Rosary and the Fathers and Brother responded. He was composed and peaceful.

Arrangements were made that Father Van Roo, SJ, would say Mass for R in the Hospital Chapel at 9:30, Tuesday morning.

Tuesday, April 19.

R was awakened from a heavy sleep and taken to the chapel where he attended the first Holy Mass since he became a Catholic. He likewise received Holy Communion at the alter [*sic*] rail with no difficulty. R promised to say ten Rosaries in thanksgiving to Our Lady of Fatima during the course of the day. When the Fathers [*unreadable*] in the evening, R had one more Rosary to say, so the Fathers and Brother joined R in his thanksgiving.

Since Monday at 11:00 PM there have been no indications of the presence of the devil.

—Dated the Feast of St. Mark, April 25, 1949.

Page 25 ends here. Page 26 ends the diary:

Follow up:

August 19, 1951. R and his father and mother visited the Brothers. R, now 16 is a fine young man His father and mother also became Catholic, having received their first Holy Communion on Christmas Day, 1950.

Typed on a different typewriter:

11/8/70   Verified residence of [**NAME DELETED**] with telephone operator...[**NAME DELETED**] lives in [**ADDRESS DELETED**] now lives in [**ADDRESS DELETED**]. Has unlisted phone number.

K. Alford

Author's Endnote

When the first edition of this book was published, several people familiar with the exorcism came forward and told me what they knew. Mostly they confirmed details in the book. Several of Father Bowdern's relatives in St. Louis told me that I had described him accurately. But I had not realized what a terrible, enduring burden the exorcism had been. They told me that Father Bowdern had suffered, mentally and physically, in silence, for the rest of his life. He was a secret hero to those few people who knew of his ordeal as an exorcist.

* * * * * *

My interest in this exorcism began when I read a two-paragraph item in the Personalities column of The Washington Post. It said that Father Walter Halloran, S.J., in an interview published by a Nebraska newspaper, had talked about an exorcism he had taken part in. Father Halloran became hard to locate after that interview. By the time I found him, he was the pastor of a church in a small town in southwestern Minnesota. He agreed to talk to me, warily at first and then warmly. We became not just a writer and a source but friends. We quickly took to each other, I think, because we were both of Irish descent and because we had a Jesuit bond-he was a member of the Society of Jesus and I had gone to a Jesuit school.

I think that Father Halloran could understand my curiosity about the exorcism as soon as I told him that I had gone to a Jesuit school. If you learn anything else from Jesuit teachers, you learn to be curious about both the sacred and the profane. And you learn that nothing, on earth or beyond, can be taken for granted.

I have admired the Jesuits for many years. I think the reader should know that. I graduated from a Jesuit high school, Fairfield

College Preparatory School, in Fairfield, Connecticut, and attended the Jesuits' adjoining Fairfield University for two years.

I was working on a newspaper and, needing to finish college by going to night classes, I transferred from Fairfield to the University of Bridgeport, from which I later graduated. My college transcript lists, as transferred from Fairfield University, a course on Roman Catholicism. The University of Bridgeport accepted the course as one in "humanities."

By the time I left the Jesuits of Fairfield University, the Catholic religion truly was part of my humanity, though not part of my everyday life. I was no longer a practicing Catholic. But I carried an image born of World War II movies: The Gestapo kicks in my door and demands to know if I am Catholic. I answer yes, not because I am a Catholic but because I had been one and my Catholicism is too deeply imbedded in me to be dismissed. Although I no longer practice Catholicism, I cannot rid myself of it, and I do not want to.

As I started doing research on this book, I came across a prayer that I had said again and again as I grew up. "St. Michael the Archangel," it began, "defend us in battle; be our protection against the wiles and wickedness of the Devil. We humbly beseech thee, O God, to restrain him, and do thou, the Prince of the heavenly hosts, cast into hell Satan and all the evil spirits who roam through the world seeking the ruin of souls." I believed that prayer, word for word. I do not believe it now. But I do believe in good and I do believe in evil.

I was an altar boy, and I learned to pronounce the strange and solemn Latin responses, answering et cum spiritu tuo when the priest said, Dominus vobiscum. Kneeling at the altar during Mass, I received Holy Communion and believed that what the priest placed on my quivering, outstretched tongue was the Body and

Blood of Christ. I went to St. Charles and St. Patrick's parochial schools and learned my religion from the enchanting or horrifying tales told by pious nuns and from the question-and-answer format of The Baltimore Catechism.

At Fairfield Prep, the Jesuits led me into another Roman Catholic world, where historical reality prevailed over holy tales, where both teacher and pupil could ask questions that did not have ready-made answers. I still went to Mass, though not as an altar boy. The Jesuits taught me Latin, not because it was then the language of the Mass but because they believed that knowledge of Latin was essential to my education. I now could translate the ceremonious murmuring of Mass into English words--Dominus vobiscum. Et cum spiritu tuo just meant "may the Lord be with you. And with thy spirit."

Under the Jesuits, the study of Catholicism became a course called apologetics, a systematic defense of Catholic doctrine and tradition. The Jesuits placed far more emphasis on a rigorous analysis of Catholicism than on saints and relics. But the saints and the relics were still there, along with the Mass and Communion. On the top of every school paper, whether the course was geometry or apologetics, I wrote A.M.D.G, the initials of Ad Majorem Dei Gloriam, For the Greater Glory of God, the motto of the Society of Jesus. On the first day of class the Jesuits told us to do that, and we always did it. That mystic foundation of Catholicism-praise to God-remained in place in every Jesuit classroom. There was a you, your physical self, learning to live in this world. And there was thy spirit, the soul, the spiritual self, the essence of your humanity.

It was from the Jesuits that I learned about agnosticism. Whenever they held up a word for first exhibit, they always showed the roots: "from the Latin for . . ." or "from the Greek for . . . ."

Agnostic was from the Greek for "unknown." I cherished the word as soon as I learned it. I immediately began prancing around as a sophomoric agnostic, feeling proud that I had made God an unknowable, an unprovable. Eventually, my agnosticism felt more comfortable, more a real part of me rather than something I had donned for some occasion.

I wrote this book as a journalist who tries to tell a story as straight and as thoroughly as he can. Never before have I felt the need to show my credentials like this. But I wanted my readers to know that what they read was written by an agnostic who was brought up Catholic, was educated by Jesuits, and still wonders about the meaning of spiritus.

Bibliography

Balducci, Corrado. *The Devil.* Translated and adapted by Jordan Aumann, O.P. New York: Alba House, 1990.

—"Parapsychology and Diabolic Possession," International Journal of Parapsychology. 8 (1966): 193-212.

Brian, Denis. *The Enchanted Voyager.* New York: Prentice-Hall, 1982.

Cortes, Juan B., S.J. and Florence M. Gatti, L.L.B. *The Case Against Possessions and Exorcisms.* New York: Vantage Press, 1975.

Faherty, William Barnaby, S.J. *To Rest In Charity*, A History of the Alexian Brothers in Saint Louis (1869-1984). St. Louis: River City Publishers, 1984. Faherty, who devotes four pages to the exorcism at the Alexian Brothers Hospital, talked to Fathers Bowdern and Kenny and had some access to the archives of the Archdiocese of St. Louis. The book bears the *imprimatur* of the vicar general of the Archdiocese of St. Louis. The book's circulation is essentially controlled by the Alexians, and its information on the exorcism is not widely known.

Gauld, Alan and Cornell, A.D. *Poltergeists.* London: Routledge & Kegan Paul, 1979.

Harney, Martin P., S.J. *The Jesuits in History.* Boston: Boston College 1941.

Huxley, Aldous. *The Devils of Loudun.* New York: Harper and Brothers, 1953.

McDonough, Peter. *Men Astutely Trained* A History of the Jesuits in the American Century. New York: Free Press, 1992.

Nicola, Rev. John J. *Diabolical Possession and Exorcism.* Rockford, Ill: TAN Books, 1974.

—*Is Solemn Public Exorcism a Viable Rite in the Modern Western World? A Theological Response.* Pontifical Gregorian Unversity, Rome, 1975.

Oesterreich, T.K. *Possession: Demoniacal & Other.* New York: University Books, 1966. *Possession*, first published in 1921 in Germany, was republished in English in 1930, with an authorized translation by D. Ibberson. University Books republished it in 1966. The book cogently examines numerous cases of possession from a psychiatric viewpoint. The book is without rival in its analysis of possession as a worldwide phenomenon.

Rapoport, Judith L., M.D. *The Boy Who Couldn't Stop Washing.* New York: Signet, Dec. 1991 edition.

Roman Ritual (Rituale Romanum), 1614. Translated and edited by Father Philip T. Weller, 1950. I was allowed to read and photocopy pages from this edition, in the Woodstock Theological Library at Georgetown University. *Nicola* assured me that the exorcism section in the 1950 edition was virtually the same as whatever edition priests were using in 1949. Comparisons of the prayers in *Diary* and the *Ritual* bore this out. No substantial changes in the *Ritual* were made until after Vatican II, which ended in 1965.

Thurston, Herbert, S. J. *Ghosts and Poltergeists.*

Sources

No other exorcism in modern times has been as thoroughly documented as the 1949 exorcism of the boy I call Robbie. The primary source for that documentation is the diary of the exorcism kept by Father Raymond J. Bishop, S.J. The diary was meant to be a record that would be used in later years by priests called upon to perform exorcisms. I have been told that the diary has been used for that purpose. But, because the Catholic Church hierarchy is reluctant to disclose information about exorcisms, the diary has been kept secret.

I obtained a copy of the diary from Father Walter Halloran, S.J., who assisted in the exorcism. He verified the diary, which, he said, was seen and approved by the exorcist himself, Father William S. Bowdern, S.J., who mentions it in 1968 letter to William Blatty, as I mention in the Prelude. The original diary, along with a formal report on the exorcism by Bowdern and a witness statement by Halloran, were presented to the Jesuit Provincial of the Missouri Province and to the Archdiocese of St. Louis. Another set of these documents, I believe, is in the archives of the Archdiocese of Washington. Several copies of the diary had been made down the years, thanks to the emergence of photo-copying machines. Blatty said that he had seen the diary, and at least portions of it apparently circulated among theologians.

The complete diary consists of 26 typewritten pages, single-spaced. (For the complete text, see page 243.) The copy I originally obtained, which had 24 pages, was fortuitously snatched from a doomed hospital building (see page 224).

The diary is one of three basic documents about the case. Two of the documents are ecclesiastical reports in Roman Catholic archives, never to be released. According to the archivist of the Archdiocese of Washington, information on the first exorcism is in the secret archives that can be opened only by the archbishop of Washington. The other official report is in a similar archive in the Archdiocese of St. Louis. A priest who has examined these documents told me that they cite forty witnesses to the possession and second exorcism. The diary notes that "there have been fourteen different witnesses to testify and verify different phenomena." Most of the witnesses are dead, but their testimony was preserved in the diary.

I have been fortunate to have had the cooperation of Father Halloran, who gave me his recollections as a participant. When I cite *Halloran* as a source, I am drawing upon those recollections, obtained in numerous interviews and conversations. Other sources that I refer to will be fully described on their first appearance and then cited with a single word.

There are minor discrepancies between what Bishop wrote and what others remembered. There are also holes in the story, and occasional absences of detail. Using the diary and other sources, I attempted to resolve these discrepancies and sidestep these holes. I evaluated the sources and, wherever there was conflict, tried to resolve it by using a system that graded the sources, from "eyewitness" (*Diary* and *Halloran*) to "account." These accounts vary from descriptions, given to others by eyewitnesses, to reconstructions, based on interviews of eyewitnesses and others. *Bober*, for example, is Father Frank Bober, who was told about the first exorcism by the exorcist himself, Father E. Albert Hughes. *Nitka* is an example of a reconstruction based, in this case, upon information gathered from the Jesuit community at St. Louis University. The sources are listed in **Citations**. Using and evaluating all these sources, I tried to produce a dispassionate, rational narrative about events that persistently challenge logic and reason.

By the time I began working on this book, only two Jesuits directly involved in the St. Louis exorcism were still alive: Father Halloran and Father William A. Van Roo, S.J. Halloran agreed to help me; Van Roo had long ago put the exorcism behind him and wanted to keep it that way. So I had one living eyewitness and the diary.

I soon learned that there were *two* exorcisms performed on Robbie. The first, begun in Maryland, ended quickly and disastrously. Available witnesses or documentation on this exorcism at first appeared to be non-existent. I knew that I had to reconstruct the first exorcism in order to understand and narrate the second, well-documented exorcism. No one, however, wanted to talk about it. "Robbie"—now a grown man living a happy, balanced, and productive life—did not respond to inquiries I directed to him. (I knew his name and had reason to believe I knew his address. I wrote to him at that address, saying that I was writing a book "about an incident that occurred in Mount Rainier and St. Louis in 1949." I also said that I was shielding the name of the person involved in the incident. I received no reply and did not press further. Nor did I attempt to contact him for this revised edition.)

Eventually, I found three extremely reliable sources for facts about that first exorcism: Father Frank Bober, who passed on to me what he was told by Father Hughes; and Father John J. Nicola, who has made a special study of the exorcism and had talked to Hughes about it. The two priests are referred to as *Bober* and *Nicola* in the citations. (An asterisk after *Nicola* refers to his book, rather than to interviews.)

Bober, as reported in the last chapter, was the last person to whom Hughes told the story of the first exorcism. Bober went over details of the story with me and was extremely helpful. Like many priests familiar with this and other exorcisms, he believes in the need to responsibly describe possession and exorcism.

Nicola, against the counsel of his superiors, became interested in demonology while still in the seminary. He has studied more than forty exorcisms. He would not discuss most aspects of the Robbie case with me because he had been allowed access to the secret archives and did not want to reveal information entrusted to him. But he did allow me to read his thesis on possession and he was extremely helpful in clarifying points about possession and exorcism.

The third source of information is a set of notes for a lecture given by Father Hughes on May 10, 1950 at Georgetown University. When I spoke to Father Joseph M. Moffitt, S.J., who invited Hughes, he remembered that someone took notes. With the help of Father Joseph T. Durkin, S.J., the eminent Georgetown historian, and Jon Reynolds, curator of Georgetown's special collections, I obtained a copy of the unpublished notes. They were written by Father William C. Reppetti, S.J., Georgetown University archivist and author of the ten-volume history, *The Society of Jesus in the Philippines*. He died in 1966.

The notes (cited as *Reppetti*) were sanitized, apparently in the 1970s, after the movie "The Exorcist" was released and Georgetown University was linked to the exorcism featured in the movie. The president of Georgetown called "Robbie" assured him that the university would not release identifying information. As part of the assurance, the names of priests in Reppetti's notes were blacked out, just in case anyone ever found them. When I went over the notes, I was able to infer that the blacked-out names were those of Father Hughes and Father Bowdern.

All quotations in the book are taken either directly from the diary or from cited sources, such as *Halloran*, who told me in his own words that he used at the time or words that he directly heard. Where I am quite sure of the gist or theme of a statement, I use italics to indicate a reconstructed quotation.

Chapter Notes

Information about audiences at "The Exorcist": "Lining Up for Horror," *Washington Star-News*, Jan. 8, 1974; "They Wait Hours to be Shocked," *New York Times*, Jan. 27, 1974; "The Exorcism Frenzy," *Newsweek*, Feb. 11, 1974.

Psychiatrists write about "cinematic neurosis": "Cinematic Neurosis: A Brief Case Report," James W. Hamilton, *Journal of the American Academy of Psychoanalysis*, Vol. 6, No. 4, 569-572 (1978); "Cinematic neurosis following *The Exorcist*. Report of 4 cases," J.C. Bozzuto, *Journal of Nervous Mental Disorders*, Vol. 161, No. 1 (1975), 43-58.

Bowdern's view of movie: *Halloran*.

Letter from Blatty: *Blatty*.

Chapter 1: "Is This You, Aunt Harriet?"

Description of "Mannheim" family: "Case Study" in *Diary* and *Halloran*. Robbie's weight and preference for board games are among the many facts in "Case Study."

"Harriet" and Spiritualism: Bishop learned about the aunt through interviews he conducted for his "Case Study." He mentions Spiritualism and the Ouija board, but does not record a seance. The information on Spiritualism comes from *Spiritualist Manual*, 1955 edition, as quoted in *Isaacs*.

Biblical references: Deuteronomy (18:10-12), Leviticus (20:27); King Saul appears in I Samuel 28:7-19.

Psychiatrist on possession: *Isaacs*.

Events of January 15-26, including quotations: "Case Study," *Diary*. Death of "Aunt Harriet," *ibid*. I verified the date of her death (and the lack of a probated will) by checking St. Louis vital statistics and court records under her real name.

Desk moving: "Case Study," *Diary*.

Incidents of flying objects and tipping chair: "Case Study," *Diary*; *Reppetti*. Also, many details come from *Diabolical Possession** by *Nicola*. In the book he does not mention Robbie's case directly, and he says he was "fabricating, changing and omitting" details to shield the identity of people involved. The case is certainly Robbie's. I showed a copy of the description to *Halloran*, who verified having heard of most details, including the description of the flipping chair and flying vase.

Remarks of psychologist and physician: "Case Study," *Diary*.

Psychologist's speculation on examination of Robbie: *Rapoport*. Also, *Schulze* says he recommended the clinic and mentions that Robbie missed the third appointment.

The Reverend Schulze: *Schulze*'s personal account of his dealings with Robbie appears in *Parapsychology Bulletin*, No. 15, Aug. 1949, published by Dr. J.B. Rhine's Institute of Parapsychology. Schulze, in a 1980 interview, also talks about the case in *Enchanted Voyager**, an authorized biography of Rhine, a pioneer parapsychologist. Rhine mentions the case several times in correspondence around this time (J.B. Rhine Papers, Special Collections Department, Duke University Library, Durham, N.C.)

Rhine also went to Washington to discuss the case with Schulze. NOTE: Since the first edition of this book, letters between Schulze and Rhine have become available. For more information on the letters, see *Schulze* in Citations below.

Chapter 2: Hunting a Poltergeist

Family's description of Robbie's condition: "Case Study," *Diary*; *Schulze*.

Family home in Mount Rainier: In 1999, in an article in *Strange Magazine*'s issue No. 20, Mark Opsasnick offers convincing evidence that Robbie lived in Cottage City, a small community adjacent to Mount Rainier. Opsasnick wrote that he had found people who said the family had lived in Cottage City for many years and that the Bunker Hill address in Mount Rainier was merely local lore. What Opsasnick did not know was that a Cottage City address appeared in the diary that I had obtained from Father Halloran. I had withheld the Cottage City address in an attempt to protect the true identity of "Robbie." Opsasnick publishes that address, along with the actual first names of Robbie and Aunt Harriet. I believed when I wrote the book in 1992 that the family had lived in Cottage City when Robbie was taken to St. Louis and that the family had lived in Mount Rainier prior to that. Several residents of Mount Rainier confirmed the 3210 Bunker Hill Road address to me, and I used in the first edition of *Possessed*, believing that this had been the home of Robbie's family before the family moved to Cottage City. Opsasnick traces the Bunker Hill Road address back to a local weekly newspaper's 1981 story on the exorcism. But it is a fact that Mount Rainier firemen in 1964 had enough belief in that address to burn the "Devil's House" to the ground, as I report in Chapter 14. Opsasnick also questions the

existence of the diary; its full text is published in this edition for the
first time. See page 243.

Martin Luther: *Oesterreich**, who cites two German works on
Luther as his sources.

"At first I tried prayer…: *Schulze* in *Enchanted Voyager**.

Spiritualism and Fox sisters: *Gauld**, *Spiritualist Manual* as cited
in *Isaacs*.

Poltergeist accounts: *Gauld**. *Oesterreich**, *Nicola*, and *Balducci**
all speculate on possible connections between poltergeist activities
and possession. All three also see possible parapsychological influences at work in some possession cases.

Schulze takes Robbie overnight: *Schulze*.

Scratches on Robbie: *Schulze*, "Case Study," *Diary*.

Zugun case: *Oesterreich**.

Schulze quote: *Schulze*.

Chapter 3: "But Deliver Us from Evil"

Biblical references: Jesus' struggle with Satan: Matthew 4:1-11,
Mark 1:12-13, Luke 4:1-13. Jesus gives power of exorcism to followers: Matthew 10:1, Mark 3:15, 16:17-18; Luke 9:1, 10:17; Acts
5:16, 8:7. Exorcisms performed by Jesus: Matthew 8:28-34, 15:21-
28, 17:14-21; Mark 1:21-28, 3:11-12, 5:1-20, 7:25-30, 9:14-29,
16:9; Luke 4:31-37, 6:18 8:26-39, 9:37-43; Acts 10:38.

Meeting with Hughes: *Bober.* For the first edition of the book, I
interviewed Father Bober, who had been told about the exorcism
by Father Hughes. Later, in an interview for the Discovery
Channel show "In the Grip of Evil," (see *Grip*), Bober gave more
details. They included the strange events in Hughes' office. *Diary*,
in "Case Study," says that Robbie did not meet Hughes. This is one
of several discrepancies in accounts about Hughes' involvement in

the case. In the previous edition, I relied primarily on *Reppetti*. (The circumstances are slightly different in "Case Study," *Nicola**, and *Schulze*. I favored *Reppetti* as the source closest to an eyewitness.) Hughes did not leave a clear-cut record on how he became involved with Robbie and how he conducted the exorcism. *Reppetti*, notes taken during a Hughes lecture on the exorcism, is hazy on details. It seems incredible that Hughes did not meet Robbie before weighing the idea of an exorcism. The confusion about Hughes' role may well stem from the priest's own confusion, induced by the shock of the attack. What happened to Hughes would so affect his mind and memory that for a long while he would not have been able to give a coherent account of his dealings with Robbie. *Nicola*, without naming Hughes, is quoted in *The Story Behind the Exorcist* by Peter Travers and Stephanie Reiff (Signet Paperback 1974): "One priest from right here in the Washington [Arch]Diocese was involved in the '49 case and did, in fact, suffer a minor breakdown as a result of it…He doesn't seem to want to talk about it, so I approach him very little." Nicola then tells the bedspring attack story and adds: "It was a deep cut, which then became infected, and his arm was in a sling for eight weeks." One unconfirmed account says that Hughes' appearance in Robbie's Georgetown Hospital room set off a frenzy even though Hughes entered disguised as a physician. No matter how the attack occurred, Hughes was not prepared for it.

Mother's conversation with Hughes: Reconstructed from account in *Reppetti*.

"Going My Way" comparison: *Bober*, quoting parishioners. Description of Hughes, anonymous parishioner, quoted in *The Sentinel* of Prince George's County (MD), Feb. 4, 1981.

As Hughes recalled the visit years later: *Bober* in *Grip*.

Robbie speaks Latin: *Nicola*, Faherty**. Other reports have the boy speaking in Aramaic, but the two eyewitness reports, *Diary* and *Halloran*, do not mention it. The speaking of unknown language was a traditional sign of diabolical possession, and, at the outset, there was a tendency to seek out this sign. *Halloran* heard Robbie speak Latin but attributed it to the boy's memorizing of Latin during the exorcism prayers. The "*O sacerdós Christi…*" phrase, however, would have come at a time when Robbie had scarcely heard Latin. And the phrase, which does not occur in any of the exorcism prayers, involved complex Latin. A person speaking it would have to have detailed knowledge of the language.

Rituale Romanum: Throughout the book, all quotations of prayers pertaining to exorcism, both in English and Latin, are from the edition of *Ritual** in use at the time. The prayers have been changed slightly since then and, as part of the Church's abandoning of Latin in liturgy, are said in the local language.

Biographical notes on O'Boyle: *Patrick Cardinal O'Boyle As His Friends Know Him*, collected and edited by William S. Abell. Privately published, 1986.

Account of Hughes' appointment as exorcist: *Reppetti*, the "unpublished, third-person account."

Background on demonology training: *Nicola*.

"Old, white-haired, wispy sort of priest": *Kelly*. No other source mentions a second exorcist, but it is possible that Hughes, a young, inexperienced assistant pastor, avoided his own pastor and sought out an older priest for help.

Georgetown Hospital: I was not allowed to check admission records. But a highly reliable source examined the records for me and confirmed that Robbie entered the hospital, under an assumed name. *Diary* makes no mention of the hospital incident, and the

Jesuit communities at Georgetown and St. Louis Universities did not know about it at the time.

Description of hospital room: *Hendrick, O'Leary.*

Attack on Hughes: *Reppetti*, which draws its information directly from Hughes, minimizes the attack. "In one of the seizures," say Reppetti's notes, "Father [blacked-out name] was holding the boy's wrist but he turned his hand around far enough to scratch the Father's arm so severely that he was unable to raise it for several weeks, and had to elevate the Host [during Mass] with one hand." The priest is obviously Hughes, since no such incident is reported in *Diary*. The "scratch" in *Reppetti*, which so seriously injured Hughes, is described as a one-hundred-stitch wound by *Nicola**, who also tells of the bedspring weapon. *Bober*, relating his recollection of Hughes' own account, also mentions the one-hundred-stitch wound and the bedspring.

Chapter 4: The Scratches Said St. Louis

"They were ready to raise the white flag": *Halloran.*

Rumors in neighborhood, move of family: Interviews with neighbors; accounts, based on *Bober*, in *The Sentinel* of Prince George's County (MD), Feb. 4, 1981 and Oct. 28, 1983. These accounts and others put the "Mannheim" family in Mount Rainier, MD. Mount Rainier volunteer firemen gave me the address where the "exorcist house" stood until the volunteers burned it down. The address coincides with the address used in the 1983 *Sentinel* article and in a *Washington Post* article on May 6, 1985, but, as stated in the Chapter 2 notes above, another address was given in *Diary*. (When Father Bishop was compiling his "Case Study," he got from the family an address that is not that of the "exorcist house," but one about half a mile away. The existence of two addresses led me to infer the move of the family to a nearby house sometime in February 1949.) Land records show that the Mount Rainier property was purchased in 1952 by a realtor using a second party's name. Records further show that since 1952 the property has had the same titular owners, though one of them told me that the actual owner wished to remain unidentified. In June 1992 the owners of record sold the lot, for $22,500, to the Maryland-National Capital Park and Planning Commission. After Robert M. Arciprete of the commission bought the lot, a staff member came into his office and told Arciprete something he did not know: "You sold the Exorcist lot!" Mount Rainier Mayor Linda M. Nalls said in 1993 that she did not know the dark history of the lot. But she hoped to bury the past by using the lot to enlarge an adjacent school playground.

Words appearing on boy's chest: "Case Study," *Diary; Nicola*; Reppetti, Halloran, Bober, Hatfield, Mann, McGuire, Nitka, O'Leary, Faherty*, Schulze*. None of the sources agree completely on the location of the words or the dates they appeared. I have constructed a sequence based primarily on "Case Study." *Schulze* made the observations in a letter, dated March 21 1949, to Dr. J.B. Rhine at his Institute of Parapsychology.

Journey to St. Louis, death of Aunt Harriet: "Case Study," *Diary*. A St. Louis newspaper death notice confirms the date of her death.

Reaction of Schulz: *Schulz*, letter to Rhine.

Religions of Robbie and relatives: "Case Study," *Diary*.

Kitchen table seance: "Case Study," *Diary*.

Move to other relatives' house and incidents there: "Case Study," *Diary*.

Chapter 5: A Priestly Blessing

Elizabeth talks to Father Bishop: "Case Study," *Diary; Halloran. Faherty**, who talked to Father Kenny, gives a slightly different account, based on Kenny's recollection. It is possible that the family would have talked to a Lutheran minister in St. Louis, and perhaps he called on Kenny. But I went with the *Diary* and *Halloran* accounts.

Descriptions of Jesuits: Personal observations; interviews with several Jesuits; *Harney**; *McDonough**.

Background on St. Louis University: Reinert quote from *McDonough**

Description of Father Bishop: *Halloran*; Society of Jesus personnel record and obituary.

"Bells for rising...": *McDonough**

Bishop visits family, gets background information: *Diary, Halloran.*

Ignatius exorcism: The exorcism is depicted in "The Miracle of St. Ignatius," a painting by Peter Paul Rubens. The painting is in the Kunsthistorisches Museum in Vienna.

Exorcism of place and treatise on exorcism: Quotation is from *Exorcism*, edited by Dom Robert Petitpierre, O.S.B. (The Findings of a Commission Convened by the Bishop of Exeter, 1972.)

Del Rio: *Disquisitionum Magicarum*, as quoted in *Gauld**.

1906 definition: A. Poulain, *Des Grâes d'oraison. Traité de théologie mystique*, as quoted, translated into English, in *Oesterreich**.

St. Margaret Mary: *The New Catholic Encyclopedia; A History of Private Life*, Roger Chartier, editor. Vol. III. Belknap Press of Harvard University Press, 1989.

Chapter 6: The Nights of the Priests

Quotes and description in bedroom: *Diary.*

Description of Father Bowdern: *Halloran;* Society of Jesus personnel record and obituary; *Faherty*.*

St. Francis Xavier Church: Personal observation and information booklet on the church.

Professed Jesuit: *McDonough*,* discussion with two Jesuits.

Xavier relic: Conversations with Jesuits; *The New Catholic Encyclopedia.* Information about Canisius and the North American Martyrs, the *Encyclopedia* and *Harney*.*

Events in house: *Diary, Halloran.*

Our Lady of Fatima: *The New Catholic Encyclopedia.*

Aunt Harriet's metal box: *Diary.* Because I have not been able to speak to any member of the family, I know nothing more about the box. Probate Court records in Missouri indicate that there was no will probated. So disposal of Aunt Harriet's possessions would have been handled informally within the family.

Bowdern's research: *Halloran* is the source of the "went right to the books" quote. What books? Del Rio would be available in the library. The infestation-obsession-possession route is well known in works on possession, and *Halloran* remembers learning of it then. Bowdern, in a 1968 letter that he had found little useful information; he says he had a diary kept because it "would be most helpful to anyone placed in a similar position s an exorcist in any future case." (See *Blatty.*)

Chapter 7: The Archbishop Gets the Case

Description of Loudun possessions: Bowdern, researching in St. Louis University's library, undoubtedly would have found references to this famous incident. *Soeur Jeanne des Anges, Autobigraphy d'une hystérique possédée,* edited, with introduction and notes, by Gabriel Legué and Gilles de la Tourette, had been published in 1886, and would be available if not for its account of the possessions, then for its psychiatric fame. For, from Gilles de la Tourette's study of possessions came the discovery of the nervous disorder that bears his name. (See last chapter.) An autobiography of Surin, based on his letters, was published in France in 1926 and would be available to Bowdern.

Warning against asking for possession: A. Poulain, S.J., writing in *The Graces of Interior Prayer,* as quoted by *Huxley*.*

Surin's description of possession: *Oesterreich*.*

Minor orders: The minor orders of porter, exorcist, and subdeacon were abolished by papal decree in 1972, but ordained priests still retained the power to perform exorcisms with permission from a bishop or archbishop. Laymen were given the right to be installed as lectors and acolytes.

Pamphlet on Iowa case: The pamphlet, *Begone Satan,* was written in German and translated by a Benedictine monk. *Halloran* says Bowdern read about the case, and the pamphlet was the only document available.

New events in house: *Diary.*

"The ones who refused...: *Halloran.*

Description of Ritter: "His Eminence Joseph Cardinal Ritter," *St. Louis Review,* 1961; *Faherty*.*

Biblical references: "roaring lion": I Peter 5:8; "For I delight in the law...": Romans 7:22-25.

Definition of possession: *Balducci [The Devil]*.*

"Nothing doing...: *Halloran.*

Chapter 8: I Cast Thee Out

Bowdern's decision about diary: Quotation is from a letter from Bowdern to William Peter Blatty. (See *Blatty.*)

Description of Halloran: *Halloran.*

Quotations and actions: All quotations by participants from now on are from *Halloran,* unless otherwise indicated. Quotations in italics, as usual, are reconstructions of conversations, from *Halloran* and other sources. The prayers, in Latin and English, are from the *Roman Ritual* (see Bibliography). The instructions give the exorcist options about the sequence of prayers. From what *Halloran* told me, Bowdern basically followed the *Ritual.* But, as the nights wore on, he undoubtedly varied the prayers. Bishop in *Diary* rarely noted what prayers were being said. All activities described come from *Diary* unless otherwise cited.

Fifty-third Psalm: In the King James Version of the Bible, this is Psalm 54. Biblical quotations in the *Roman Ritual* come from the Douai version of the Bible, used by Roman Catholics until the 1960s.

Scratches and marks on Robbie's body: *Diary, Halloran, Faherty*, Nicola*, Mann, McGuire, Nitka, Reppetti, Schulze.*

Spitting: *Diary, Halloran, Faherty*, Nicola*, Reppetti.*

Robbie sings: *Diary, Halloran.*

Chapter 9: "He's Going! He's Going!"

Bowdern's view of exorcism: The assessment comes from *Halloran* and from the letter Bowdern wrote to *Blatty.* The remark about his not making "things easy for himself" comes from *Faherty*.*

Fasting: *Halloran.*

Biblical reference: Matthew 17:20.

Chapter 10: The Sign of the X

Bowdern preparing for Mass: Roman Catholic liturgy of the time.

Bowdern knew he was the prize: A widespread belief, in Roman Catholic literature about possession, is that the exorcist, not the demoniac, is the target of the demon. Modern Catholic theologians do not agree on this.

Urinating: *Diary, Halloran, Nicola**. Prodigious amounts of urine are reported repeatedly in this case, as in others.

Schulze attempt at intervention: *Scholze*

Description of Alexian Brothers: *Faherty*, Hatfield.*

Visit by Bubb: "Professor Bubb and the Paranormal," by John M. McGuire, *St. Louis Post-Dispatch*, May 9, 1988. Also, *Halloran.* A physicist at Washington University confirmed Bubb's interest in the paranormal.

Prayers said by Robbie: Information about first Confession and first Communion is based on information in *The Little Key of Heaven,* a collection of prayers for Catholic children of first Communion age, published by the Catholic Publications Press. The little book was used throughout the United States in the 1930s and 1940s. If Robbie did not use this one, he used one quite like it.

Description of Van Roo: *McGuire, Halloran.* Van Roo declined to be interviewed for this book.

"I heard this wild, idiotic laughter": Father Lucius F. Cervantes, S.J., quoted in *McGuire.*

Chapter 11: Messages

Writing on sheet: *Diary.* I have quoted accurately from the *Diary* account of this incident, but I did not use the actual name of the female relative. I have been unable to learn how this relative, a woman, was related to Robbie. The actual name does not appear in the death notice that lists the next of kin of "Aunt Harriet."

Information on baptism: *Handbook of Christian Feasts and Customs* by Francis X. Weiser, S.J. New York: Harcourt, Brace & World, 1952.

Incident on way to church and aftermath: *Diary, Nicola*, Faherty*, Nitka.*

Chapter 12: A Search for a Quiet Place

Robbie's daytime spell: *Diary.*

Quotation from psychiatrist: *Isaac.*

"Billy, Billy. You will die tonight": *Diary*. No harm came to the young cousin.

Events on train: *Diary, Halloran*. Van Roo quotation: *McGuire.*

Schulze reaction: *Schulze.*

Bowdern meets Hughes: *Diary. Reppetti* mentions the meeting but there is no indication that Hughes told Bowdern about the attack in Georgetown Hospital. *Halloran*, who witnessed much of the exorcism and was filled in by Bowdern about the rest, did not know about the attack until I told him about it. I believe that first Hughes, and later Bowdern, wanted to keep the attack secret to protect Robbie from being taken from their care and given psychiatric treatment.

Failure to find place for Robbie: *Diary*. There is no mention of O'Boyle's apparent disinterest in the case; I inferred this.

H E L L and S P I T E: *Diary, Cortes**

I will not go…": *Reppetti.*

Cave or pit description: *Reppetti, Diary.*

At least twenty scratches: *Diary.*

half a pint of spit: This vivid estimate appears only in *Reppetti.* Although the subject of Hughes' lecture at Georgetown was his own participation in Robbie's case, Father Reppetti's notes show that Hughes provided details of events in St. Louis. This information would have come from Bowdern, who met Hughes in Maryland, and from the ecclesiastical report on file in the Archdiocese of Washington. Several sources speak of such a Washington file, even though Archbishop O'Boyle is said to have ordered that no written report be made on the case. Father Joseph M. Moffitt, S.J., who attended the lecture, told me that Hughes read from a document about twenty pages long. Coincidentally, this is the estimated length of Bowdern's ecclesiastical report to Archbishop Ritter. I believe that Ritter sent a copy of the St. Louis report to O'Boyle and that it is this report, with scant reference to Maryland events, that is in the secret archives of the Archdiocese of Washington. Thus, Washington would have an archival record of the case but O'Boyle's order prohibiting a written report would still have been obeyed.

Holding towel as shield: *Cortes*, Reppetti, Nitka.*

H E L L and C H R I S T on Robbie's chest: *Diary.*

***I'll* keep you up…**: I put into first-person words recorded in the third-person in *Diary.*

Events prior to return to St. Louis: *Diary.*

Actions of Hughes' pastor: *Diary, Reppetti.*

Robbie's "unfathomable knowledge" of priests' lives: *Nicola*, Mann, Nitka*; Hughes' quote, *Reppetti. Halloran* does not confirm this.

References to other Jesuits: Jesuit personnel records and obituaries.

Chapter 13: The Demon on the Fifth Floor

Description of hospital: *Faherty*, Hatfield.*

"He looked terrible…: Dr. Bowdern's recollections are in *McGuire.* His son, Father Bowdern's nephew, Ned Bowdern, confirmed the quotation when I talked to him. *Halloran* does not recollect that Bowdern was ever on a bread-and-water fast (also called a "black fast"). But it is the belief of the Bowdern family that Father Bowdern did make a black fast. He obviously did lose weight. He may have secretly decided to intensify his fast as the exorcism wore on.

Description of events in hospital: *Diary.*

Summoning of pediatrician: The incident was recalled to me by the pediatrician's son, whose recollection is the basis for the reconstructed quotations. The son said that he did not know of his father's involvement in the exorcism until the movie "The Exorcist" premiered in 1973. After seeing the movie, the physician told his son that he did not like it because it did not tell the true story. He then broke his silence.

"How do you like that for a nutcracker?": *Halloran.*

I am the devil…: I put third-person words in *Diary* in first-person. The later "I will not let" etc. quotation is taken directly from *Diary.*

Trip to White House: *Halloran.* I visited White House and walked the path of the Stations of the Cross. Background information about White House came from the gracious Matt Palmer, director of buildings and facilities, and from literature he provided me. Father Bowdern was retreat master at White House from 1956 to 1959.

Incidents in hospital room: *Diary, Faherty*, Hatfield.*

"My legs are hurting": *Halloran.*

Robbie hears *Tre Ore*: *Diary.*

Statue of St. Michael: *Diary, Faherty**. The statue is now in a small museum at the Alexian Brothers U.S. headquarters in Elk Grove Village, Illinois.

Chill in room, Bowdern in overcoat: *Faherty*, Nitka.* Halloran does not recall hearing about the chill. But Holy Thursday was his last day he was directly involved in the exorcism. As he tells it, on the morning of Good Friday, "the provincial got word that I was involved in this thing. So he called up the university and told the minister [the Jesuit in charge of the discipline of scholastics] to tell Halloran to get off. So I was off."

Doctor not in "state of grace": *Nicola**. Asked about this incident, *Halloran* said he did not remember it. "If it happened when I was not present," he told me, "I am sure Bill [Bowdern] would have told me. Bill had a great sense of humor."

Incidents with Father Widman and Brothers Theopane and Emmet: *Diary, Reppetti.*

"I mean one BIG word...": *Diary.*

Van Roo recollection: *McGuire.*

Incidents in hospital room: *Diary, Nitka, Reppetti, Hatfield.* According to *Diary*, Robbie complained that the medals were burning him, but, the diary says, "the medals were not taken off. Father Bowdern forced a small reliquary crucifix in R's hand when he was in a spell."

Spit "with uncanny accuracy"...tongue like a snake: *Nitka*, with Father John G. O'Flaherty, S.J., almost certainly the eyewitness source. *Halloran* also attests to Robbie's incredible accuracy—always with his eyes closed.

Robbie speaks with beautiful, rich voice: *Nitka, Reppetti, Faherty*.*

Robbie's vision: *Reppetti, Faherty*, Nicola*, Nitka*. The sources do not agree in detail. I based this primarily on *Faherty**, who, as a historian of the Alexians, had access to the best witnesses about events in the hospital. *Halloran* points out that, technically, a vision is an apparition that can be seen objectively by others; what Robbie had was a dream or an inner vision.

Explosion like gun: *Faherty**

Chapter 14: The Secret Unlocked

Locked room: Jesuit and Alexian sources.

Schulze learns about conversion: *Reppetti.*

Schulze lecture: *Schulze*, 1949.

Schulze-Rhine letters: *Schulze.*

Story leaked: The three-paragraph appeared on the front page of *The Catholic Register* on Aug. 19, 1949.

O'Leary recollection: *O'Leary.*

Blatty background: Blatty gives his account in *William Peter Blatty on The Exorcist from Novel to Film* (Bantam Books, 1974). A Jesuit's letter to Blatty, with the name of the writer blanked out, appears in the book. The letter writer is Bowdern. I have a copy of the letter. (See *Blatty.*)

Incidents on movie set: Interview with Bermingham.

Maniacal laughter: Thomas J. Mullen, a former priest, who was at the camp at the time. Mullen was quoted in *The St. Louis Post-Dispatch.*

Finding of diary in old building: *Halloran.* I checked this story out through a lawyer who has possession of the diary pages found by the worker. The lawyer has talked to people involved in the discovery and made a written report to me. The details of the discovery are taken from this report. Information about the furniture going to a nursing home: "Tearing Down a Devil of a Rumor," *St. Louis Post-Dispatch*, July 12, 1988.

Steubenville, Ohio, incident: *Faherty**, in a footnote, mentioned the correspondence between the Ohio bishop and Archbishop Ritter. Another priest who has seen correspondence on the exorcism also knew about the inquiry from Ohio. But I was unable to find any further references to it in Steubenville newspaper or library files.

Information on Jesuits' lives: Jesuit personnel records and obituaries.

Information on Father Hughes: *Bober, Kelly*, "The Priest Behind 'The Exorcist', *National Catholic Register,* June 5, 1983.

Burning of "The Devil's House": Interviews with Robert J. Creamer, a former City Council member, and with volunteer firemen and neighbors who wished to remain anonymous. Also, *The Washington Post,* May 6, 1985.

Examiner's report to Ritter: A Jesuit who did not take part in the exorcism but who, because of his official duties, was familiar with the case and the Ritter report.

Halloran verdict on Robbie's possession: *Halloran.*

"Difference between ancient conception of demonic possession and...mental disease: *Nicola* in his dissertation on possession.

Judaic attitude toward possession: I discussed this with two rabbis, one Orthodox and the other a Hasidic. They agreed that possession and the *Dybbuk* are no longer part of Jewish belief. This was also borne out by *The Encyclopedia of Judaism* (Macmillan, 1989). Exorcism in ancient times was an accepted folk practice. The Roman historian Josephus reported on a Jew named Elazar who performed exorcisms a number of times in Roman civilian and military officials.

Biblical references: "destroy the works of the devil": I John 3:8; "But if I cast out devils by the Spirit of God, then the kingdom of God is come unto you": Matthew 12:28. [note to editor: text should be changed so that biblical quote coincides.]

Cortes' disbelief in possession and exorcism: *Cortes**. Several Jesuits I talked to suggested that I read Cortes. After doing so, I concluded that the consensus among those Jesuits was that they tended to agree with most of his conclusions, and that this was, implicitly, a modern theological view. Cortes had access to ***Reppetti***, but, for reasons unexplained in the source notes of his book, he saw only a portion of ***Diary***. "A Jesuit friend, however," the Cortes source notes say, "has read the entire diary and given me his recollections of the rest of it and of a talk he had in 1949 with a priest who assisted the exorcist." Cortes also read a short document by a Jesuit who apparently attended the Hughes lecture with Reppetti. "We find as the most reliable documents," Cortes concluded, "those written by the Jesuits."

Rapoport on possible causes: *Rapoport:* interview at the National Institute of Mental Health, where she is chief of the Child Psychiatry Branch. Also, her book (see Bibliography). The definition of scrupulosity is from the ***New Catholic Encyclopedia***.

Tourette syndrome: *Rapoport*. See also Arthur K. Shapiro and Elaine Shapiro in ***American Journal of Psychotherapy*** (July 1982). They think that the syndrome may be linked to exorcisms they analyzed back to 1489.

Nicola on Church's attitude: *Nicola*.

Thurston quotation: See Bibliography.

Citations

Blatty: Letter, dated October 17, 1968, from Father Bowdern to William Peter Blatty, author of *The Exorcist* and screenwriter of the movie of the same title. I have a copy of the letter. Blatty quotes the letter, with the name of the letter writer deleted, appeared in *William Peter Blatty on the Exorcist from Novel to Film* (New York: Bantam, 1974).

Bober: Interview with Father Frank Bober; also videotaped interview in *Grip*.

Grip: "In the Grip of Evil," a documentary of the Robbie exorcism produced by Henninger Media Development, with Brian Kelly, producer. I was a consultant and co-author of the script. The documentary was first telecast on the Discovery Channel in 1997.

Halloran: Interviews with Father Walter Halloran, S.J.

Hatfield: "Ghostly True Tales Are Part of Haunted Hospital Lore," by Scott Hatfield, *Advance for Medical Technologists*, Oct. 23, 1989. This account of the exorcism in the Alexian Brothers Hospital was given to me, along with *Mann* and *Nitka,* when I asked for information from religious and lay officials of the Alexian order. So I assumed that the three sources were considered accurate. I was also given *Faherty**, another source obviously considered accurate. He is a distinguished Jesuit historian.

Hendrick: Tom Hendrick, television correspondent, who produced a short news film about exorcism for Fox Television. *O'Leary* gave the hospital-room description in the film, which was part of a series titled "Beyond the Senses." *Boder* and *Nicola* also appear in the film and do not contradict the description of the hospital room. The film, a copy of which Hendrick kindly gave me, was aired in May 1986.

Isaacs: "The Possessive States Disorder: The differentiation of involuntary spirit-possession from present diagnostic categories," a dissertation by T. Craig Isaacs. Abstracts International 1986 June Vol 46(12-B, Pt 1) 4403.

Kelly: Winfield Kelly, who later became Prince George's County Executive and Maryland Secretary of State. Kelly knew about the exorcism from neighborhood gossip and believed at the time that this was the source for Hughes' sickly appearance.

Mann: "Setting the Exorcism Record Straight," by Mary Mann, *South Side Journal*, St. Louis, MO, March 14, 1990. (The article appeared originally in *The University of St. Louis News* and contains several quotations from Jesuits familiar with the exorcism.)

McGuire: "The Exorcist Revisited," by John M. McGuire, *St. Louis Post-Dispatch*, April 17, 1988.

Nicola: Interviews with Father John J. Nicola. Nicola carefully avoided direct discussion of this specific case with me. But, as noted above, he is quoted about it in *The Story Behind the Exorcist*.

Nitka: "A Tale of Sound and Fury, Signifying Exorcism," by Beth Nitka, *St. Louis University News*, April 24, 1981. Beth Nitka was an undergraduate when she wrote this story for the student newspaper. The story has become a quasi-official account of the exorcism; a copy of it was given to me by both Jesuit and Alexian sources, with the implication that it was a truthful account. Nitka does not attribute the many quotes in the story to anyone specifically. "It was all pretty hush-hush," she told me. I was later informed by a Jesuit that Nitka's source was the late Father John G. O'Flaherty, S.J., who was present at the exorcism for several days. Nitka, without disclosing her source, said that at the conclusion of her interview she asked the priest if he believed in possession. "All I have to tell you, young lady," he said, "is that you'd better believe in the devil."

O'Leary: "'The Exorcist': Story That Almost Wasn't," by Jeremiah O'Leary, *Star-News* (Washington, D.C.), Dec. 29, 1973. O'Leary told me he got his account of the hospital-room scene "second-hand" from a priest he spoke to in August 1949.

Rapoport: Interview with Judith L. Rapoport, M.D., author of *The Boy Who Couldn't Stop Washing** and chief of the Child Psychiatry Branch at the National Institute of Mental Health.

Reppetti: Notes taken by Father William C. Reppetti, S.J., Georgetown University archivist, when Father Hughes spoke at Georgetown University on May 10, 1950. According to Father Joseph M. Moffitt, S.J., a theologian who invited Hughes to Georgetown, Hughes spoke from what looked like a report about twenty pages long. He retained the report, but Reppetti took notes as Hughes read from it. Father John J. Nicola, who talked to Hughes about the case, said that Archbishop Patrick A. O'Boyle of the Archdiocese of Washington ordered Hughes not to write down anything about the case. Presumably, this injunction did not extend to an ecclesiastical report that was placed in the Archdiocesan archives. Hughes, also presumably, read from that report.

Schulze: Interview with the Reverend Luther Miles Schulze in **The Enchanted Voyager***; Schulze's account, given anonymously, in **The Evening Star** (Washington, D.C.), Aug. 10, 1949; **Washington Post**, Aug. 10, 1949; **Times-Herald** (Washington, D.C.), Aug. 11, 1949. Schulze letter, dated March 21 1949, to Dr. J.B. Rhine, Department of Psychology, Duke University. This letter was used in *Grip*. Schulze gives an account of events in his bedroom in his letter to Rhine, beginning a lengthy correspondence about Robbie.

Schulze quotations in Chapter 14 are from these letters. They were obtained by Sergio A. Rueda, who received a grant from the Institute of Parapsychology to investigate the exorcism. Rueda made the letters available for the producer of *Grip* and appeared on the video.

*See **Bibliography**.

INDEX